# WELFARE AND SOCIETY
## STUDIES IN WELFARE POLICY, PRACTICE AND THEORY

*Series Editors*:
Matthew Colton, Kevin Haines, Tim Stainton and Anthea Symonds
School of Social Sciences and International Development,
University of Wales Swansea

*Welfare and Society* is an exciting series from the University of Wales Swansea, School of Social Sciences and International Development in conjunction with Ashgate, concerned with all aspects of social welfare. The series publishes works of research, theory, history and practice from a wide range of contemporary applied social studies subjects such as Criminal Justice, Child Welfare, Community Care, Race and Ethnicity, Therapeutic and Intervention Techniques, Community Development and Social Policy. The series includes extended research reports of scholarly interest as well as works aimed at both the academic and professional communities.

# Listening to the Welfare State

*Edited by*

MICHAEL SELTZER
*Oslo University College, Norway*

CHRISTIAN KULLBERG
*University of Örebro, Sweden*

SØREN PETER OLESEN
*National School of Social Work, Aarhus, Denmark*

ILMARI ROSTILA
*University of Jyväskylä, Finland*

# Ashgate

Aldershot • Burlington USA • Singapore • Sydney

Published by
Ashgate Publishing Ltd
Gower House
Croft Road
Aldershot
Hants GU11 3HR
England

Ashgate Publishing Company
131 Main Street
Burlington, VT 05401-5600 USA

Ashgate website: http://www.ashgate.com

**British Library Cataloguing in Publication Data**
Listening to the welfare state. - (Welfare & society)
   1. Welfare state  2. Scandinavia - Social policy  3. Scandinavia
   - Social conditions - 20th century
   I. Seltzer, Michael
   361.6'5'0948

**Library of Congress Control Number:** 00-111543


ISBN 0 7546 1565 0


Printed in Great Britain by
Antony Rowe, Chippenham, Wiltshire

# Contents

# Notes on Contributors

**Ilkka Arminen** (Ph.D.)

Researcher, Department of Sociology, University of Helsinki, Finland. He has studied therapeutic interaction in both professional and lay settings. His research interests include also the methodology of the study of institutional interaction.

**Elisabet Cedersund** (Ph.D.)

Senior Lecturer, Department of Health and Environment, Linköping University, Sweden, and Research Associate, Department of Communication Studies, at the same university. She has conducted research on and written about bureaucratic discourse, constructions of financial problems in social welfare interviews, narratives in social work and communication in educational settings.

**Hannele Forsberg** (Ph.D.)

Assistant Professor of Social Work, University of Tampere, Finland. Using social constructionist perspectives, she has studied and written extensively about families, children, and social workers as well as child protection professionals.

**Lars-Christer Hydén** (Ph.D.)

Professor, Department of Communication Studies, Linköping University, Sweden. He is a social psychologist and has studied and published about conversational interaction in medicine and social welfare agencies, illness narratives and life history, as well as narratives in social work documents.

**Arja Jokinen** (Ph.D.)

Assistant Professor of Social Work, University of Tampere, Finland. She is co-author of the first textbook (in Finnish) on discourse analysis as well as co-editor of *Constructing Social Work Practices* (Ashgate 1999). She has studied and written about client-helper interaction in a variety of social welfare settings as well as the social construction of homelessness.

**Kirsi Juhila** (Ph.D.)

Professor of Social Work, University of Tampere, Finland. Her research interests include the application of discourse analysis and the social construction of homelessness. She is currently working on a project focused on social problems work and social worker-client interaction in different social work organisations. She is co-editor of *Constructing Social Work Practices* (Ashgate 1999).

**Christian Kullberg** (Ph.D.)

Research Associate, University of Örebro, Sweden. A former social worker, he has conducted research and written about gender and social work, equal pay policy implementation, social work evaluation and inter-organisational co-operation.

**Anna Leppo** (MA)

Researcher at the Finnish Foundation for Alcohol Studies (STAKES) and Editorial Secretary of *Acta Sociologica: The Journal of the Scandinavian Sociological Association.* She has conducted an ethnographic study of a 12-step addiction treatment program in Finland. Her research interests include ethnographic and interactional studies of addiction treatment.

**Søren Peter Olesen** (MA)

Senior Lecturer, National School of Social Work in Aarhus, Denmark. He has studied and written about conversation analysis, unemployment, and labour market policy implementation. He is currently affiliated with CARMA, The National Centre for Labour Market Studies at the University of Aalborg, Denmark.

**Ilmari Rostila** (Ph.D.)

Professor of Social Work, Department of Social Sciences and Philosophy, University of Jyväskylä, Finland. He has done conversation analytical research on talk-in-interaction between social workers and clients at Finnish social work agencies. He is currently conducting social work evaluation studies.

**Michael Seltzer** (Ph.D.)

Associate Professor, Oslo University College, Norway. A cultural anthropologist and sociologist, he has studied and written about family therapy, bilingual education, racist discourses and social work education. He is co-author of a book (in Norwegian) about financial counselling in social work.

**Eero Suoninen** (Ph.D.)

Assistant Professor of Social Psychology, Department of Sociology and Social Psychology, University of Tampere, Finland. He has written about research methods and client-helper interactions in various welfare and therapeutic settings. He is co-author of the first textbook (in Finnish) on discourse analysis.

## Åse Vagli (MA)

Senior Lecturer in Sociology at the University of Tromsø, Norway. She has studied in social welfare institutions for the elderly as well as persons having substance abuse problems. She is presently completing her Ph.D. dissertation - an ethnographic study of a Norwegian child protection agency.

## Sanna Vehviläinen (Ph.D.)

Researcher, Department of Education, University of Helsinki, Finland. She has written about interaction in psychodrama groups as well as adult education counselling situations. She recently completed a study based on conversation analyses of counselling encounters in career training programs in Finland.

# Foreword: Listening to Talk at Work in the Nordic Welfare Systems

MICHAEL SELTZER AND CHRISTIAN KULLBERG

## Introduction

This anthology is about the welfare systems of Denmark, Finland, Norway and Sweden. The aim of its fourteen contributors is to examine how these systems operate at street-level: that is, at those sites where professional helpers encounter persons seeking help, financial assistance and other welfare services. The researchers presenting in the following pages approach talk-in-interaction and related social behaviour at the core of these meetings from three closely related though different perspectives. Though their academic training represents a variety of disciplines ranging from social psychology, linguistics, sociology, social work and cultural anthropology, they share one main goal. This is to mobilise their skills as investigators of social behaviour in face-to-face situations to present a body of knowledge about the routine, everyday workings of the welfare systems of Finland and the Scandinavian countries. As the following will show, this knowledge derives from systematic ethnographic, conversation and discourse analyses of the authentic conversations taking place at many sites in these systems.

From the outset, it must be made clear that this book makes no claims to have attended fully to the vast literature about social policies of the Nordic welfare states. In the first place, these writings are too immense to be handled effectively in a single volume. In addition, much of this literature is comprised of statistics and policy issues involved with the macro-level operations of national systems whose core features comprise what hereafter will be referred to as the Nordic Welfare State (NWS). Rather than researching questions at this level, this book's contributors have investigated the mundane, naturally occurring situations at the micro-level of these systems. It is here that the NWS and its many institutional branches is "talked" into being in the many public encounters taking place between helpers and users at social welfare and probation offices, child protection agencies, family therapy clinics, employment and labour market counselling programs, rehabilitation clinics and other sites.

This book, centring on talk-at-work at these locations, is divided into four parts. Prior to part one, this forward first presents a synopsis of the contributions comprising the book's main body. This is followed by a discussion of traditional welfare state research and its limitations as well as a summary of the three interrelated methods of ethnographic description, conversation and discourse analyses serving as the shared source for data upon which this book is based. Part one then opens with two contributions - one from Sweden and the other from Finland - taking up issues involved with the study of authentic conversations in research on the welfare state as well as the ways in which meaning may be constructed in talk between professionals and clients. Part two shifts focus to examine how talk-in-interaction takes place at points where the well being of children becomes the concern of welfare state professionals. Here, two contributions from Finland and Norway provide a comparative perspective on talk at child welfare agencies. In part three, attention is shifted to the roles of the Danish and Finnish welfare systems in counselling the unemployed and others participating in different programs linking them to the labour markets. In the book's final part, contributors from Finland and Sweden examine the role of talk-in-interaction in institutional contexts. Here, a shared research concern is the study of ways in which order and organisation is produced through talk-in-interaction at social work agencies in Sweden and Finland as well as a substance abuse clinic in Finland. A second shared concern here is with the effects of different ways of talking in organisations on the sense of self among clients as well as helpers. The book then concludes with a brief summary of some of the highlights of the picture of the NWS emerging from studies focused on the talk at work taking place in the many public encounters constituting its most routine and everyday activities.

**The Book and Its Contents: A Synopsis**

In the book's first chapter, the Swedish researchers Christian Kullberg and Elisabet Cedersund provide an overview of research focusing on encounters between social workers and clients carried out in the Nordic countries in recent years. The examples chosen are taken from publications by colleagues in the field (some of them, like Lars-Christer Hydén, contributors to this book) as well as from their own studies. With a point of departure in the concept of the multi-strategic approach developed by the British sociologist Derek Layder (1993), Kullberg and Cedersund concentrate on three themes they regard as central to our understanding of the work that street-level bureaucrats within the welfare institutions do.

The first theme discussed concerns *social interaction* understood as interpersonal negotiations taking place within social welfare institutions. Attention here is directed towards studying how the various levels of context, setting and activity are created and recreated in interaction. The second theme concerns the various *moral aspects* that appear in conversations within social work. The prime concern here is with the concept of self and how the individual self - with special focus on the client's own sense of selfhood - may be constructed in the discourse. The third theme concerns *gender aspects* of conversation in social work. Here, the authors attend to the ways in which the gender constructions of social structure and society as a whole - in both private and public spheres - may be created and reinforced in institutional environments of the type studied.

In chapter two, a Finnish research team comprised of Arja Jokinen, Kirsi Juhila and Eero Sunoninen, examine talk-at-work in the NWS from a social constructionist perspective. In using a theoretical approach influencing much of the contemporary literature of the social and behavioural sciences, the contributors see the interaction between professional helpers and clients as "conversational" encounters consisting of negotiations. According to their understanding of helping work in the welfare state, the negotiating taking place at these meetings can be seen in terms of three interrelated components and perspectives. These they describe as: institutional context, interactional positions and meanings. Using material drawn from conversation analyses of two different interactions between professional helpers and clients (family therapy and correctional care interviews), the authors apply their notion of negotiational work. From their analysis of these encounters, they draw the conclusion that interactional positions and meanings are not determined by the kinds of context in which negotiation may take place. On the contrary, their findings demonstrate that professional helpers, in positioning and viewing the topics that are dealt with in encounters respond to the kind of positions assumed by their clients. In doing this, they combine different strategies to achieve the kinds of problem- and solution-centred tasks serving as their goals.

In chapter three, Hannele Forsberg explores the place of the child in child welfare work in a Finnish setting. This is an interesting question since Finland (as well as the other Nordic countries) is perceived as being greatly concerned with children's rights as well as prioritising the child's own view and involvement in matters concerning her/his own welfare. Focusing on social welfare offices and family support centres, Forsberg employs an ethnographic approach to the conversations occurring at these sites. Central to her research is the question: How is the position of children interpreted in relation to those of parents and professionals in the interaction between child protection professionals and their clients? This question is examined in terms of three different interaction frames (Goffman 1974): the first a legally informed frame of children's rights; the second, a family-centred frame of action, and a third based on the notion of children's peer culture. Following her analysis, Forsberg concludes that despite official rhetoric emphasising children's involvement in Finland, the typical mode of dealing with child protection is one primarily involving parents. In actual practice, this means that children often are positioned as "side-participants" and in this sense are given a "passive participant identity". Only when parents are treated as incapable of assuming parental responsibility or are regarded in other ways as questionable carers for their children are the views and voices of children heard. In contrast, the interactional frame of children's peer culture provides children with a platform for developing their own mode of interaction and opportunities for their views to be heard. In dealing with children in this frame, professionals are provided with chances to meet children acting on their own.

In the book's fourth chapter, Åse Vagli explores the talk-in-interaction at the centre of the daily life of a Norwegian child protection agency. In doing this, she approaches the agency in the role of an ethnographic fieldworker. As a participant observer, Vagli's principal concern has been collecting material by listening to and observing interactions between the professional helpers at this site. Her main focus has been on how child welfare decisions are made as well as on the logic linking the meanings of the talk involved in these decisions to this specialised institutional context. In her investigation, Vagli found that a general trait of professional talk in this context was a collective attempt to legitimate the child protection work being done. Processes of legitimisation, she concluded, appeared to serve the purpose of establishing a occupational identity for the professionals as well as protecting them and making bearable the stresses of the "risk situations" lying at the core of much child protection work.

In chapter five, Søren Peter Olesen combines qualitative and quantitative findings from an ongoing study of 32 public encounters between 8 employment officials and 32 unemployed persons at employment offices in Denmark. In addition to making observations and tape recordings of these encounters, Olesen also interviewed both sets of participants about their perceptions of the encounters after these meetings had taken place. By comparing data drawn from the encounter situations with the unemployed person's own evaluation of how they felt their service-seeking had been satisfied by these meetings, Olesen identified several distinctive patterns of interaction. These involved different ways of talking and acting on the part of the employment officials as well as the characteristics comprising action-plan talks regarded by the unemployed as being either satisfactory or non-satisfactory. In describing how the needs of the unemployed person - particularly face-saving needs - are dealt with by officials charged with implementing labour-market policies at street-level, Olesen shows how both qualitative and quantitative approaches to talk-in-interaction complement each other. This, he claims, provides us with richly detailed accounts of conversations constituting the building blocks of welfare state operations at the micro-level.

In chapter six, Sanna Vehviläinen presents an account of the ways in which counsellors in Finnish career guidance training respond and give support to adult students who talk about problems and problematic circumstances. Her conversation analysis of this "troubles-talk" is presented against the particular institutional environment where these interactions between counsellor and student take place and the kinds of constraints on talks created by this setting. Vehviläinen finds that counsellors in interactions with the students presenting troubles use two different means of action, or orientations, in dealing with troubles talk. The first of these she calls an *activating orientation*, and the second, a *help giving*. In the case of the former, counsellors promote self-directedness among students bringing up problems, while in the latter counsellors actively orient themselves to the task of helping students with their troubles. Vehviläinen concludes that both orientations may be understood as rather "neutral" but active ways professionals choose to give support and help provide solutions to problems. In the activating orientation, the counsellor acts as a co-constructor of the solution and indicates that the matters dealt with are a concern for the student's future agenda. In the help-giving orientation, the counsellor uses advice giving to eliminate the student's worries. This is achieved by offering advice and help as well as normalising the troubles presented by the student.

In the book's seventh chapter, Ilkka Arminen and Anna Leppo draw from their study of a Finnish rehabilitation clinic for persons having substance-abuse problems. Their main concern is with how professional staff deal with a recurring problem in this treatment milieu. The authors focus especially on the communicative strategies used by professional helpers working with clients who publicly confess their willingness to solve their addiction problems, but who, in interaction, express positive attitudes toward substance use. The authors employ both ethnographic and conversational analytic perspectives in examining this problem and their account represents in this respect an experiment of how these methods may be combined. Their findings indicate that the kind of confrontational work professional helpers have to pursue in order to deal effectively with problems and keep clients on the right track is a highly delicate and sensitive activity. Even though professionals in their talk with each other sometimes describe themselves as successful in trying to change attitudes among clients, Arminen and Leppo suggest that many changes, in reality, seldom involve quick processes. In addition, they demonstrate that working with client attitudes in face-to-face interaction is a delicate collaborative construction achieved by the participants' constant attuning themselves and their face-saving strategies to each other.

In chapter eight, the Swede Lars-Christer Hydén presents a wide-ranging account focused on communicative work in the institutional context of the NWS. His central concern here is with the interactional processes involved with establishing identity in these settings. By using encounters between social workers and clients in the social welfare office as his point of departure, Hydén investigates how modes of production of identity are tied to specific contexts. He shows how professional helpers and their clients in these institutional settings establish, display and communicate their identities in three ways. These, he characterises, as indexing, categorising and symbolic placement. Hydén concludes that social workers, unlike most clients, possess possibilities to move beyond the constraints of administratively and professionally imposed roles and thus develop more "genuine" relationships with clients. For clients, on the other hand, it is much more difficult to use their identities as tools or "strategic resources" in their interaction with social workers. In encountering social workers, clients often find themselves positioned where only a specific part of their identities are displayed - often in extremely limited and impersonal ways. Even though all clients enter these institutional settings as whole persons with problems, Hydén shows that many end up as bearers of only those aspects of these problems defined as relevant by the institution in its processing of them.

In the book's final chapter, Ilmari Rostila builds on data drawn from tape-recorded encounters between social workers and clients in Finnish social welfare office. His account, based on conversation analysis of these materials and focused on the question - social work or bureaucracy? -

draws attention to important differences in these public encounters. Using the notion of "alignment", Rostila indicates how participants may organise their talk co-operatively either as single topic conversations focused only on money-matters or as conversations consisting of various topics of talk. His findings show how participants often utilise considerable skill and a high degree of co-ordination to construct jointly their encounters to fit either the idea of 'social work' or 'bureaucracy'. These kinds of interactions Rostila then compares to encounters where no such shared alignment is present.

## The Nordic Welfare State: Ideals and Realities

The welfare state, both as ideal and institution, long has been the focus for great interest and considerable debate throughout the industrialised and industrialising nations of the world. For many decades during this century, much of this attention has centred upon the welfare states of the Nordic countries of Denmark, Finland, Norway and Sweden. Undoubtedly, one reason for this relates to the widespread perception that these nations possess service-delivery systems representing the most advanced, effective and just versions of the welfare state. At the same time, however, these systems long have had their critics on both the right and left sides of the debate about the place and role of the welfare state in the modern and post-modern world (see, for example, Eriksen & Loftager 1996; Svallfors & Taylor-Gooby 1999; Huntford 1971).

Behind the many claims, counter-claims, policy statements, white papers and related documents about the NWS's various arrangements for providing care, employment and other forms of support, there exists a shared base in the everyday social activities taking place between the state's representatives and clients/users seeking service. These face-to-face encounters between such street-level bureaucrats (Lipsky 1980; Prottas 1979) and service-seekers or those required to attend such meetings are, of course, the end stations where social policies are to be implemented. It is at these sites where members of the public are positioned on the receiving end of various policies, programs and interventions of the NWS. From an interactional perspective, however, these public encounters are, in the final analysis, sites where conversations naturally occur between actors. More often than not, the general focus of these talk-in-interaction situations is on problems of various sorts. Often, these are presented by members of the public seeking assistance on their own volition, or those required to seek help, or otherwise in need of expert aid. In recent years, as has been forcefully argued by many theorists (Beck & Ritter 1992; Beck et al. 1994), the numbers of those seeking expert help has increased dramatically. This, it is maintained, results from the proliferation of risks in modern societies making everyday life a project requiring expert advice from professional helpers of the state as well as the private sector.

No matter the reasons bringing them to the welfare state's helpers, each individual arrives at these meetings as a whole person with one or many problems (Satyamurti 1980). Consequently, talk at these encounters often focuses directly upon the meaning of the problem for the person experiencing it as well as for the professional helper required to attend to it. No matter whether talk is about the respective meanings of problems for clients or helpers or involves other issues, these conversations appears to represent a principal, if not the prime, social activity of the welfare state in its everyday, street-level operations. At a higher level of abstraction, the talk-in-interaction at these encounters may also be seen as representing a key to the understanding of how the massive social arrangement that is the welfare state actually functions in practice.

Since talk occupies so central a place among helpers and help-seekers in various settings, it stands to reason that recording, observing and otherwise studying conversational activities represents a major avenue to learning about how the welfare state accomplishes or fails to accomplish its many institutionalised goals. As already noted, this approach has been central to the work carried out by the social and behavioural scientists who have contributed to this book. Their descriptions and analyses have shared a methodological point of departure focused on listening to and observing conversations naturally occurring in the course of the everyday operations of these various agencies, offices and clinics making up the NWS.

In attending to talk-in-interaction here, these researchers have employed a small set of closely related but distinct methods for studying the authentic conversations taking place here - both among and between clients and professionals. These methods - ethnographic description, conversation analysis and discourse analysis - often provide, as will be shown in the following, the kinds of deep and detail-rich descriptions of communicative work rarely elicited by interview and other techniques. Another strength of these methods is that they provide a check on the classic sociological problem involving contrasts between what people claim to do in interaction and what they actually do. Still another reason for using these methods with their common focus on authentic conversations is that research employing interview techniques often fails to take into consideration such specific contextual conditions (prerequisites) or ecological factors that are at hand in helper-client encounters. As Charles Briggs (1986) has shown, this means that interviewers seldom adjust their methods to such factors as specific language use and "communicative genres" as well as norms specific for the group interviewed. Still, a further reason for employing an authentic conversation focus can be understood as an attempt to shed some light over questions of how, when and why public officials use theory in meetings with their clients. As the following chapters suggest, the data of "thick description" (Geertz 1972) provided by studies of authentic conversations adds extra depth to our knowledge of the rationales the helping professions choose to define, direct and legitimate their actions in face-to-face meetings with clients.

## The Authentic Conversation as a New Focus for Welfare State Research

In approaching authentic conversations in the welfare state with these three methods, this book's contributors have collected different kinds of data. Some have been extremely objective in terms of reproducing in fine detail interactional events, while others have been much more impressionistic and generalised. Yet, whichever tool chosen to collect and to analyse conversational and related materials, all researchers reporting here have occupied a common listening post. Here, they have focused their research attention to varying degrees on the utterances, turn-takings and paralinguistic features of talk-in-interaction. In attuning themselves to this shared task, they have listened and/or observed the forms of talk transpiring in these settings. This listening - and to a lesser extent, observing - of these situations made the search for this book's title a relatively easy one: it is a book made possible by listening to conversations in the Nordic Welfare State and its various agencies.

As Christian Kullberg and Elisabet Cedersund describe in their opening chapter, the locales described in this book may be conceived of as the microlandscapes of interaction in the Nordic welfare systems. As they point out, these locations until quite recently have been little explored and poorly mapped. Indeed, throughout much of the history of the welfare states of Finland and the Scandinavian countries, relatively little research attention has been devoted to its many conversational territories.

The main thrust of research on the workings of the welfare state in the Nordic countries - as elsewhere in Europe and North America - long has been and continues to be focused on macro-level issues. Here investigators have attended to large scale questions often those involving pressing social problems, such as poverty and unemployment, as well as implementations of policies for providing a host of social and health services to those segments of the population defined as being in need and or at risk. Set against this historical background, the contributors to this volume as well as many of their colleagues and mentors may be understood as pioneers. By shifting the scope of the research gaze to sites other than those involving macro-level social policy and administrative concerns, they have alerted us to the everyday workings of the welfare system taking place on the smaller street-level stages where clients and helpers come together. In attending to these long-neglected zones, this book's contributors and other pioneers have begun to produce a reliable map of the many regions of this immense and relatively unknown territory by examining it with the help of tools first developed in cultural and social anthropology, sociology, psychology and linguistics. Though possessing different origins, these tools have, as we shall see, a number of features in common.

In directing research attention to microlandscapes of interaction, this book's contributors and others like them have broken with a number of time-honoured traditions in welfare state research. Rather than follow the pathways laid out by earlier generations of investigators whose primary research tools have been that of the social survey, the questionnaire and the interview schedule, researchers focused on talk-in-interaction have employed tape recorders, video cameras and participant-observational techniques to explore these facets of the welfare system. As innovators in this field, they have gone behind the statistical representations of clients and helpers long serving as the main source of knowledge of the welfare state's workings. As the following contributions illustrate, this move broadens our knowledge of the welfare state's human components - particularly its clients. The reader of this book will hear authentic voices of a diverse body of professional helpers and their clients. Heard in the following pages will be the voices of children and their parents, the unemployed, persons on probation and in vocational training schemes, clients of institutions treating substance abuse, and others on both the receiving end and service-providing side of welfare state policies and programs.

## The Nordic Welfare State and Its Researchers

In order to gain an appreciation of the break with past research practices as well as the move toward giving voice to clients and professionals, some of the key features of the Nordic welfare states and how these traditionally have been studied need to be briefly discussed. With good reason, many throughout the world today look to the welfare systems of Denmark, Finland, Norway and Sweden as models of how highly industrialised societies can provide high quality social services to those in need of assistance. Even though these four nations differ in terms of their histories and cultures, the welfare delivery systems they have developed during the past century share many features. These commonalties in core structures and functions make it possible, as already noted, to speak of a shared Nordic welfare system - the NWS. Despite national differences, this may be thought of as a basic set of ideologies and practices for the delivery of social services shared by Denmark, Finland, Norway and Sweden. Staffed by a corps of professional helpers working to assist persons seeking or required to seek assistance for a wide range of problems, this system is regarded by many as a major, if not the crowning, achievement of social democratic policy making and bureaucratic practices. When operating effectively, the NWS may be thought of as an arrangement for equitably providing economic and other benefits to persons in need of help and/or incapable of providing for themselves. In contrast to welfare service delivery systems in other industrial societies, the welfare benefits made available in the Nordic countries are conceived of as political rights, rather than forms of charity.

Though similar in many respects to welfare systems developed in other countries, the NWS possesses certain historical and political features making it specific to Finland and the Scandinavian countries. Though Germany and Great Britain had considerable influence on the early development of the welfare policies and practices of these countries, the Nordic welfare apparatus may be understood as the product of a set of specific and interrelated economic, political and social processes (Stjernø 1995).

In the first place, it would be an oversimplification to view the NWS as solely the sum of social planning and policy implementation carried out by successive governments in the Nordic countries during the 20th century. Though some scholars oppose such a view (Edlebalk et al. 1998), many view this system as the continually evolving product of a lengthy struggle for equitable care and financial assistance waged by organised labour and social democratic and other political parties of the Nordic countries. Secondly, the NWS is unique among the world's welfare systems in its solid financial base: on the whole, more than 30% or more of the total GNP of the Nordic countries is devoted to financing the NWS. No other welfare delivery system in the world comes anywhere near approaching this figure. Not surprisingly, this results in the employment of many persons to carry out the work of the welfare state: the social and health services employ from 8 to 14% of the workforces of the Nordic countries. Thirdly, as one of its central goals, the NWS has a welfare model aimed at insuring full rights for all citizens. While some believe that this goal has been attained, questions about the fairness and effectiveness of the institutional welfare model in practice have been raised in recent years by feminist and sociological researchers (Marklund & Svallfors 1986; Hernes 1987; Bergqvist 1990).

One way of framing the limitations and benefits of the NWS is to examine its links to the coming of modernity to Denmark, Finland, Norway and Sweden. While it is clear that the condition of modernity was thrust upon Danish, Finnish, Norwegian and Swedish societies by capitalism and industrialisation, it is equally clear that this development was closely linked to the processes involving the evolution of the NWS. Guided by the notions of rational planning and empiricism, the policy makers of the emergent NWS moulded and refined the workings of a modern bureaucratic organisation designed to provide a wide range of social and financial services. As these services expanded under the umbrella of an institutional welfare model insuring full rights for all, they came to cover a many needs for health, housing, employment, income maintenance as well as to provide care for families, children, the elderly and other segments of the population.

**Research Discourses in the Nordic Welfare State**

The development of these many services have tended to follow a set of standardised procedures and these, too, have been much influenced by the values and ideals of modernity. One such ideal, that of positivism, played and continues to play a central role in co-evolution of the NWS and its research apparatus. In identifying problems in society, suggesting policies for addressing these, evaluating the effectiveness of programs implemented to solve them, the welfare system requires research organisations capable of carrying out systematic investigations resulting in quantitative data. In order to obtain these figures, ties have been established between welfare services and various research institutions both in and outside the state bureaucracy.

The co-operative projects resulting from these links have tended to follow routinised patterns throughout the welfare state's history. Many of these patterns have been heavily influenced by idealised pictures of policy formulation and implementation promoted by welfare state planners and prominent in official policy literature. Often, a key role in the operations of these policy processes has been occupied by state-sponsored statistical and research agencies. Given the great size and vast scope of these activities, the personnel charged with carrying out this kind of research work have come to comprise, together with policy makers and practitioners, the three main groups making up the staff of the welfare state. Traditionally, these researchers have used a variety of tools designed to measure and count social phenomena. The social survey has been a mainstay of this kind of work. Historically, it has roots beginning with the pioneering research carried out in industrialising Europe by LePlay, Sundt and the anonymous authors of multitudes of parliamentary reports, white papers and similar publications. Questionnaires and interview schedules, too, have played substantial roles in research carried out in the welfare states of the Nordic countries.

Owing to the immensity of these kinds of research activities, there has accumulated through time a massive amount of information about the NWS. With the advent of computerised data retrieval systems, it is today an easy task to gain access to an impressive array of statistical material about the Nordic societies. In addition, these data are supplemented by multitudes of publications containing data drawn from questionnaire and interview queries directed at populations about how they experience their lives, where they live, what they do, and so on. These accounts provide a great range of details about unemployment, poverty, wealth, childcare as well as many other factors involved in determining the quality of life in Danish, Finnish, Norwegian and Swedish societies.

In relation to the structures and functions of the welfare system itself, these data have yielded through time a highly detailed, statistically solid picture of how the NWS works - particularly at the macro-level of its operations. Today there exists an extensive literature documenting and measuring income maintenance schemes, employment policies, childcare programmes and many other areas of welfare policy and practice. This has been especially true of problem areas and those programs implemented to solve or otherwise to alleviate hardship among the citizenry of the Nordic countries. Reports of all sorts have been compiled describing the effects of various programs of the NWS aimed at providing assistance, care and other benefits to persons designated as being in need or at risk.

Yet, in so far as these research reports touch upon more micro-level operations of welfare systems, their data - more often than not - have been drawn from accounts furnished by welfare states practitioners. These report about how they go about implementing policies, carrying out their duties and the kinds of problems they encounter in their work. It is clear, however, that these and other research reports involving the everyday street-level workings of the welfare system leave much to be desired in terms of methodological rigour and reliability. Though there undoubtedly are many factors accounting for these weaknesses, a handful appear to play a major role in explaining these deficiencies.

Primarily, the day-to-day face-to-face operations of the NWS seldom have been subjected to research efforts corresponding in scope, method and detail to those carried out at the macro-level of state functioning. Even though many studies have touched upon encounters between agency practitioners and their clients, much of the data yielded by these investigations has been of a questionable nature. When analysed in depth, these studies often appear to be based on findings having highly subjective and sketchy character.

In the main, the kinds of data emerging from these micro-level studies have been of two basic sorts. On the one hand, the bulk of findings have been heavily one-sided in that their data have been elicited through questionnaire and interview situations often involving only one set of actors -the welfare state's professional helpers. Furthermore, descriptions of these public encounters, though often quantified in terms of numbers of clients seen and kinds of problems reported by clients, have relied heavily on representations of clients constructed by professionals. Usually when clients have spoken in the research literature, they have done so in ways mediated by professional helpers.

In addition to this bias built in these accounts, much of what is reported by professionals about their meetings with clients has been presented in anecdotal form. More often than not, what is presented about these interactions takes the form of tales told by professional helpers about themselves, their clients and what occurs in their meetings. When voices of clients have been heard in these accounts, their utterances occur most often in reports or notes made about their actions by the professional helper. Clearly, it is this latter group who long have enjoyed a monopoly in deciding what to report about clients. For clients, on the other hand, their main role in much of the literature has been as objects to be represented in fairly standardised forms: they have tended to exist in monologues and anecdotes produced by professionals about them and the lives it is claimed they live.

Until quite recently, professionals' own version of these meetings and their representations of themselves and the clients they have met dominated much of the research literature focused on client-professional interaction. It was not until the 1970s, that the voices of clients representing themselves first began to be heard in ways not mediated by professional helpers. This occurred with the publication of *The Client Speaks: Working Class Impressions of Casework* written by Mayer and Timms. Here, researchers finally provided a platform for clients to represent themselves.

As Kullberg and Cedersund note in their opening chapter, when clients gained voice the narratives they presented about their encounters with social workers contrasted markedly with what long had been presented as research knowledge about interaction at these meetings. It is noteworthy, too, that these accounts forced on the research agenda a long overlooked fact: namely, that descriptions of encounters between clients and social workers when told from either perspective had to be understood as impressionistic, rather than factual, descriptions of the talk-in-interaction at these meetings.

Not many years after the publication of *The Client Speaks* in Great Britain, a somewhat similar study focused in part on client accounts of their meetings with social workers was published in Norway (Guttormsen & Hoigaard 1978). The findings of this book, based on research carried out by a criminologist and psychiatrist at a suburban social welfare agency in Norway, were mirrored not long afterwards in a research report drawing from client descriptions of their experiences with social workers in Sweden (Sunesson 1979). In both these accounts, clients described their meetings with social workers as painful, humiliating and degrading.

These exceptions aside, the research descriptions of client-helper interactions in the NWS remained relatively unchanged until the 1980s: these were still ones privileging the voices and views of professional helpers while simultaneously silencing their clients. What was known about client-staff interactions at welfare agencies was usually that which professional helpers chose to reveal about these meetings. And as noted in the 1980s by Marianne Ranger, a Swedish researcher embarking on her own observational study of a Norwegian social welfare agency, found that social workers overwhelmingly described their own behaviour in these encounters using such positive terms as: "supportive, stimulating, warm, willingness to help . . ." (1993, 23).

The scarcity of studies focused on the micro-level of the welfare state was not fully acknowledged until after the mid-1980s. Beginning then, research devoted to social work as well as the implementation of the public policy by bureaucratic administration posed the question of *how to study* what was actually going on in the "outermost capillaries of the public bureaucracy" (Esping 1984, 72). Among political scientists interested in implementation, however, the question has often revolved around *how* or *to what extent* public policy is actually effectuated in micro-level settings (Lundquist 1987; Rothstein 1994). With the exception of similar questions posed about social workers as policy implementers (Åström 1988), the primary concern among social welfare researchers has been devoted to authentic interaction and conversations between social workers and clients and the implications of these interactions for understanding social work as profession.

In many respects, the situation in social work research up until the late 1970s was remarkably similar to the one long dominant in the field of psychotherapy. Beginning with the writings of Freud and continuing through much of this century, the picture of what took place in meeting between therapists and their clients has been one constructed by the therapist. What was presented in the literature as being heard in the therapy room had as its source the therapist's gaze. To read about the conduct of therapy and its processes was to share the perceptions of psychiatrists and psychologists about what transpired in their meetings with clients. The voice of the professional dominated nearly totally the literature: if clients were heard to speak in these accounts, their voices were processed through the medium of their therapists. Occasionally, autobiographical accounts like that by Beers (1923) presented versions of therapy as experienced by clients. Yet with the few exceptions of such accounts, descriptions and narrative produced by therapists of happenings in the therapy room were the main source of textbooks used to train generations of students in the practice of therapy.

It is not surprising that this mode of describing encounters with clients was mirrored for many decades in the literature of social work. This, after all, is the one area of welfare state operations most often framed to include therapeutic goals. Given the long-standing dominance of psychoanalytic and related models in social work education, it seemed only natural that authors of social work textbooks framed their meetings with clients within the ruling paradigm of the therapeutic profession social workers were supposed to emulate. As a result, generations of social work students were educated to conduct and to report on their practice in accordance with the ways in which textbooks represented the actions and motives of both professional helpers and their clients. Typically, textbook accounts of talk-in-interaction between social workers and clients described these processes as seen and interpreted by social work professionals. These focused especially on the authors' own descriptions of what clients said and did as well as their own actions. Thus, for a great part of social work's history, client behaviour in these meetings was often described negatively using such terms as immaturity, resistance and related psychoanalytic framings. Not surprisingly, the social work textbook accounts focused on the negative aspects and other deficiencies of the client "other" in face-to-face encounters often served as a neat contrast defining the social worker's maturity, tact, and insights.

As Kullberg and Cedersund describe in their opening chapter, these earlier modes of research have been replaced by new ways of conducting investigations at the street-level of the NWS in the course of the past two decades. A key factor in this shift has been the multidisciplinary focus on studying talk-in-interaction as it occurs in meetings between social workers and clients. Beginning in the 1960s with the pioneering work of the sociologist Don Zimmerman on interaction at public assistance agencies in the US (1966), the movement away from impressionistic and univocal representations of social worker-client interaction has gained momentum - especially in the 1980s and 1990s. These developments, which may be understood in the main as the turn to studying authentic conversations, were often cumulative efforts involving researchers from a number of fields including social work as well as sociology, anthropology and linguistics.

What united these investigators coming from diverse disciplines was a single shared perspective. Rather than relying on accounts of client-helper interactions based on perceptions and impressions authored by the latter, these researchers increasingly took as their focus naturally occurring encounters between those seeking help from the welfare services and those charged with providing such assistance. This new perspective aimed at collecting data through direct observations as well as audio- and videotaped recordings of helper-client conversations at diverse sites in the welfare system. For researchers focusing on authentic conversation, the main goal became one of seeking to capture in the greatest detail possible the structures and dynamics of these encounters.

Seen in relation to the history of earlier research on the NWS, these shifts were, in many ways, revolutionary. If one employs Thomas Kuhn's seminal work about changes in science, these new approaches broke with the methodological traditions of "normal" science and its rules of "normal" research on the micro-level operations of welfare agencies. Once interactions between clients and social workers began to be seen and their voices heard in authentic conversations, many discrepancies appeared in prevailing understandings of welfare state functioning. When these newer research accounts were compared to established accounts of and theories about social service delivery systems, a number of contradictions appeared. This happened not only in relation to the welfare states of Nordic countries, but in other welfare systems as well.

Obviously, it is premature at this early stage to claim that these developments have led to a new paradigm replacing the old and that a revolution in the science of the Nordic welfare states has occurred. Nonetheless, there are many signs indicating that older and established pictures of the micro-level operations of welfare systems are seriously flawed. As we shall see in the following chapters, what emerges from these new approaches to helper-client interaction is considerably more complex and contradictory than earlier accounts of what happens when those seeking help meet the welfare state's professional helpers. Clearly, these new accounts show that passive, flawed and otherwise deficient clients are relics of the past. In their stead, we find persons actively constructing meaning and solving problems while working together with welfare state professionals. This is extremely well documented in the material presented by Vehviläinen and Olesen from their respective studies, in Finland and Denmark, of counsellors interacting with persons who are unemployed or in labour market training programs. Similarly, rather than the omniscient professional helpers portrayed in textbooks, we find persons pondering often crucial decisions such as those described in touching detail by Vagli. In looking at these child protection workers in Norway, she found social workers whose talk about child welfare decisions is clouded by many fears and doubts. As all contributors to this book have found at their respective research sites, detailed examinations of authentic conversations reveal that the street-level landscape of the welfare state is a complex mosaic filled with struggles and conflicts of many sorts as well as uncertainties and contradictions.

It would be a major mistake, we believe, to see the emergence of these new sets of knowledge about the NWS solely as the work of enlightened research pioneers. Certainly, much of the work on authentic situations done by those contributing to this book and their precursors is highly original and empirically solid. However, to over emphasise these qualities is to skirt dangerously near to the "great scientist" model of change Kuhn so effectively challenged in *The Structure of Scientific Revolutions*. If we are to do justice both to his theory and the work of those involved in the shift to authenticity, it is necessary to look at these developments in terms of the intellectual history of the late 20th century.

Undoubtedly, many transformations in the conduct of micro-level research of the NWS may be linked - as Kuhn would have it - to the many anomalies in time-honoured theories of social welfare brought to our attention by this new wave of investigators of face-to-face interaction and authentic conversations. In the following pages, Forsberg together with Jokinen, Juhila and Suoninen in Finland as well as by Hydén in Sweden make clear that textbook portrayal of the professional helper working smoothly to help clients deal effectively with their various problems is greatly flawed. Instead of this stereotypic figure smoothly handling equally stereotypic textbook clients, what actually take place in face-to-face meetings are processes involving many conflicts and contradictions. These are particularly well described in Arminen and Leppo's description of the clash between two cultures in treatment centre for substance abusers as well as in Rostila's discussion of the constant tension between professional and bureaucratic orientations impacting on social worker - client talk. Similarly, Forsberg's description of the practice of child protection at different sites in the Finnish welfare system provides a richly detailed account of conflicts and other problematic issues involving client work. Like the other contributors to this volume, these researchers show in their studies of interaction how face-to-face meetings between helpers and clients are always ripe with potentials for doing good as well as serious harm to all conversational participants.

It can be claimed that the accounts presented here as well as those produced elsewhere by researchers employing similar methods reflect not only changed research strategies, but also certain intellectual developments of recent decades. The findings presented here, like those found in similarly framed accounts of other areas of contemporary society, may also be seen as a product of a dramatically changed context stemming from a series of interrelated developments in late 20th century history. Central to this intellectual climate has been a series of developments described with a range of terms. Here, we have chosen to refer to them as post-structuralism, social constructionism and a move toward defining practice as that which can be observed in conversations occurring when physicians, therapists and other professionals encounter persons seeking help.

Perhaps one key factor influencing the turn to authenticity in research on welfare services has been the influence during recent decades of post-structural and post-colonial theories on the social and behavioural sciences.

In certain respects, the manner in which welfare state clients traditionally have been defined and represented in the literature parallel how non-western "others" long served as the representational mainstay of dominant discourse of the West. As Leslie Margolin (1997) has argued, silenced clients represented by social workers have had a lengthy history as a central artefact of the profession, its practice and its texts. As objects of the social worker's privileged perception, what Foucault (1975) described as *the gaze* clients were without voice and existed only as essentialised objects to be defined, dissected and discussed by social work professionals and textbook authors. Margolin argues that this silencing of one actor in the client-social worker dyad and the privileging of the voice of the other made it possible for generations of social workers to mask many of their assumptions and claims to power. Moreover, this was extremely effective because it was often accomplished in a benign appearing way, or as Margolin puts it, "under the cover of kindness".

As claimed by many post-structural and post-colonial thinkers from Foucault to Spivak (1988), the authority of the expert depends much on keeping the other silent. If, however, the other gains voice and thus the power to represent herself/himself, this then becomes a serious threat to the power and legitimacy of those who previously enjoyed a monopoly of voice and representation. No longer can they as self-proclaimed experts make unchallenged interventions into the lives of these others - whether these be clients, colonised peoples abroad and at home, women and children. Once this happens, those ideological edifices Foucault called "regimes of truth" can begin to crumble. Time-honoured knowledge about "others" then is often shown to little more than a collection of stereotypes serving the self-image of the professional as well as self-fulfilling prophecies of many sorts and other prejudices masked as scientific truths.

Once both sets of actors in two person interactions - rather than one - start to represent themselves, a different kind of knowledge about the two and their relationship begins to be generated. When previously muted and passive objectified persons begin to voice their concerns and become acting subjects capable of representing themselves and their interests, their uniqueness and variation come to the fore and long-standing essentialist views of them as members of a homogenised group lose much of their validity. Transformations of this sort - especially those involving women and colonised peoples - have punctuated much of the latter half of the 20th century. Thus when positioned in terms of recent history, the turn by welfare state researchers to authentic conversations involving the voices of all actors in naturally occurring encounters is not an altogether unrelated development.

These changes, too, may be linked with what can be thought of as the social constructionistic turn in the social sciences. This, too, has been a recent and fundamental transformation moving the human sciences away from long-standing understandings where persons were often constructed and positioned as rather passive objects rigidly embedded in and programmed by unyielding social constellations. This view, characterised as the "over-socialized conception" of human beings (Wrong 1961), had little to say about human imagination and creativity. On the contrary, it tended to emphasise that society's members were programmed like robots to react in set patterns to various stimuli. In opposing this view, advocates of social constructionist views seemed to argue that the proper human metaphor was that of the pilot, rather than the robot. Their view of social life was one privileging human subjects actively involved, like pilots navigating through life, in using their creative imaginations to make choices and create differing realities. The constructionist paradigm, developing concomitantly in philosophy, linguistics, psychology and sociology, made some of its most substantial inroads in psychotherapy. Rejecting constructions of therapy as something done by active therapists to rather passive clients or interventions made by experts into the lives of persons more acted upon than acting, constructionist thinkers advanced alternative notions. Prominent among these was the view that the therapeutic encounter is basically a process of meaning construction involving both parties in the talk-at-work taking place in the therapy room. Therapy, therefore, become no longer something to be defined by therapists alone. Instead, it was something talked into existence by persons bearing labels as therapist and client. By situating talk at the core of therapeutic processes, the constructionist perspective directed researchers and practitioners to attend to the ways conversation and its paralinguistic accompaniments worked to created various definitions of reality in the therapy room (Riikonen et al. 1997).

Much of the groundwork for this shift began to be laid in the 1960s as psychotherapists increasingly began to work with whole families rather than individuals. Owing in great part to the influence of ethnographic research where observations of interaction were a keystone of fieldwork, studies of therapy in general and family therapy in particular increasingly based themselves on direct observations of therapist-client interaction. Today, videotapes and audio recordings have supplemented observations and all have become a central part of therapeutic research and training. As this mode gained dominance in therapy, it began to spread to research and practice fields of other helping professions. In social work, where psychotherapy already had a long history as the profession to be emulated, the use of observations of social worker-client encounters in both training and research gained ground-especially after the first ethnographically framed approaches to welfare agencies began to appear (Ranger 1986, 1993; Pithouse 1987; White 1997).

## Observation and Participation: The Ethnographic Approach

Perhaps the first published observational account of authentic conversations between social workers and clients in the NWS was presented in the early 1980s by Marianne Ranger, a Swedish social worker and researcher. In preparing for her study of a municipal social welfare office in Norway, Ranger received training in naturalistic observational techniques developed by the cultural anthropologist Jules Henry in his pioneering studies of families, schools, mental hospitals and old people's homes in the US (1963, 1971). Ranger's point of departure - original at that time - was that social work was not what social workers reported that they did with their clients. Instead, social work was that which could be observed in the conversations naturally taking place between social worker and clients. In keeping with this view, the subtitle Ranger chose for her study, first published in 1986 and revised in 1993, was "client conversations at a social work agency".

Beginning with Ranger and continuing on through research carried out in England by Pithouse (1987) and White (1997) as well as by a number of this book's contributors (Vagli, Forsberg, Arminen and Leppo), ethnographic students of the welfare state have joined the systems they wish to study. In their roles as field workers, researchers taking this approach have been required to take the classic position of anthropologists who are extremely curious, but woefully ignorant, outsiders interested in learning about how group members structure, organise and make meaningful their relations to one another. In this and related ways, as we shall see, ethnographic researchers try to get as close as possible to the activities - especially those involving talk - of the groups they wish to learn from.

The term ethnography, meaning literately writing about a people, captures succinctly the main thrust of this way of learning from a group about its constructions of the world. Like other ethnographic writings, such accounts of the welfare state draw from the field worker's day-to-day contacts and observations of the helpers and service seekers constituting the groups whose lifeways are being explored. Listening here is just important as observing since all field workers naturally become audiences for the narratives group members tell about their lives, troubles, joys and sorrows. Indeed, the ethnographic investigator of the welfare state seldom hears a practitioner or client say that "my identity is such and such". Instead, the identities persons construct for themselves occur in talk-in-interaction - often in storied or narrative forms. As Hydén points out in his chapter on identity construction in welfare contexts, the communicative work carried out in the institutional settings of the welfare state often serves both to create and reinforce the narrative and other identities of the actors meeting in these settings.

As illustrated impressionistic detail in Vagli's chapter describing talk in a Norwegian child protection agency and in Arminen and Leppo's account of the interaction at a treatment centre in Finland, an underlying principle of ethnographic listening is that the ideas, beliefs and practices of a culture borne by any group can be understood as "speaking itself" in the tales told by its members. Though what is recorded by the field worker listening to and observing scenes from welfare state settings is clearly influenced by her/his own selective perception, prejudices and other subjective factors, this often may be offset by the kinds of deep knowledge provided by the ethnographic approach. This involves especially the tacit knowledge shared by those persons with whom the field worker has come to know through long-term contact. It can be argued with some justification, of course, that information yielded by such research - with its subjectivity and diminished methodological rigor heavily influenced by the selective perceptions of the ethnographer - can never measure up to the calibre of data gathered with the help of video cameras and tape recorders. That being said, however, a strong case can be made - as illustrated by this book's contributions - for the fullness and richness of detail these approaches can yield. Most of these contributors, it can be claimed, have ethnographic techniques, both explicitly and implicitly, in getting close to the people they have studied.

This is especially so when their approaches resemble what Malinowski first termed "native" ethnography in his preface to *Facing Mount Kenya: The Tribal Life of the Gikuyu* (1938). This book, written by his student Jomo Kenyatta, exemplified for Malinowski the kinds of knowledge produced when "natives" trained in anthropological methods returned to study the groups claiming them as members. In the following pages, among the "natives" returning to study former work sites are Sanna Vehviläinen, a former vocational counsellor in Finland, and Christian Kullberg, who formerly worked as a social worker at Swedish welfare agencies. Much like Ranger, who also returned to study the social services once employing her, these contributors appear to add an experiential dimension to their accounts of listening to the welfare state.

It can also be claimed that what may be framed broadly as ethnographic approach influences contributions to this book sharing conversation analysis as their explicit methodological point of departure. This is perhaps best exemplified in the reports made by Olesen, Rostila, Jokinen, Juhila and Suoninen. These and other researchers have been required by their research to be in close and lengthy contact with welfare personnel and clients they have studied with the help of conversation analysis. Consequently, even though their primary research interests have been elsewhere, they have become knowledgeable about the larger social contexts of the conversations they analyse. In being so positioned, these researchers like others reporting here have followed in the footsteps of Erving Goffman, perhaps the pre-eminent investigator of talk-in-interaction. As Goffman explains about what often happens to those taking this approach to health and social institutions in his preface to *Asylums* (1959), surely the classic ethnographic study of life in a key institution of modern society:

> It . . . is my belief that any group of persons - prisoners, primitives, pilots, or patients - develop a life of their own that becomes meaningful, reasonable, and normal once you get close to it, and that a good way to learn about any of these worlds is to submit oneself in the company of the members to the daily round of petty contingencies to which they are subject.

## Conversation and Discourse Analyses of the NWS

As Kullberg and Cedersund point out in their overview of interactional studies of the social welfare in the NWS, the one method clearly influencing much of this work in recent decades has been that of conversation analysis. Beginning at the University of California in the 1960s, this methodological approach has had a major impact on many fields. Conversational analysis, or CA, takes as its point of departure ordinary conversations and the ways these are organised. As Psathas (1995) notes, the CA approach alerts us to the fact that all conversations, or talk-in-action as he puts it, are meaningful and possesses a natural and routinised order that researchers can discover and analyse.

In the first instance, this entails investigating the mechanisms underlying and maintaining this order. As Heritage notes, the research objective of such investigations "is to describe the procedures by which speakers produce their own behaviour and understand and deal with the behaviour of others" (1988, 128). Most importantly, this is to be accomplished without preconceived categories and classifications. Rather than ordering data to fit theoretical schemes, investigators using CA take an inductive approach and conduct a search for patterns to be found in naturally occurring conversations. This is well illustrated in the accounts in the following pages provided by Jokinen, Juhila, Sunonin, Olesen, Vehviläinen, Arminen, and Leppo. As exemplified in Rostila's concluding chapter, such searches often focus on sequences of turn takings in conversation as well as paralinguistic features of the conversationalists' actions.

Pioneers in CA research were much inspired by ethnographic field work and collected data through observations of talk in various settings (Goffman 1963; Garfinkel 1967). As tape-recording instruments become smaller, lighter and more portable, it became much easier to carry out analyses of talk-in-interaction: conversations could be easily stored and made alive again when needed by investigators interested in monitoring in detail the flow and minutiae of interaction. This, in turn, led to a greater research sensitivity to "what happens" in conversation. Tapes allowed investigators to scrutinise the flow of talk in small segments and to identify what participants did in their respective talking turns in a chain of turns. In this way, researchers could begin to discern major patterns in conversational activities. They could show, for example, how some first speaker, by uttering his/her turn of talk, creates a relevant context for the next speaker. This speaker than does something as a response to the previous turn of talk and her/his turn may be interpreted as a response to the previous turn as well as her/his understanding and analysis of it. In the third turn the first speaker is in a position, by her/his response, to affirm, modify or even correct the understanding of the second speaker about what the first speaker had meant by his/her turn.

Analyses of these sequences and other features of talk-in-interaction demonstrate a claim fundamental to the CA approach: namely, that every turn as well as every other action in conversation both *shapes* and is *shaped* by context. This double contextualisation, as noted by Garfinkel (1967) and Heritage (1984), is of particular importance when looking at talk in institutional settings. This means that people in conversation are actively involved in creating institutions. As Heritage (1984, 290) puts it: "within these local sequences of talk, and only there, that . . .institutions are ultimately and accountably talked into being". In this sense, all institutional settings - not just those of the NWS examined in the following chapters - may be understood as contexts created through conversations between and among professional staff and their clients.

CA in a very real sense is a set of methods for studying *methods* used by human beings in constructing institutional as well as other kinds of realities. By employing the transcription systems commonly used in CA for describing utterances in talk-in-interaction in various institutional settings, it then becomes possible to see how things get done differently in this or that particular context. Thus, a comparison of Vehviläinen's account of how troubles talking by clients was dealt with by counsellors in Finland with the findings drawn from Olesen's study of counsellor-unemployed interaction in Denmark reveal difference in the methods used to get things done in these settings. When this comparison, in turn, is related to the kinds of talk-in-interaction among social workers and clients in Finland described by Rostila, this further shows how practitioners using different methods in talk succeed or fail in getting different institutional tasks done. As evidenced in contributions made by others using CA approaches, once data of these sorts have been gathered, one can start to define in a strict sense the characteristics involved in the creation-through-talk of various institutions.

As earlier noted, there is considerable overlap involving the use of ethnographic and conversational analytic approaches to talk at various sites in the welfare system. In this book, for example, it is extremely difficult to characterise one or another chapter as purely CA or purely ethnographic in terms of methods through which data have been collected. In many respects, much the same can be said of a third approach, that of discourse analysis, used to study language in various settings. Though none of the contributors to this book characterise their research as purely discourse analytic, certain of the key ideas and assumptions central to this approach run through many of the descriptions and analyses they present.

Discourse analysis, broadly defined, consists of methods for examining the ways talk and texts construct the world we carry in our heads. Those who employ the variety of approaches comprising these methods often differ in their disciplinary backgrounds and perspectives, but all share an interest in examining the role of spoken and written language in the production of the subjects, objects and experiences making up our socially created reality. With its multidisciplinary roots in philosophy, cultural anthropology, semantics, sociology, psychology and other approaches, discourse analysis - or DA - is viewed by many as one of the broadest but most poorly defined fields focused on how language constructs and orders much of our lives (Schiffrin 1994, 5; Tannen 1989, 8; Stubbs 1983, 12).

In the first presentation of discourse analysis to a professional audience by the linguist Harris (1951), the field was narrowly defined as a set of methods for examining relationships between units in language - above the level of the sentence - without reference to speakers, context and meaning. Today, however, few hold such a restrictive view and broadly apply the term discourse to cover conversation analysis, ethnographies of communication and other approaches to language (see, for example, Schiffrin 1994). If discourses, loosely defined, are sets of terms and categories both constructing and positioning particular events, objects and actors in relation to one another, it is clear that many of this book's contributors - like students of language in social settings everywhere - are analysing discursive processes.

Some of the following chapters, however, take a more clearly defined discursive analytic approach then others. Thus by focusing on social welfare agencies in Sweden, Hydén makes visible certain of the key processes through which language at welfare agencies construct senses of self and identities for both social workers and their clients. Similarly, Forsberg identifies certain discursive practices - or ways of acting and talking about children - representing different ways the child may be constructed by professionals to support or negate certain versions of happenings. Writing about talk in similar settings in Norway, Vagli's analysis of the discursive practices occupying a central place in the everyday operations of a child welfare agency suggests how these ways of talking function to provide moral justification for actions taken by these professional helpers. For Kullberg and Cedersund, too, discursive practices in social work agencies play an important role in producing and sustaining distinctive constructions of client identity - both along moral as well as gender-related lines. Even though the main thrust of Arminen and Leppo's chapter is conversation analytic, they also show how competing discourses involving substance use and abuse are an ever present feature of the contacts between bearers of staff and inmate culture in a treatment institution. Somewhat similarly, the conversation analyses at the centre of Vehvilianen and Olesen's accounts of counselling are also supplemented with discursive analytic findings. In Vehvilianen's case, this involves her identification of distinctive ways of talking and acting among counsellors dealing with trouble discourses produced by clients. In Olesen's chapter, too, he makes visible a number of ways in which counsellors manufacture particular versions of reality and how some of their clients, in turn, react to these constructions with their own ways of talking into existence other versions of social reality.

As the findings yielded by ethnographic, conversation and discourse analytic approaches presented here show, the actual delivery of services in the welfare state often do not coincide with the official service delivery goals of various institutions. Portions of Olesen's account of client experiences of their treatment in the Danish employment system of 1990s are strongly reminiscent of accounts first presented by welfare clients in the British welfare state of the 1970s described by Mayer and Timms (1979). In coming full circle, these similarities in client discourse and their contrasts to the ways the same encounters are represented in accounts made by professional helpers point to a still another important feature of discourse analysis. This involves the fact that discourses are at all time competing for hegemony. Thus, one way of evaluating their respective claims is through deconstructive research aimed at identifying the interests served and strategies employed in the construction of different versions of events, persons and processes.

**Conclusion**

Given this understanding of how discourses may be analysed critically, it seems that all contributions to this book may be considered to be deconstructive in one way or another. This, of course, relates to the fact that the research findings presented in the following pages often are at odds with the versions of client-helper interactions long dominating the texts and talk produced by social workers and related welfare state professionals. The accounts presented in this volume by researchers who have listened to and observed talk-in-interaction in the NWS obviously qualify as another set of discursive constructions of the actors and events in these situations. In one way or another, all contributors - some more explicitly than others - acknowledge this. Yet, as readers will discover, they include in their chapters transcripts of conversations and/or observations drawn from various sites in the welfare systems.

Though each contributor makes her/his own interpretations of these data, it is in the final instance left up to the readers of this book to create their own discourses about the events, actors and processes they find represented in these transcripts and observations. In one way, this positioning of the reader as a listener to and witness at welfare state encounters is consistent with the main methodological thrust of ethnographic field work as well as conversation and discourse analyses. This is the claim that meaning and order of all social arrangements can be discovered and analysed by closely examining what transpires when actors in these situations meet and interact. As the following chapters demonstrate, such examinations often can be most directly accomplished by simply listening to, observing and recording the talk-in-interaction comprising the centrepieces of these encounters.

## Bibliography

Beck, U. and Ritter, M. (1992) *Risk Society*. London: Sage.
Beck, U., Giddens, A. and Lash, S. (eds.) (1994) *Reflexive Modernization*. Cambridge: Polity Press.
Beers, C. (1923) *Mind That Found Itself: An Autobiography*. Garden City, New York: Doubleday.
Bergqvist, C. (1990) Myten om den universiella svenska välfärdsstaten. *Statsvetenskaplig tidskrift* (3), 223-233.
Briggs, C. (1986) *Learning How to Ask*. Cambridge: Cambridge University Press.
Edlebalk, Per Gunnar, Ståhlberg, Ann-Charlotte and Wadensjö, Eskil (1998) *Socialförsäkringarna. Ett samhällsekonomiskt perspektiv.* Stockholm: SNS Förlag.
Eriksen, E. and Loftager, J. (eds.) (1996) *The Rationality of the Welfare State.* Oslo: Scandinavian Universities Press.
Esping, Hans (1984) Göra individuellt förnuft av de allmänna reglerna, uppgift för gräsrotsbyråkrat. *Tiden* (2), 72-78.
Foucault, M. (1975) *The Birth of the Clinic: An Archaeology of Medical Perception*. New York: Random House.
Garfinkel, H. (1967) *Studies in Ethnomethodology*. Inglewood Cliffs: Prentice Hall.
Geertz, C. (1972) Deep Play: Notes on the Balinese Cockfight, *Daedalus* (101), 1-37.
Goffman, E. (1959) *Asylums*. New York: Doubleday-Anchor.
Goffman, E. (1963) *Behavior in Public Places*. New York: Free Press.
Goffman, E. (1974) *Frame Analysis*. New York: Harper and Row.
Guttormsen, G. and Hoigaard, C. (1978) *Fattigdom i en velstandskommune.* Oslo: Universitetsforlaget.
Harris, Z. (1952) Discourse Analysis, *Language* 28:1-30.
Henry, J. (1958) Naturalistic Observation of Family Cultures, unpublished paper presented at the 1958 Symposium on Naturalistic Observation, American Anthropological Association Annual Meeting, Washington, D.C.
Henry, J. (1963) *Culture Against Man.* New York: Random House.
Henry, J. (1971) *Pathways to Madness.* New York: Random House.
Heritage, J. (1984) *Garfinkel and Ethnomethodology*. Cambridge: Polity Press.
Heritage, J. (1988) Explanations as accounts: A Conversation Analytic Perspective. In Antaki, C. (ed.) *Analysing Everyday Explanation: A Casebook of Method.* London:Sage.
Hernes, H. (1987) *Welfare State and Woman Power*. Oslo: Norwegian University Press.

Huntford, R. (1971) *The New Totalitarians*. London: Allen Lane-Penguin.
Kenyatta, J. (1938) *Facing Mount Kenya: The Tribal Life of the Gikuyu*. London: Secker & Warburg.
Lipsky, M. (1980) *Street-Level Bureaucracy*. London: Sage.
Lundquist, Lennart (1987) *Implementation Steering. An Actor-Structure Approach*. Lund: Studentlitteratur.
Margolin, L. (1997) *Under the Cover of Kindness: The Invention of Social Work*. Charlottesville: University of Virginia Press.
Marklund, Staffan and Svallfors, Stefan (1986) Välfärd efter prestation - om arbetstvång inom socialförsäkringen. *Nordisk sosialt arbeid* (4), 6, 17-31.
Mayer, J. and Timms, N. (1979) *The Client Speaks: Working Class Impressions of Casework*. New York: Atherton Press.
Pithouse, A. (1987) *Social Work: The Social Organisation of an Invisible Trade*. Aldershot: Gower.
Prottas, J. (1979) *People-processing: the Street-Level Bureaucrat in Public Services Bureaucracies*. Boston: Lexington.
Psathas, G. (1995) *Conversation Analysis. The Study of Talk-in-Interaction*. London: Sage.
Ranger, M. (1986) *'Er det bare meg som roter sånn?'Klientsamtaler på et sosialkontor*. Oslo: Universitetetsforlaget.
Ranger, M. (1993) *'Er det bare meg som roter sånn?' Klientsamtaler på et sosialkontor*. (2nd edition). Oslo: Universitetetsforlaget.
Riikonen, E., Smith, G., Gergen, K., and McNamee, S. (1997) *Re-imagining Therapy*. London: Sage.
Rothstein, Bo (1994) *Vad bör staten göra? Om välfärdsstatens moraliska och politiska logik*. Stockholm: SNS Förlag.
Satyamurti, C. (1980) Discomfort and defence in learning to be a helping professional, paper presented at annual meeting of the International Association of Schools of Social Work, Sussex University, England.
Schiffrin, D. (1994) *Approaches to Discourse*. Oxford: Blackwells.
Spivak, G. (1988) *In Other Worlds*. London: Routledge.
Stjernø, Steinar (1995) *Mellom kirke og kapital*. Oslo: Universitetsforlaget.
Stubbs, M. (1983) *Discourse Analysis*. Chicago: University of Chicago Press.
Sunneson, S. (1979) *Sosialt arbete i forandring*. Stockholm: Methodybyrå.
Svallfors, S. and Taylor-Gooby, P. (eds.) (1999) *The End of the Welfare State? Responses to State Retrenchment*. London: Routledge.
Tannen, D. (1989) *Talking Voices: Repetition, Dialogue and Imagery in Conversational Discourse*. Cambridge: Cambridge University Press.
White, S. (1997) *Performing Social Work: An Ethnographic Study of Talk and Text in a Metropolitan Social Services Department*. Unpublished PhD dissertation. University of Salford.
Wrong, D. (1961) The Oversocialized Conception of Man in Modern Sociology. *American Sociological Review* (26) 2, 183-193.
Zimmerman, D. (1966) *People Work and Paper Work. A Study of a Public Assistance Agency*. Unpublished Ph. D. Dissertation, Department of Sociology, University of California at Los Angeles.
Åström, Karsten (1988) *Socialtjänstlagstiftningen i politik och förvaltning. En studie av parallella normbildningsprocesser*. Lund: Lund University Press (Dissertation).

# Part I
# Authentic Conversation and the Construction of Meaning in the Microlandscapes of Interaction in the Welfare State

In the following two chapters, five authors (two from Sweden and three from Finland) attempt to provide us with pictures and analyses from some of the multitudes of face-to-face encounters where the Nordic Welfare State's professional helpers meet the users of its services. These chapters, however, make no claims to be definitive answers to questions about the role and functions of these welfare systems.

Rather, the prime goal shared by these authors is of a much more exploratory and expository nature. By examining various features of the topography of the microlandscapes of interaction at social welfare agencies, probation offices and family therapy clinics, their chapters provide a set of lucid summations of what may be going on at these sites. In moving behind the assumptions and ideals of the welfare state, they show in detail that central to the ways in which welfare services are conducted are interpersonal negotiations between street-level bureaucrats and their clients about meaning, morality, and gender. In examining the conversational realities of the everyday operations at these sites, these five authors add their bit to the development of an empirically-based, reflective approach to theory and practice of the Nordic welfare state.

# 1 Images of Encounters in Social Work - with a Focus on Social Interaction, Morality and Gender

CHRISTIAN KULLBERG AND ELISABET CEDERSUND

## Introduction: The Encounter Between Social Workers and Clients from a Multistrategic Approach

This chapter is written to report the results of research conducted in Nordic countries for the past decade on the encounter between social workers and clients within social services. The focus of the report will be upon research studying authentic conversations between social workers and clients.[1] In our opinion, research that uses data from authentic situations is a highly significant contribution to the predominant methods (interview or survey studies). However, those methods which break with the accepted repertoire, have until recent years been a relatively underestimated means of gaining knowledge about the work performed within society's welfare institutions and the encounters that take place between society's street-level bureaucrats and citizens/clients.[2] There are as yet relatively few studies of social work based upon data from the interactional level that use, for instance, ethnographic or conversation analytic methods to process the production of meaning that the daily work entails.[3] Encounters between clients and social workers are influenced by a number of different factors. Hydén (1996a, 181) claims that it is reasonable to distinguish the following types of influential factors: *political frameworks and prerequisites, norms and guidelines, organisational prerequisites, models for case management, the professional collective* and *factors related to the individual*. Marklund, Nordenstam & Penton (1984, 12ff) present a model of the encounter that contains similar concepts: *social conditions, prevailing ideology, subculture* and *living situation*. If one summarises the elements the authors present, it appears that the factors they mention can be sorted into the following main categories: *background factors, contextual factors* and the *interaction*.

Regardless of which basis of division is chosen to define the conditions of the interaction between social workers and clients, it is easy to see that many different types of research can contribute to understanding of that which takes place in the encounter. We divide the various approaches into three main categories.

A first type of research approach entails the study of how various cases can be categorised based upon quantitative data obtained through register studies or interviews on an overarching structural or cultural level. This premise may involve, for instance, the types of *services rendered* (see Stjernø 1982; Hydén 1993a), or the *case types* (see Bernler & Johnsson 1993; Kullberg 1994) that occur. Research of this kind may also concern *social workers' explanations* (see Olsson 1993) or *general beliefs* about social welfare (see Berglind & Puide 1976; Halleröd 1994). Using comprehensive survey studies, the researcher can also study the social worker's guiding principles when making decisions related to social welfare (see Gustavsson, Hydén & Salonen 1990; Hydén, Kyhle Westermark & Stenberg 1995; Hydén 1996a) or the implementation in practice of the norms and values that laws and other regulations prescribe (see Åström 1988).

A second research approach involves using interview data to analyse *preconceived notions about* or *experiences and perceptions* of social work and the social problems dealt with by social workers and their clients (see Mayer & Timms 1970; Kempe 1976; Puide 1985; Nilsson 1989; Gunnarsson 1993).

Finally, a third approach is oriented towards analysing the *specific conditions*, or *frameworks*, within which the work is done (see Pithouse 1987; Arnstberg 1989) and to study the *texts and conversations* that are the "media" through which the standard procedures of social work (Hydén 1987) come to expression (see Pithouse 1984; Pithouse 1987; Pithouse & Atkinson 1988; Cedersund 1992a; Fredin 1993; Kullberg 1994, 1996, 1997; Berg Sørensen 1995; Kåhl 1995).

In our synthesis of the research, the main focus lies, as mentioned, on the last of the three approaches; more specifically upon studies of the interaction itself. In our opinion, however, a focus on the interplay between the actors within social welfare institutions should be complemented with data from other levels. Research that gathers data from authentic situations at the interactional level and which seeks to describe and explain a phenomenon as complex as the encounter between the social worker and the client demands a multistrategic approach. The British sociologist Derek Layder (1993) has defined what he calls a research map for the various levels from which such a multistrategic approach may depart. Layder's ambition is to capture "the multifaceted nature of the empirical world" (ibid., 7). He describes the dimensions or levels that he has developed as tools for studying social reality thus:

> The approach to research outlined...is meant to convey the 'textual' or interwoven nature of different levels and dimensions of social reality....These levels and dimensions are in fact, the elements which form the basis of the research map....They are: the self, situated activity, setting, context and history (as a dimension applicable to them all) (1993, 7).

Thus, Layder's point of departure consists of five separate, analytically distinguishable levels: in addition to the self level, contextual level, and situated activity level, the author distinguishes a setting level with its environment-specific or ecological conditions, and a historical level which is possible to link to the other four levels.

This perspective aligns well with our previous statement that the encounter between social workers and clients may be understood as being influenced by the three main factors of background, context and the interaction itself. One of the differences is that Layder's map is more elaborated than our categorisation. Just as previous research about other types of institutional environments (e.g. Fisher & Todd 1986) has shown how social structure is created and recreated via social interactions between professionals and laymen, research maps of the kind formulated by Layder (1993) also need to be used in studies of social work and its thus rather vaguely sketched landscape. Deeper explanations of social work, its settings, actors, action patterns and social structures, are necessary so that a sufficiently detailed picture can be drawn.

The researchers to whom we refer here also begin with the premise that reality must be understood via a multidimensional image; the precept of many of the studies was a combination of descriptive and analytical levels.

## Images of Encounters in Social Work

In our review of studies carried out within the Nordic welfare states, we will use the research map formulated by Layder (1993). Our review is intended to provide an overall image where it proves that a number of themes are described in several of the studies. The largest and most well-developed theme concerns *social interaction* in social welfare institutions and the interpersonal negotiations that take place. The focus here is directed towards studying how the various levels of context, setting and activity are created and recreated in the interaction between them. The data for these studies of interaction is primarily language and communication. Various properties and phenomena in the encounter are analysed, from individual utterances in conversation to more comprehensive and summarising descriptions that show how social welfare issues are processed linguistically.

A second theme discernible in the studies concerns the various *moral aspects* that appear in conversations within social work. Interest here is primarily focused on the concept of self and how the individual self (primarily the client's) is constructed in the discourse.

A third theme has to date been the subject of relatively little research in the Nordic context. This theme concerns *gender aspects* of conversation in social work. The primary focus here is the concept of context, which is to say how the social structure and society as a whole, in both public and private life, are created and recreated in institutional environments of the type studied.

### The Encounter between Social Workers and Clients via Studies of Social Interaction and Structure

Many of the studies to which we refer in this section were directed towards studying social interaction in encounters between social workers and clients. These studies concern conversation in social work and how it is constructed with respect to form and content. The focus is often upon interviews of the type that take place in social services offices. There are studies on interviews from Denmark (e.g. Berg Sørensen 1995), Norway (e.g. Ranger 1986; Oltedal in press), Finland (e.g. Rostila 1994, 1995, 1996; Jokinen & Juhila 1997), and Sweden (e.g. Fredin 1993; Cedersund & Säljö 1994; Kullberg 1994, 1996, 1997; Hydén 1996). However, in some of the studies, consultative and decision meetings at social services offices were also analysed (e.g. Kullberg 1994; Jokinen & Juhila 1997). In most of the studies, both the interviews and meetings concerned applications and assessments related to financial assistance, but other types of social services cases also occur, e.g. conversations concerning substance abuse problems or family/parental difficulties with children and child rearing (e.g. Rostila 1997; Jokinen & Juhila 1996).

As mentioned, there have been few studies of the encounter between social workers and clients from either a Nordic or international perspective. With respect to describing client-oriented social work, the classic study carried out by American sociologist Don H. Zimmerman (1966, 1969) is the precursor to the Nordic works. Zimmerman focuses on case management of financial assistance to individual clients within what is called a public assistance agency in the American context.

One of Zimmerman's aims is to look at the relationship between formal regulations and the activities that occur in this type of bureaucratic organisation (Zimmerman 1966). The study of interaction at the public assistance agency is combined with descriptions of its social structure and the agency as environment. Zimmerman shows the action patterns that occur in the form of "practicalities of bureaucracy". If we compare Zimmerman's study of American society from the 1960s with current research on encounters in social work, certain differences emerge with respect to both the types of data and the way that material is processed and interpreted. While Zimmerman has a number of different data types gathered at the public assistance agency (primarily observations, interviews, recorded client interviews and formal and informal meetings between social services staff), Nordic research has concentrated more upon analysing recorded and transcribed conversations. Certainly, a desire still exists today to connect the social interaction environment and social structure in a way that can be compared to Zimmerman. Contemporary Nordic researchers do, however, have a much sharper focus on the conversational level and have stated why this is of particular interest. Erik Fredin (1993), one of the Swedish researchers within the field, describes the motivation thus:

Conversation with the client seeking assistance from social services at some stage of the process is a condition for the client obtaining assistance; if this condition is not met, social work is made nearly impossible (1993, 1, translated from Swedish).

In expanding on this he adds:

I should thus like to propose that it is not primarily through language that social work takes place but rather "in the language". This does not mean only that one talks in social work, which is after all a trivial matter.... a social reality is constructed - for good and ill - in the linguistic encounter between the social worker and client, which becomes "real" in the instant that the parties embrace one another's symbolic world and act in accordance with it (1993, 2, translated from Swedish).

Fredin points out that the language is a central ingredient and an indispensable tool for achieving the aims of the organisation. Talk in social work supply the researcher with vital information on the encounter between social workers and clients.

Contemporary Nordic studies of conversations within social services have a clearer orientation towards what occurs *in* the conversation than their precursors, an approach that is facilitated by practical conditions that are better today, simply due to the existence of easy to handle technical equipment for audio and videotaping.[4] However, to formulate one's research mandate as the desire to describe the "practicalities of bureaucracy" as Zimmerman (1966) does is still within the domain that contemporary researchers of encounters in social work may regard as their scholarly territory.

The challenge during recent years has thus been to more purely begin with the conversations that occur within social services and to regard these conversations as an important ingredient in the practicalities that exist within social services. The intention here is to find methods for studying the microprocesses that take place, for instance, in the encounter between social workers and clients. It is important here to explore the relationship between the micro and macro levels, between talk and structure as they occur in the practices of social work. In this way, studies of talk constitute a new and powerful tool that can provide greater understanding of the meaning, complexity and dilemma of social work.

## Theoretical and Methodological Approaches in Studies of Encounters in Social Work

The theoretical basis and methods in the studies recounted in this section follow different research traditions, which, although related, are still different in nature. Based upon dialogue theory, Fredin (1993) carries out a detailed interactional analysis. Berg Sørensen (1995) has also taken this perspective in his research; for Sørensen, the methodological approach entailed applying the method to a relatively large body of empirical material. Dialogue-oriented studies are primarily concerned with exploring the dynamics of conversation and the relative strengths of the partners in dialogue. Thus, they are directed at describing and demonstrating the properties of the encounter's *social participant structure* and how the dialogue in the encounter takes shape. Research of this kind encompasses a *topic analysis* of conversations: which topics occur in conversation and how the transition between topics takes place. Another central aspect concerns which *perspective* dominates during the various phases of a conversation. Does what may been called the social services perspective dominate the encounter, or does the individual client's or the layperson's perspective emerge in the conversation? (Fredin 1993, 2-3).

A second line of research on encounters in social work is made within a tradition usually referred to as conversation analysis (Rostila 1997, 117). Here as well, the data consists of recorded and transcribed conversations between social workers and clients. However, conversation analysis is often based upon much more detailed transcriptions and analyses than is the case with dialogue analysis of the kind described above. The studies carried out by the Finnish researcher Ilmari Rostila (1997) exemplify research with a conversation analysis design. Rostila describes the conversation analysis approach and how it is applied within the research tradition he pursues:

In conversation analysis, talk is studied as sequentially organised social action. This means that all talk is analysed as comprising a turn of talk that responds to a previous turn of talk...The study describes in detail how social workers and clients, using different practices or sequential patterns of talk, carry out the institutional tasks and activities and, in doing so, construct the social meaning and character of the encounters. The way the client's identity is presented is highly consequential to his or her interests. Different ways of organising the encounter give the participants different possibilities for presenting their identities (1997, 117).

Conversation analytic studies focus primarily on the activity level (cf. "situated activity" in Layder, 1993). Conversations are viewed as "turns of talk" - but this is coupled here to the connections that exist between activity and various ways of *organising* the encounter. Rostila's work shows how the levels are associated and how the organisation of the encounter contributes to the formation of the client's *identity*.

A third type of study of the encounter between social workers and clients that will be addressed here may be called *discourse analytic* (see van Dijk, 1985). This category includes many different types of studies and can thus not be said to constitute a homogeneous research orientation. Use of the term discourse implies that both conversations and written material that appear and are produced in encounters in the social services office may be used as data and analysed. As examples of research with this orientation may be mentioned studies by the authors of the present chapter (e.g. Cedersund 1992a, 1992b; Kullberg 1994, 1996). Discourse analysis quite often includes a focus on social structure, for instance, the organisation of the work performed by staff within street-level bureaucracies (Lipsky 1980) or how the gender system is reproduced in the interaction (Hirdman 1988, 1990).

## Studies of Topics, Phases and Sequences in Talk

Even though studies of the interaction between social workers and clients are founded to a certain extent upon diverging traditions with respect to theory and method, most emphasise the occurrence of certain observable and similar phenomena. One of these is that encounters between social workers and clients tend to be relatively similar when it comes to the form and general layout of the conversation. This applies both when conversations between social workers and clients are studied in detail and when research on conversations is done from a more overarching perspective. The occurrence of regularity in the layout of the conversations is not surprising, considering that the content and structure of conversations within other institutional contexts also has proven to follow similar, more or less fixed, patterns (see the concept of speech genre in Bakhtin, 1986).

The fundamental patterns described by researchers have focused upon various aspects of conversations between social workers and clients. The following have been the primary objects of study:

1   the *phases* of conversation and how certain overarching *themes* recur in conversation
2   *the topics* touched upon once or more during the conversations between social workers and clients
3   *the perspectives* taken by the partners or their *orientations* during conversation
4   types of *utterances* or different *sequences of utterances* the partners contribute during conversation.

Studies of the aspects mentioned above have been directed at both regularity and variance of the conditions.

## Phases

Analysis of the encounter between professionals and clients in social services contexts shows a fundamental pattern of division into phases of this kind of conversation. Kullberg (1994), who studied conversations during social welfare case management, describes the division into phases using a schematic structure, as shown in Figure 1 below.

---

Greeting phase

Introduction phase

General circumstances phase

Form phase

Calculation and notification of decision phase

Administrative procedures phase

Concluding phase

---

**Figure 1  Phases of Conversation between Social Workers and Clients**
(modified based on Kullberg 1994, 51)

The figure above indicates the different phases of a typical conversation. The phases encompass the various topics to be discussed from the initial conversational phase wherein the social worker and the client exchange greetings and get acquainted, to the last, where the social worker signals that the conversation is over. It should of course be stressed that a phase division of this type, compiled in the form of a schematised model, is a simplification, a kind of ideal type of speech in actual conversation. Nor should the model be interpreted to mean that the various phases always succeed one another in a regular pattern. Returns to an earlier phase are not unusual and certain changes in the order of the phases also occur. Identification of a phase division can provide a picture of the fundamental structure of conversation, although the properties of the individual conversation cannot of necessity be recounted in every detail. Rather, it gives a general idea of how this kind of conversation is laid out.

Other researchers (e.g. Cedersund 1992b; Fredin 1993) who have studied phases in conversations between clients and social workers have found similar regularities with respect to the conversational phase division in broad terms. As previously mentioned, this kind of structuring is similar to the fundamental structure shown in conversations between experts/officials and laymen/citizens in other institutional environments. In these studies, the phases have proved to contain at least the three following basic building blocks: an introductory phase, a phase in which the matter in question is discussed, and a concluding phase (Linell 1990a, 1990b). Thus, this essentially agrees with the recounted conversations within social services, although the phase in which the matter in question is discussed is divided into a number of subphases with more specific content.

Kullberg (1994) compares the phase division that was the result of the empirical study with an ideal procedure for social services cases formulated by Egelund and Halskov (1986). This ideal procedure is presented as including the following phases: 1) description, 2) assessment, 3) planning and 4) follow-up (Egelund & Halskov 1986, 57ff). Kullberg stresses that there are similarities between his own findings and the ideal model to which he refers.

The ideal phase division differs regarding some aspects from Kullberg's empirical study. The difference has to do with the planning phase and the follow-up phase, which occur in the ideal model, but not in the empirical material. In the conversations included in Kullberg' s study, social workers do not discuss goals that should be set with clients, nor how such goals could be achieved. Since the clients in Kullberg's study contacted social services to get temporary economic assistance, a discussion of planning and follow-up were perhaps not considered necessary conversational phases. However, differences of this kind are interesting findings and may be included as grounds for discussion between researchers and practitioners; discussions which may conclude with reflections and thoughts about preferred versus realised working methods. The research on phases in conversations in social work may provide a basis for discussion of whether ideal structures differ in any critical way from the actual work performed in the practice of social work. In this way, our notions or images of social work can be founded upon descriptions of what actually occurs in the encounter between social workers and clients, rather than solely upon our opinions of how the work *should* proceed.

**Topics of Conversation**

While the phase division of conversation between social workers and clients follows relatively uniform patterns, research directed at identifying and describing topic division in conversation has been a considerably more difficult methodological task. To illustrate the point, we can mention here Fredin's (1993) study of twenty-one social worker/client conversations. Upon analysis of these conversations, it appeared that about one hundred topic sequences occurred and that they in turn could be grouped into about thirty topics, of which about half occurred one or more times (113). The following topics and aspects of topics were common: money, work, housing, medical treatment, child care, substance abuse, education, health care, dental care. Fredin also finds that the analysed conversations show a form of topic hierarchy:

> ...the fact that the conversations are essentially about fixing, providing or assisting clients with something. Thus, we may call the client's *problem situation* and how it is defined at that point in time an overarching topic. To fix the client's problem situation entails e.g., financial assistance, help finding a job, housing, child care, education, dental care, etc. (Fredin 1993, 114, translated from Swedish).

Fredin recounts a conversation given the overall designation "economic and psychosocial support measures". Analysis of this conversation shows that it contains the following predominant *main topics*: housing, money, narcotics abuse, work. These main topics take up almost eighty per cent of all responses that occur in the conversation. The main topics can thus be said to constitute a framework for the conversation and to provide a structure for the way in which the conversation is organised. This is also a pattern that is well in line with the analysis of other parts of Fredin's material. In this respect, Fredin depends upon *quantitative* measurements where the number of responses in each topic is counted, but also upon which topics are of great *relevance* for the encounter's direction and causes seen from the perspective of one or both of the speakers (115-116).

**Perspectives and Orientations**

Another theme which may be regarded as a separate analysis unit, but which may nevertheless be related to the analysis of topics and sequences of topics (see below), concerns the issue of *whose perspective* prevails when various topics are discussed.

Fredin (1993) gives examples of how deeper analysis can reveal how one topic may be seen from several different perspectives. In his interpretation of perspective, Fredin approaches the heading we chose for the preceding section - images of encounters in social work:

> The concept of perspective is metaphorical to a certain extent; it conjures up a visual notion of a person who looks at something from a certain point of departure; a point of departure that thus illuminates certain aspects of the topic or point of a conversation from a certain angle or towards a horizon (1993, 144).

In his account, Fredin shows how the perspectives expressed by the participants in a conversation relate to one another and how they successively change during the course of the conversation. He identifies perspectives which gradually converge or diverge, as well as dominating perspectives. In a fourth type of analysis, the concept of *perspective dissonance* is introduced (Fredin 1993, 174-175). One occasion where this occurs and which is analysed in depth is the following excerpt from a conversation between a female social worker and a male client. The excerpt was taken from the main topic, which concerned the client's housing situation.

*Excerpt 1  (From Fredin 1993, 170, translation from Swedish).*

Social worker: Okay so housing is taken care of
Client:          Uh-huh
Social worker: And you do know that to get help with the rent you have to bring in an approved sublease
Client:          But I don't have one I've said that all along [IRRITATED] I haven't been able to get one, you know
Social worker: But you have =
Client:          = What the hell am I supposed to do I have to have some place to live, you know
Social worker: But then you are going to have to arrange THAT if we are going to give you assistance for
Client:          But then then now it's like this I got two thousand and one hundred from the social security office on Friday and then I paid the rent, so now what the hell am I supposed to do huh I can

In the example above, we see that the social worker is trying to conclude the topic of housing - "Okay, so housing is taken care of" - and adds an utterance that contains a message about the conditions for obtaining financial help with the rent: "And you do know that to get help with the rent you have to bring in an approved sublease" However, the client does not accept the conditions stated by the social worker for granting assistance. He dismisses the social worker's argument by objecting to the demand to show a sublease and then adds his own, alternative perspective to the topic of housing: "what the hell am I supposed to do I have to have some place to live, you know...I can't bloody well live on the street if I I get a job now can I" The diverging perspectives in the quoted conversation show how the encounter comes to contain a clear conflict between the parties. The struggle in the conversation ends up between what Fredin (1993) calls an "authority perspective" and an "everyday life perspective" (171). Neither of the parties demonstrate any particular willingness to take the other's perspective. In his analysis of diverging perspectives, Fredin also uses the concept of "voice" (Bakhtin 1986), which other researchers studying conversations in social work have found useful in depicting the parties' different points of departure and how they are expressed in conversation (see Cedersund & Säljö, 1993).

Another aspect related to the issue of perspective is what orientations can be discerned in conversation between social workers and clients. Two Norwegian researchers within social work use this term to describe what occurs in the conversation between social workers and clients. Marianne Ranger (1986) begins with an overarching and holistic analysis of attitudes and fundamental action patterns of social workers towards the clients they encounter. Siv Oltedal (in press) has a somewhat more elaborated analytical approach and allows the concept of orientation to encompass variations in the conversation's *form, content* and *function.*

Ranger's (1986) work is based upon an observation study of thirty-one conversations between caseworkers and clients at a social services office in Oslo. A clear conflict emerges in the study between ideals and reality in social work. Ranger shows that the conversations studied can be divided into two different types of orientations, the *administrative* and the *client-oriented.* The latter can be said to fulfil the ideal for how the work should be performed as taught at universities, while the former has more of the characteristics expected from conversations between laymen and professionals within government agencies in general.

In the administrative-oriented conversations it is characteristic that the caseworker makes a routine categorisation of the problem from an administrative respect without making this clear to the person seeking assistance. The caseworker also asks specific questions or interrogates the client. She/he ignores direct questions from the client and withholds and limits information that could lead to open negotiations about the client's need for social welfare. The caseworker also simplifies and limits assistance without recounting the prerequisites for receiving aid. Finally, she/he declines to gather information beyond that which confirms the administrative categorisation.

The caseworker's orientation influences the conversation so that the working process is simplified; social workers come to stress fulfilment of administrative regulations rather than seeing the clients as acting topics. In addition, conflicts and misunderstandings are common in these conversations and distrust and hostility often arise between the speakers due to the misunderstandings.

Client-oriented conversations are characterised by the caseworker's awareness of her professional role, position of power and her opportunities to influence the client. The caseworker works at a calmer pace, with insight into the client's difficulties, and communicates openly about objective circumstances as well as her own values. This orientation influences conversation so that clients gain better knowledge of the administrative process. The orientation also yields greater understanding between the caseworker and client as well as fewer conflicts and misunderstandings.

The empirical material for Oltedal's study (in press) is made up of seventeen encounters between social workers and clients, studied upon two occasions. The conversations were taped and subsequently analysed. Most of the conversations took place at the social services office. The material includes interviews with the participating clients and social workers. In light of microsociological aspects and the formation of theory on the profession, the author identifies five analytically differentiable orientations: *rights orientation, counselling orientation, research orientation, co-operation orientation* and *general orientation*. The first four of these are addressed in more detail in the study. Oltedal points out variations in form, content and function between the orientations. Among other things, specific topics of conversation appear to be bound with each of the separate orientations. Thus, for instance, the issue of money is associated with rights orientation. When it comes to variations in form between the different orientations, it appears that the professional dominance that usually occurs in conversations between officials and clients is not equally prominent in all orientations. The interview format's questions (from the social worker) and answers (from the client) are most common in the rights orientation, whilst the counselling orientation is characterised more by longer statements from the social worker and short (minimal) responses from the client. There are also differences in function among the orientations. For instance, the function of the rights orientation is that the social worker interprets the client's legal rights to obtain financial assistance, whilst the counselling orientation functions to a greater extent as a means for the social worker to attempt to get the client to take actions that may be to his or her benefit, such as looking for a job or moving to different housing.

## Utterances and Sequences of Utterances

Another aspect connected to perspectives and orientations that was studied during conversations between social workers and clients is the utterances that occur in conversation and how different sequences of utterances influence the direction of the interaction as it proceeds. Such influences have, for instance, been studied when the conversation begins or is "opened" (Rostila 1996) and when certain important topics are discussed (Kullberg 1994). The latter issue will be discussed in the section *Gendering Processes in Social Work*.

The Finnish researcher Ilmari Rostila (1996) studied "mutual alignment" and "non-alignment" - the occurrence or lack of an orientation towards the counterpart in the conversation and his or her perspective and interests - in the encounter between the social worker and the client. The study shows how this can be connected with the sequencing of the conversation. The study (Rostila, 1996) shows that when mutual alignment can be said to occur in the encounter between the social worker and the client, the conversation is often begun by the social worker initiating a topic that concerns the client's need for assistance. Immediately after the greeting phase (see Figure 1 above), the social worker may, when this kind of sequencing occurs, use a question to put the client's living circumstances in focus. This opening of the conversation is done in a way that clarifies the client's need for assistance. When the conversation is characterised by non-alignment, it is instead the client who initiates a topic that concerns his or her need for assistance. In these cases, the social worker demonstrates unwillingness to continue with the initiated topic through a reorientation, which means that another question is put in focus. The way that the conversations are sequenced - for example, if it is the social worker or the client that brings up a particular topic - proves in Rostila's study to also have an effect upon whether the client's need for assistance will be examined during the course of the conversation.

Rostila's findings may be compared with the results from Cedersund's (1992b) study of conversations within Swedish welfare case management. In that study, the occurrence of early conversation related to the client's application for financial assistance and the completion of the form that is the basis of the application (the social welfare form) is interpreted as a manifestation that the social worker is taking the client's petition for financial assistance seriously. In the conversations where form-related topics are addressed only later in the conversation, the procedure can be perceived as a form of delay and postponement strategy emanating from the social worker.

In studies of conversations in Swedish social welfare offices, sequencing of client stories has also been the topic of analysis (Cedersund 1992b; Cedersund & Säljö 1994). A pattern emerges here where the client, often early in the conversation, tells a coherent story about the situation and the problems and difficulties that led to the need for assistance.

A consistent element that emerges during the kind of detailed analysis recounted above is that the official (the social worker) functions as a kind of supervisor or "gatekeeper" (Ericsson & Schultz 1982), controlling which topics are addressed, the order in which they are discussed and when it is time to conclude a topic. This is a type of "orchestrating" (see Dingwall 1980) of the encounter, which is also seen in other kinds of institutional talk.

**Conversations in Social Work as Negotiations**

The encounter between the social worker and client within social welfare institutions may be described as a phase in the transformation of sociopolitical issues to institutionally delimited problem definitions and measures that are the hallmark of modern society (see Blumer 1971; Spector & Kitsuse 1977; Holstein & Miller 1993). In other words, conversations at social services offices are held within a part of society where social problems at the microlevel of society are addressed. Based upon theories of street-level bureaucracies, one can therefore make a somewhat simplified claim that the most important task of social workers, like other street-level bureaucrats, is to categorise the individual's specific circumstances according to the criteria established by the public authority.

According to Lipsky (1980) and Hasenfeld & Steinmetz (1981), however, the street-level bureaucrat or social worker does not have sole influence over the outcome of the case; the citizen or client also has influence. In order to achieve their aims, the street-level bureaucrat and the citizen are always dependent upon one another. The rules prescribed by the public authority do not in fact provide the social worker with any indisputable grounds for decision. Instead the work entails constantly allowing the rationalities that control everyday life and the rules and prescriptions of the authorities to infringe upon one another in order to determine which measures should be taken. The result of this process has no ready answers, but rather depends upon the assessments made by the social worker from case to case. The social worker is constantly engaged in a *negotiation* between the various logics or rationalities based upon the *institutional world* and the understanding of how a responsible person should behave, which is anchored in the *life-world*.

Nordic researchers have paid attention to this element of negotiation encompassed in the encounter between the social worker and the client within the context under discussion. Jokinen & Juhila (1997) propose that the decisions made within social work may be derived from the negotiations that occur among social workers and between social workers and clients. These negotiations fundamentally concern a struggle over how the client and his or her problems shall be understood and categorised (see also the section *Social Work as "Moral Practice"* below). In other words, the negotiations encompass a process in which the client's own interpretations and statements about his or her situation are highly significant.

Fredin (1993) shows (as previously mentioned) that the negotiations that occur in social worker/client conversations vary a great deal. The extent of variation depends, among other things, upon which topics are discussed; there is always a space where definition of the situation at hand is open to negotiation.

According to Linell & Fredin (1995), these negotiations can be of two kinds:

First, we negotiate *outcomes*. In the case of social work, this concerns first and foremost matters like levels and kinds of financial assistance, decisions on therapy and medical or other treatments, future contacts between the parties, and so on. Second, in the process of accomplishing this, there are other kinds of negotiating going on: we negotiate *means* for making progress in the tasks of achieving results. These means, in turn, may be said to fall into two major analytic categories, those concerning social relations and those concerning descriptive and administrative categories used in the interpretation and evaluation of matters talked about (314).

From a conversation analytic perspective, these conversations on outcomes and means to achieve the expected outcomes consist of linguistic negotiations. These linguistic deliberations between social workers and clients are, according to Linell & Fredin (1995), comprised of negotiations on *linguistic categories* and assumptions and *preconceived notions about reality*, and that there is a constant interplay between these levels. The linguistic expression used here is significant for how the words and concepts are interpreted and the definitions affect the language that is used. This relative openness between the levels is also a means of explaining how the client's, or life-world's, logic can gain influence over, or take root in, the logic of the authority figure or system world. The negotiations that occur between social workers and clients thus fundamentally concern a struggle over how the client and his or her problems shall be understood and categorised. A pivotal issue in this process of the production of meaning has to do with the client's moral character and his or her possible rights to social welfare. The next section addresses this issue.

## Social Work as "Moral Practice"

Taking Ervin Goffman (1968, 1973) as one's point of departure, the question of what shall be regarded as a moral issue is given a very broad definition. The moral dimension encompasses the entire frame of reference from which the individual judges him/herself and the ways that others judge him or her. Based upon this, one may claim that the client's encounter with the social worker (like, for that matter, all other interpersonal encounters to one extent or another) contributes quite clearly to constructing the identities of the participants - that is, their self images and social standings - from a moral aspect. Social work and other social programmes involve moral issues from another aspect as well, however. These institutions are moral practitioners of a sort. One of these organisations' primary mandates is to maintain the borders between what is permitted and desirable in society and that which is undesirable (see Beckman 1981). That the very basis, or substance, of many of the encounters taking place within these kinds of institutions is to determine issues of moral character means that the *structure* of conversation in many cases (but far from always) will be based upon one of the interacting parties (the social worker) having greater rights to investigate and question the other's actions (see Kullberg, 1994).

The fact that social welfare assessments encompass a moral dimension is a thesis pursued by many researchers (see Rees 1976, 1978; Pithouse 1987; Pithouse & Atkinson 1988; Midré 1990). Midré asserts that three factors or dimensions have been pivotal for how society's responsibility for those who cannot support themselves has been understood during various periods. These dimensions, which have been emphasised to various extents during different epochs are 1) *the moral dimension*: whether the person in need of assistance *wants* to support himself or herself or not, 2) *the resources dimension*: whether the individual *can* support him or herself or not, 3) *the market dimension*: whether the client *is allowed to* support him or herself on the current labour market. Historically, the three dimensions working together have played a role in the social worker's judgement of the individual seeking assistance. According to the author, clients who are perceived as having the will to support themselves, but who for various reasons (for instance, due to a handicap or other impediments) cannot nor are given the opportunity to work, have been traditionally perceived as the *deserving* needy (Midré 1990, 183). However, those clients who are judged as being unwilling to support themselves, even though they have the resources to do so and have had the opportunity to get a job on the market, have been perceived as *undeserving* needy (Midré 1990, 183).

The social worker's examination of the client's application entails, as previously mentioned, an encounter between two logics or rationalities or interests that are distinct to a certain extent. Here meet the forms of understanding that distinguish the institutional world and the citizen's life-world (Cedersund & Säljö 1993; cf. Habermas 1981). This means that the social welfare process must to a certain extent always encompass an encounter between different moral explanation models. That the client's own explanations are judged as being morally acceptable actions may appear unacceptable from an institutional or authority perspective, and vice versa.

Hydén (1991, 1993b, 1996b) and Kullberg (1994), among others, have based their analyses upon these circumstances. One of the authors' fundamental thoughts is that examination by Swedish social workers of the client's right to financial assistance cannot be made solely based upon existing formal regulations, but rather that diverse aspects of the cause for the client's economic predicament are always evaluated in practice. The latter entails an investigation of the moral arguments that speak for and against the client being granted assistance.

According to Hydén (1991), the social worker examines the social welfare situation based upon two special aspects when determining whether assistance shall be granted. *Legitimacy* is examined in relationship to the rules in effect for social welfare and to the client's *credibility*. The social worker's examination of legitimacy in the social welfare situation means that she or he tries to determine whether the client's economic situation depends or does not depend on circumstances over which he or she has control. An individual who was laid off due to lack of work thus has legitimate grounds for needing social welfare. Conversely, an individual who quit his job does not have the same clearly legitimate grounds. His unemployment is considered self-inflicted. The social worker's examination of the client's credibility entails an attempt to assure herself that the information provided may be considered correct. Verification of pay stubs, rental contracts and other documents function as a means of certifying the client's credibility. Such verifications also function as a means of ensuring legitimacy, since the client's income and expenses determine whether he/she is entitled to social welfare.

Kullberg (1994) builds further upon Hydén's (1991) results and states that the question of whether the client can make a legitimate claim to financial assistance in relationship to existing eligibility rules for social welfare can be more precisely defined (see Figure 2 below).

| Legitimacy | | Credibility |
|---|---|---|
| **Formal aspects** | **Personal-moral aspects** | |
| Actual economic circumstances. | What the client has done and/or is doing to support him/herself. | Whether the information provided by the client is true. |

**Figure 2  Legitimacy and Credibility in the Social Welfare Eligibility Assessment**

According to Kullberg (1994), the social worker must, in addition to the matter of credibility, establish the client's legitimate reasons for needing assistance from two different aspects. The first kind of legitimacy the social worker examines is what is designated as the *formal aspects* of the application, that is, whether the client has sufficient income or whether the client can support him/herself. Among other things, this includes verifying the client's income during the period upon which eligibility for social welfare is based. This is a matter of determining the actual economic circumstances of the case. The second type of legitimacy to be established has to do with whether the client has previously taken or is currently taking adequate measures to avoid the social welfare situation, that is whether the economic problems are self-inflicted or not. In this case, the social worker judges what the client *as a person* has done or not done, is doing or is not doing, to contribute to his or her own support. Kullberg (1994) calls the part of the assessment that concerns what the client is doing to support him/herself the personal-moral aspect of the cause of the social welfare situation. This concerns the perception the social worker has of the client and the perception the client has of him/herself as a person with a legitimate or illegitimate claim for assistance.

Excerpts 2 and 3 below, taken from Hydén (1996b), exemplify how conversations about, or investigations of, job situations may unfold in the encounter between the social worker and the client. The excerpts were taken from the part of the social welfare eligibility assessment that concerns the general circumstances (see the section *Studies of Topics, Phases and Structures*) that must be investigated in order to determine whether social welfare will be granted. The conversation concerns the circumstances around the welfare dependency, which must always be investigated in this type of conversation in addition to the formal aspects (i.e., the client's income in relationship to the established income norm). The later investigation of whether an actual need for assistance exists is seldom determined at the stage of conversation from which the excerpts are taken, but is rather part of the formal assessment constituted by the eligibility calculation itself (see the section *Studies of Topics, Phases and Structures*).

*Excerpt 2  (From Hydén 1996b, 852-853).*

| 1 | S: | Why did you have to leave your last job? |
|---|---|---|
| 2 | C: | I quit |
| 3 | S: | You quit? |
| 4 | C: | Mmm |
| 5 | S: | Yes |
| 6 | C: | Because of my unstable income |
| 7 | S: | Yes |
| 8 | C: | My income varies between five thousand and ten thousand crowns a month |
| 9 | S: | Yes |
| 10 | C: | Because I'm a freelancer and I work on commission |

| 11 | S: | Mmm |
|----|----|-----|
| 12 | C: | Fixing lights and sound recording equipment and things like that |
| 13 | S: | Mmm |
| 14 | C: | Driving cars and fixing things and I can work for a week and then be off for [ ... ] |
| 15 | S: | Uh-huh |
| 16 | C: | Then I work for two days and am off for two months then work a month and be off for two days |
| 17 | S: | Yes [.] |
| 18 | C: | I need a different job that gives me a stable income every month |
| 19 | S: | Mm |
| 20 | C: | 'Cause I've got some things I have to pay for |
| 21 | S: | Yes |
| 22 | C: | In order to survive, and now I never know if I'll earn one thousand crowns or five thousand [ ... ] |
| 23 | S: | Well I think I'm beginning to understand now [cough]. Well, it is like this. If you quit a job voluntarily we are usually very tough we usually [. . .] |
| 24 | S: | Have a benefit free month [. . .] |
| 25 | S: | Since you didn't quit because you didn't like your job |
| 26 | C: | No, absolutely not it was a great job |
| 27 | S: | Mmm |

In the example (excerpt 2), the client meets with understanding from the social worker for the choice he has made:

> The client claims that the job he had was "great" but that his work periods were irregular and his income unstable. Consequently, he had problems supporting himself. In order to stabilise his financial situation, he quit the job with the intention of finding a new one....When the social worker finally sums up her impressions of the client's story, she does so by evaluating it according to the rules for social welfare eligibility....The social worker states the rules and describes the normal procedures in cases in which a client quits of his own accord, and by doing so contributes to defining the moral status of the client. She sums up with an open question, "since you didn't quit because you didn't like your job," and receives a reply in the negative form from the client (Hydén 1996b, 853f).

Thus, the social worker finds the reason that the client quit his job to be acceptable in the given example. In the second example (excerpt 3), however, another client is not met with the same understanding for his actions:

*Excerpt 3 (From Hydén 1996b, 855).*

1  S:  Why are you unemployed when you could get a job?
2  C:  What the hell, I was at this clothing company that paid seven thousand five hundred crowns a month [$1.200]. Do you think I could like a job like that?
3  S:  Well, you have to choose between living on social welfare benefits
4  C:  No=
5  S:  =Two thousand sixty crowns [$450] plus the rent for the apartment
6  C:  There are other jobs I'm looking into so we have to wait and see
7  S:  There is something important and fundamental which you yourself touched upon
8  C:  Yeah
9  S:  It's this about rejecting a job offer 'cause you think seven thousand five hundred crowns is too little [ . . . ]
10  S:  'Cause we can't accept that you turn down job offers or weed out jobs
11  C:  No, but this rejecting, well I didn't turn it down, I went to an interview
12  S:  No, but you're not out looking for certain kinds of jobs
13  C:  Well, I'm going to a new interview today

The example shows that:

The client presents his everyday standards when he tells the social worker that he will not accept a low salary. The social worker responds to this by stating the eligibility rules, but in so doing she criticises the client's moral standards as being illegitimate. The client senses this criticism and immediately attempts to mitigate his position by reframing his rejection of the job as an initial interview and saying that he is going in for another interview the same day....The social worker not only formulates a different moral standard, but she supports her moral standard by an indirect threat: if the client does not accept her moral standards, he will not be eligible for social welfare (Hydén 1996b, 856).

Both excerpts provide significant examples of the joint work performed by the social worker and client when it comes to clarifying whether there are legitimate grounds for economic assistance based upon personal-moral aspects.

The clients in both of the conversations are in relatively similar situations. Both report a more or less active choice to decline jobs that would provide them with income. In other words, this circumstance speaks against either of them being considered entitled to social welfare according to the eligibility assessment. Neither of them has taken adequate measures (jobs they started which they could have kept in order to avoid being in the social welfare situation). Despite this, the conversations develop in different ways. The client in the interaction from which excerpt 3 was taken does not receive the same support. Instead, his view of reality is called into question when the social worker puts forth an alternative interpretation and when she places direct demands for how he must act.

Both conversations clearly show that the social worker's investigation of the matter of the client's possibilities to receive financial assistance contains a moral dimension. As street-level bureaucrats, social workers are involved in attempting to find possible ways to link the public authority's formal rules with the client's specific circumstances (see Prottas 1979; Lipsky 1980; Johansson 1992). As shown, this cannot be done without discussing the client's moral character, that is, whether he/she has acted in a way that fulfils expectations in his or her situation (see Rees 1976, 1978; Pithouse 1987; Pithouse & Atkinson 1988; Midré 1990).

These studies of interaction between social workers and clients may be compared to conclusions from a study of linguistic interaction among social workers at a decision meeting as they discussed the reasons for client problems and determined whether the clients were entitled to assistance in cases that involved petitions for assistance over and above the established norm (see Kullberg 1994, 139 ff). This study shows that social workers in this working form as well are engaged in discussions about the client's moral character and whether applicants can be considered as having taken adequate measures to avoid the social welfare situation. However, the negotiations in these meetings do not take place with the client, but rather between the social workers gathered in a meeting. The results of the study show that those clients who are portrayed in the conversations in the decision committee as being *responsible* for their situations (that is, where it appears in the conversations that the clients did not "wish" to do anything about their problems) were granted social welfare significantly less often than those who were portrayed as victims (conversations where it appears to a greater extent that the clients had no possibility of doing anything about the problems in question themselves).

One explanation for client problems being treated this way may be sought in the circumstance that the task of bringing the client's life-world and institutional frameworks into line with one another places the social worker before a number of conflicting demands or a *dilemma* (Kullberg 1994, 24ff). This dilemma is founded in the (internal) *conflicting objectives* encompassed in the Swedish Social Services Act. In his or her practical work, the caseworker must deal with two conflicting demands: *on the one hand* to take the legal or juridical side of the case into consideration and to attempt to comply with the existing *general* laws, regulations and instructions. On the other hand, the social worker shall also consider the client's needs and the *unique* social conditions that apply in his or her situation.

Since the cases addressed during the decision meetings were applications for assistance over and above the established norm, one can say that the cases where the decision committee denied assistance to the client (and where they mainly talked about the clients as if they were responsible for their situations) represent action that entails holding fast to the general regulations. For the same reason, one can say that the cases where the client was granted assistance (and clients the decision group talked about as victims of circumstance) are cases where the attitude entails taking the client's needs and his/her specific living conditions into account.

Thus, to deny assistance may be regarded as an action that stresses the general institutional principles, while granting assistance may be regarded as an acknowledgement of the importance of taking the client's unique living conditions into consideration. In other words, one could assert that the decision committee's manner of speaking about clients as victims or as being responsible for their own situations quite simply is the social worker's means of choosing paths of action in the dilemmatic situation they must deal with when converging the client's life-world and institutional frameworks.

However, these two perspectives are not completely divergent. There is a common ground for both worlds in the mutual point of departure that the individual is responsible for his/her economic situation (see Hydén 1993c, 1996b). Social work in the modern, industrialised world is based, in other words, upon a practice that may be described as *victim-blaming* (see Ryan 1971). In Kullberg's (1994, 205ff) opinion, this premise in the Swedish Social Services Act and the public consciousness may make it seem understandable that social workers use both a "responsibility model" and a "victim model" to explain the causes of individual economic difficulties. Both explanatory models are natural consequences of social services having been founded upon the assumption that differences in living conditions between different groups or individuals in society shall be ameliorated through assessing and deciding upon assistance to the individual.

## Gendering Processes in Social Work

The last theme that we shall address in our description of encounters in social work has to do with the question of whether and how gender order is reproduced in conversations between social workers and clients.

The order between the sexes, designated the "gender system" by the Swedish researcher Yvonne Hirdman (1988, 1990), may be understood as a more or less routinised, constantly recurring "production of meaning," which is executed by both women and men with reference to differences between the sexes that are so taken for granted that they are perceived and understood as natural (Goffman 1977; West & Zimmerman 1987). The active mechanisms in the maintenance of gender order are a *hierarchisation* and a *segregation* between the men and women.

Established practices and perceptions about the meaning of masculine and feminine exist within all social institutions. Based upon Acker (1991), one can assert that the organisation of all spheres in society (paid employment, family, etc.) are genderised and that there is a need for a systematic theory surrounding the process that creates these conditions.

The question of what happens when sociopolitical frameworks, social legislation and other reforms shall be put into daily practice within the authorities mandated to administer the welfare society (e.g., social services offices, social insurance offices, et al.), and what significance this transformation of public decision has for the upholding or changing of the gender system is a question that has been addressed at a relatively late stage, even from the international perspective (e.g. Todd 1983; West & Zimmerman 1985, 1987; Waitzkin 1991). There is a small but growing number of Nordic studies that problematise the issue of how women and men are treated within these types of institutions, such as the social insurance system (see Bäckström & Eriksson 1989; Bäckström 1994; Hetzler 1994), within the Swedish health care system (see SOU 1996, 133) or within social welfare institutions (e.g. Gunnarsson 1993; Kåhl 1995; Kullberg 1994, 1995).

The issue of gender differences has also been addressed in Nordic research for which authentic data is used to study the encounter between social workers and clients. Kullberg (1994, 1995) has conducted a study of the work of caseworkers in two different areas. One is the caseworker's conduct and conversations with respect to the topics of paid employment and children (family) in encounters with social welfare clients who are single fathers and mothers. The encounters studied are "interviews" at the social services office regarding financial assistance. The second area involves the caseworker's way of presenting arguments and making decisions in decision meetings on cases involving amounts above the norm where the clients are men and women with varying problem pictures. Outcomes from the social worker's encounters with female and male clients show that the conversations proceeded in very different ways depending upon the client's gender, which was reflected in both the conversation's structure and content.

When the topic of paid employment was discussed in conversations with men, social workers took the initiative. The social workers controlled the interaction and a great deal of the conversation was taken up by the social worker's questions, directives and statements about the man's unemployment. All of these speech actions were aimed in different ways at trying to ascertain whether the man had legitimate reasons for being in need of social welfare. They attempted therewith to determine whether the man had taken adequate measures to avoid needing assistance. In conversations with female clients, paid employment was a rare topic of conversation. The social workers asked few questions and the conversations had a statement-statement character rather than a question-answer character. The same thorough examination of the causes of welfare dependency did not occur in these conversations, as was the case with male clients. The social workers instead tended to investigate the issue in a more formal way and thus restricted themselves to the economic calculation to a greater extent. The results thus show that when client's visited the social services office, social workers put more emphasis upon men obtaining means to support themselves as soon as possible than they did with women. They also examined what legitimate reasons the men had for being in the welfare situation more thoroughly than was the case in conversations with women.

When the topic of children was discussed with male clients, the dialogue was in most cases part of the formal investigation conducted by the social worker aimed at determining the amount of the welfare grant. In four cases, however, the interacting parties tried to introduce talk about the topic from another perspective. In two of these cases, the clients initiated a line of reasoning that involved a wish to get closer to their children, but the social workers did not respond to their attempts. Instead, they abruptly steered the conversation back to the institutional procedures and continued to investigate the circumstances that needed to be investigated in order to evaluate the client's application. In the two other cases, the social worker took the initiative to the line of reasoning about the client's children. In both cases, however, the social worker seems to be giving a picture of a father who is somewhat distanced from his children. For instance, in one of the conversations, the social worker seems to be defending the inevitability of a father losing touch with his children when they get older. In the second conversation, the social worker is clearly anxious to encourage the client to contact his children. Despite this, what she actually says is that children usually wonder who their father is and that they: *...usually want to know about their origin.* This could also be seen as the social worker in question painting a picture of a rather absent father. As she puts it, a father appears primarily to be someone whom it could be "interesting to meet" and not someone who is responsible for his children's well-being in their daily lives.

Results from the part of Kullberg's (1994) study that had to do with decision meetings show that the participating social workers talked about the causes of the problems of male clients in such a way that they are described as responsible for their own problems to a greater extent than the female clients. The economic difficulties of female clients were instead presented in such a way that they appear to be victims of their problems to a greater extent than the male clients. Moreover, male clients were granted social welfare at these meetings to a significantly lesser extent than female clients.

The fact that, as Kullberg (1994) found, female social workers could control the conversation on both topics with male clients, linguistically and with respect to content, may be compared with the study conducted by Berg Sørensen (1995) in Denmark, where the initiative-response analytic method of conversation analysis was used (see Linell & Gustavsson 1987) to study the dominance relationship in conversations between social workers and male and female clients respectively. It appeared in the study that social workers were more dominant in their interaction with male clients than they were with female clients. Male clients spoke less and did not dominate the interaction to the same extent as female clients. The men also contributed more to wrapping up the conversation. They both gave and received less feedback. Conversely, female clients overlapped and interrupted the social workers more frequently.

The results from the Danish study are the opposite of what one might expect in light of similar international studies of interaction within various institutional environments (see West 1984; West & Zimmerman 1985). However, the similarities with the results from Kullberg (1994) are striking. Berg Sørensen (1995) comments on the first of these facts as follows:

> These observations are in clear opposition to other studies of the connections between gender, interaction style and linguistic usage, which have shown that men purportedly have the most aggressive and least considerate interaction style, while women purportedly have a more humble, self-effacing role as those who, heedless of personal costs in the form of reduced prestige, sought to ensure harmony and equilibrium; see the previously discussed study by Zimmerman, West (1975) as well as, among the more recent studies, that by Holmes (1993), where it was found that women were, from every observed angle, both the most pleasant and most competent communication partners (250).

Berg Sørensen (1995) has also investigated whether there are differences between how male and female social workers act in the encounter with clients of both genders. The most important result from this part of the study is that male social workers had a relationship that could be characterised more as a "relationship of respect," while the women's way of conversing was more in the nature of a "caretaker relationship" (Berg Sørensen 1995, 248). Characteristic of the first of these attitudes was that the men more frequently adjusted their speech according to the client's manner of speaking and were more removed from what may be termed bureaucratic usage. The way that female case workers conducted conversation was characterised by a style anchored in the bureaucratic organisation, while elements of closeness and involvement in the topics brought up by clients also occurred. According to Berg Sørensen (1995), differences between male and female case workers were not as prominent as they were with respect to clients.

Fredin (1993) has also employed initiative-response analysis to study gender differences in social workers and client conversations (a total of sixteen conversations were analysed). This study also seems to confirm that conversations between female social workers and female clients are somewhat more symmetrical (or linguistically equal) than those between female social workers and male clients. The results also show that conversations with male clients contain significantly more communicative disturbances than equivalent conversations with female clients. The disturbances mean, for example, that the speakers ignore one another's contributions to the communication, do not pay adequate attention or misunderstand one another.

Fredin (1993) also draws a topic-related comparison between conversations that are more equal (symmetrical) and those that are more unequal (asymmetrical), and finds that the conversations of a more equal nature deviate somewhat from the others with respect to the topics discussed. Conversations of a symmetrical nature are not directed towards economic or social problems, which may be termed traditional topics of conversation within social welfare institutions.

In conclusion, existing Nordic studies of social work show that there are differences in how women and men are treated and how their cases are handled. The studies referred to can be said to confirm that the practice of social work encompasses a number of separate, more or less intricate and sophisticated methods (see West & Zimmerman 1987), which social workers and clients jointly use to maintain the gender system. One way that the differences discussed here are manifested is through linguistic interaction. Yet another distinguishing element highlighted primarily by Kullberg's studies (1994, 1995), is that attribution of responsibility for social problems seems to have a connection with the client's gender.

**Summarising Comments**

The aim of this chapter was to provide an overview of Nordic research concerning the encounter between social workers and clients. The examples we chose were taken from our own studies of authentic conversations and from publications by colleagues in the field. We used a research map designed by Layder (1993) for the abstract, which meant that several levels and dimensions of conversations in social work were in focus. In the latter half of the section, the significance of context was clarified via studies of gender order in conversations between social workers and clients. In another section, the moral dimensions of conversations in social work were analysed. The research summarised here has shown how the client's self is discursively created, something made possible through the connection of conversation data with both contextual and historically-based perspectives. In the opening paragraphs of the chapter, it is shown how social interaction may be understood as a kind of negotiation process between the parties to the conversation. The interplay between participants in the encounter in the social welfare institution was said in the introduction to be dependent upon relevant background and contextual factors. Via Layder's (1993) research map, these various aspects have contributed to greater understanding of what takes place in the encounter.

What then is the image we have formed of encounters in social work via studies of authentic conversations? Has the picture we have drawn come to describe the studied object encounters between social workers and clients from a "worm's eye view" as it could be termed in the context of art history. Do the properties in the dialogues become strangely magnified so that they impede deeper understanding of, for instance, the social processes and various forms of the exercise of power which can occur in encounters of this kind? Have certain peripheral and insignificant details in the conversations come into excessive focus through taking this approach? The reader must naturally be the judge. However, we should like to assert that the multistrategic approach predominant in the studies to which we referred, made possible by study of the "small things" - patterns in conversation - has yielded insight into the "large things" in the areas studied as well, for instance with respect to the relationship of citizens to public authorities in modern society. Via a research approach that switches back and forth between a worm's eye view to a bird's eye view, some aspects of the studies of what social workers and clients say and how they act during the encounter in social work provide us not primarily with knowledge about the outcomes or opinions about the interactions, but also with greater insight into *how* the work is done. Using these methods, we can depict how observable changes in social services praxis also affect meaningful conditions in the lives of the people concerned.

## Notes

1   The report does not claim to include all conceivable aspects of current research, nor to refer to all literature that has been produced. Instead, the aim is to refer, based upon our own research horizon, to a selection of particularly interesting angles of approach.

2   We use the term "welfare institutions" to refer to institutions within the social security system and the social welfare system.

3   See Hydén (in press) for a review of completed studies.

4   Zimmerman (1966, 389) emphasises in his account of his study carried out in the 1960s that he had difficulties obtaining audio recordings of sufficient quality to transcribe and analyse the recorded conversations.

# Bibliography

Acker, Joan (1991) *Hierarchies, Jobs, Bodies: A Theory of Gendered Organisations.* In Lorber, Judith and Farell, Susan, A. (eds.) *The Social Construction of Gender.* Newbury Park: Sage Publications.

Arnstberg, Karl-Olov (1989) *Socialarbetare. En etnologisk analys.* (*Social Workers. An Ethnological Analysis*) Lund: Studentlitteratur.

Bakhtin, Michail, M. (1986) *The Problems of Speech Genres.* In Holquist, Michael and Emerson, Caryl (eds.) *Speech Genres and Other Late Essays.* Austin: University of Texas Press.

Beckman, Svante (1981) *Kärlek på tjänstetid. Om amatörer och professionella inom vården.* (*Love on Duty. On Amateurs and Professionals within the Health Care System*) Stockholm: Arbetslivscentrum.

Berg Sørensen, Torben (1995) *Den sociale samtale - mellem klienter og sagsbehandlere.* (*The Social Conversation - between Clients and Case Workers*) Århus: Forlaget Gestus.

Bernler, Gunnar and Johnsson, Lisbet (1993) Den sociala journalen. In *En studie i akter - deras struktur och funktion.* (The Social Journal. In *A Study of Case Files - Their Structure and Function*). Göteborg: Göteborg University Department of Social Work (Report 1993:7).

Berglind, Hans and Puide, Annika (1976) Synen på socialhjälpstagarna. In H. Berglind (ed.), *Ideal och verklighet i svensk socialvård.* (The View of Welfare Recipients. In *Ideals and Reality in Swedish Social Services*) Stockholm: Wahlström & Widstrand.

Bäckström, I. (1994) *Rehabilitering för män? En undersökning om arbetsrehabilitering av långvarigt sjukskrivna kvinnor och män.* (*Rehabilitation for Men? A Study of Occupational Rehabilitation of Women and Men on Long-term Sick Leave*) Umeå: Umeå University Department of Social Work, Report No. 37.

Bäckström, I. and Eriksson, N. (1989) *Rehabiliteringsgrupper till vilken nytta? - En studie av fyra lokala rehabiliteringsgrupper och deras klienter* (*What Good Are Rehabilitation Committees? - A Study of Four Local Rehabilitation Committees and Their Clients*). Umeå: Umeå University Studies in Sociology, No. 97.

Blumer, Herbert (1971) Social Problems as Collective Behavior. *Social Problems* (18), 298-306.

Cedersund, Elisabet (1992a) *Talk Text and Institutional Order. A Study of Communication in Social Welfare Bureaucracies.* Linköping: University Studies in Arts and Science, 78 [Dissertation].

Cedersund, Elisabet (1992b) *Från personligt problem till administrativt beslut* (*From Personal Problems to Administrative Decisions*) Linköping: University (Studies in Communication, 33).

Cedersund, Elisabet and Säljö, Roger (1993) Bureaucratic Discourse, Conversational Space and the Concept of Voice. *Semiotica* (97), 79-101.

Cedersund, Elisabet and Säljö, Roger (1994) Running a Bit Low on Money. Reconstructing Financial Problems in the Social Welfare Interview. In Walter M. Sprondel (ed) *Die Objektivität der Ordnungen und ihre Kommunikative Konstruktion. Für Thomas Luckmann.* Suhrkamp Verlag, pp. 226-260.

Dingwall, Robert (1980) Orchestrated Encounters: An Essay in the Comparative Analysis of Speech-exchange Systems. *Sociology of Health and Illness* (2), 2, 151-167.

Egelund, Tine and Halskov, T. (1986) *Socialt arbete i praktiken* (*Social Work in Practice*) Lund: Studentlitteratur.

Ericsson, Fredrick and Schultz, Jeffrey (1982) *The Counselor as Gatekeeper. Social Interaction in Interviews.* New York: Academic Press.

Fisher, Sue and Todd, A.D. (eds.) (1986). *Discourse and Institutional Authority. Medicine, Education and Law.* Norwood: Ablex.

Fredin, Erik (1993) *Dialogen i socialt arbete.* (*The Dialogue in Social Work*) Linköping: University (Studies in Communication, 36) [Dissertation].

Goffman, Ervin (1968) *Stigma: Notes on the Management of Spoiled Identity.* Harmondsworth: Penguin.

Goffman, Ervin (1973) *Totala institutioner. Fyra essäer om anstaltslivets sociala villkor* (*Total Institutions. Four Essays on the Social Conditions of Institutional Life*) Stockholm: Rabén & Sjögren.

Goffman, Ervin (1977) The Arrangement between the Sexes. *Theory and Society* (4), 301-331.

Gunnarsson, Evy (1993) *I välfärdsstatens utmarker. Om socialbidrag och försörjning bland ensamstående kvinnor utan barn.* (*On the Fringes of the Welfare State. On Social Welfare and Support among Single, Childless Women*) Stockholm University: School of Social Work (Report on Social Work No. 64).

Gustavsson, Björn, Hydén, Lars-Christer and Salonen, Tapio (1990) *Beslut om socialbidrag i storstäder.* (*Decisions about Social Welfare in Large Cities*) Stockholm: Social Welfare Service of Stockholm (R & D Report 141).

Habermas, Jürgen (1981) *Theorie des kommunikativen Handelns.* Frankfurt: Surkamp.

Halleröd, Björn (1991) *Den svenska fattigdomen. En studie av fattigdom och socialbidragstagande.* (*Swedish Poverty. A Study of Poverty and Social Welfare Recipients*) Lund: Archives.

Hasenfeld, Y. and Steinmetz, D. (1981) Client-Official Encounters in Social Service Agencies. In C. T. Godsell (ed), *The Public Encounter. Where State and Citizen Meet.* Bloomington: Indiana U.P.

Hetzler, Antoinette (1994) *Socialpolitik i verkligheten. Den handikappade och försäkringskassan.* (*Social Policy in Reality. The Handicapped and the Social Insurance Office*) Lund: Bokbox Förlag.

Hirdman, Yvonne (1988) Genussystemet-reflektioner kring kvinnors sociala underordning. (The Gender System - Reflections on the Social Subordination of Women). *Kvinnovetenskaplig tidskrift* (3), pp. 49-63.

Hirdman, Yvonne (1990) Genussystemet. In *Statens offentliga utredningar, 1990:44. Maktutredningens huvudrapport.* (The Gender System. In *Official Reports of the Swedish Government: 44. The Main Report of the Study of Power*) Stockholm.

Holmes, J. (1993) New Zealand Women Are Good to Talk To: An Analysis of Politeness Strategies in Interaction. *Journal of Pragmatics* (20), 91-116.

Holstein, James A. and Miller, Gale (1993) Reconsidering Social Constructionism. In Holstein, James A. and Miller, Gale (eds.) *Reconsidering Social Constructionism. Debates in Social Problems Theory.* Hawthorne, NY: Aldine de Gruyter.

Hydén, Lars-Christer (1987) *På spaning efter det sociala arbetet.* (*On the Trail of Social Work*) Stockholm: Social Welfare Services of Stockholm (R & D Report 65).

Hydén, Lars-Christer (1991) *Moral och byråkrati. Om socialbidragsansökningar.* (*Morality and Bureaucracy. On Applications for Social Welfare*) Stockholm: Social Welfare Service of Stockholm.

Hydén, Lars-Christer (1993a) Vad får man från 'socialen'? Social insatser vid socialbyråer i Stockholm. (What Do You Get from the Welfare Office? Social Programmes at Social Services Offices in Stockholm) *Sociologisk forskning* (30), 3, 63-81.

Hydén, Lars-Christer (1993b) The Social Worker as a 'Moral Worker'. In Gunnarsson, B.-L., Linell, P. and Nordberg, B. (eds.) *Text and Talk in Professional Contexts. Selected Papers from the International Conference "Discourse and the professions".* 26-29 August, 1992, Uppsala.

Hydén, Lars-Christer (1993c) The Social Construction of Juvenile Delinquency. *Young* (1) 2-10.

Hydén, Lars-Christer (1996a) Att besluta om socialbidrag. Förändringar av beslut och attityder till socialbidrag 1990-1994. (Making Decisions about Social Welfare. Changes of Decisions and Attitudes towards Social Welfare) *Socialvetenskaplig tidskrift* (3) 3, 180-194.

Hydén, Lars-Christer (1996b) Applying for Money. The Encounter between Social Workers and Clients - A Question of Morality. *British Journal of Social Work* (26), 843-860.

Hydén, Lars-Christer (in press) *Att samtala om socialbidrag. En översikt av socialbidragshantering. En antologi om socialbiddrag. (Talking about Social Welfare. An Overview of Social Welfare Case Management. An Anthology on Social Welfare)* Stockholm: Board of Health and Welfare, Centre for Evaluation of Social Work (CUS).

Hydén, Lars-Christer, Kyhle Westermark, Pia and Stenberg, Sten-Åke (1995) *Att besluta om socialbidrag. En studie i 11 kommuner. (Making Decisions about Social Welfare. A Study of 11 Municipalities)* Stockholm: National Board of Health and Welfare, Centre for Evaluation of Social Work, CUS publication, 1995 (1).

Jokinen, Arja and Juhila, Kirsi (1997) Social Work as Negotiation. Constructing Social Problems and Clienthood. *Nordisk sosialt arbeid*, 17 (3), 144-151.

Kempe, P. (1976) Varför drar man sig för att söka hjälp? (Why Do People Hesitate to Ask for Help?) In H. Berglind (ed), *Ideal och verklighet i svensk socialvård. (Ideals and Reality in Swedish Social Services)* Stockholm: Wahlström & Widstrand.

Kullberg, Christian (1994) *Socialt arbete som kommunikativ praktik. Samtal med och om klienter. (Social Work as Communicative Practice. Conversations with and about clients)* Linköping University: Linköping Studies in Arts and Science (115) [Dissertation].

Kullberg, Christian (1996) Swedish Fathers and the Welfare State Institutions. In Björnberg, Ulla & Kollind, Anna-Karin (eds.) *Men's Family Relations.* Stockholm: Almqvist & Wiksell International.

Kullberg, Christian (1997) Arbete eller socialbidrag? Socialsekreterares samtal med och om kvinnliga och manliga klienter. (Work or Social Welfare? Social Workers' Conversations with and about Male and Female Clients) In Bladh, Christine, Cedersund, Elisabet and Hagberg, Jan-Erik, *Kvinnor och män som aktörer och klienter. En antologi som skildrar tidigt 1800-tal och framåt. (Women and Men as Actors and Clients. An Anthology Depicting the Early 1800s and Forward)* Stockholm: Nerenius & Santérus Förlag.

Kåhl, Ingela (1995) *Socialarbetarkåren- den lindansande professionen. (Social Workers - the Tightrope-walking Profession)* Lund: Bookbox Förlag [Dissertation].

Layder, Derek (1993) *New Strategies in Social Research.* London: Polity Press.

Lindquist, Anna-Lena (1990) Utvecklingstendenser och utvecklingsmöjligheter i socialtjänstens arbete med vuxna missbrukare och klienter med psykiska problem. (Development Tendencies and Development Opportunities in Social Services Work with Adult Substance Abusers and Clients with Psychological Problems) In G. Aronsson and H. Berglind (eds.) *Handling och handlingsutrymme. (Action and Scope for Action)* Lund: Studentlitteratur.

Linell, Per (1990a) De institutionella samtalens elementära former: om möten mellan professionella och lekmän. (The Elementary Forms of Institutional Conversations: On Encounters between Professionals and Laymen) *Forskning om utbildning*(4), 18-35.

Linell, Per (1990b) The Power of Dialogue Dynamics. In Markova, I. and Foppa, K. (eds.) *The Dynamics of Dialogue*. New York: Harvester Wheatsheaf.

Linell, Per and Fredin, Erik (1995) Negotiating Terms in Social Welfare Office Talk. In Firth, Alan (ed) *The Discourse of Negotiation. Studies of Language in the Workplace*. Great Yarmouth: Pergamon.

Linell, Per and Gustavsson, Lennart (1987) *Initativ och respons. Om dialogens dynamik, dominans och koherens. (Initiative and Response. On the Dynamics, Dominance and Coherence of Dialogue)* Linköping: University Studies in Communication: 15.

Lipsky, Michael (1980) *Street-Level Bureaucracy. Dilemmas of the Individual in the Public Service*. New York: Sage.

Marklund, Staffan, Nordenstam, K. and Penton, R. (1984) *Socialvärlden. Om mötet mellan socialarbetare och client. (The Social World. On the Encounter between Social Worker and Client)* Stockholm: Liber.

Mayer, J. E. and Timms, N. (1970) *The Client Speaks. Working Class Impressions of Casework*. London: Routledge & Kegan Paul.

Maynard, D. W. (1988) Language, Interaction, and Social Problems. *Social Problems* (35), 4, 311-334.

Midré, Georges (1990) *Bot, bedring eller brød: om bedømming og behandling av sosial nød fra reformasjonen til folketrygden. (Help, Improvement or Bread: On Assessment and Treatment of Social Need From the Reformation to Social Security)* Oslo: Universitetsforlaget.

Nilsson, G. (1989) *Fattigliv. (Life in Poverty)* University of Lund: School of Social Work.

Olsson, Erik (1993) "Naiv teori" i socialt behandlingsarbete. ("Naive theory" in Social Case Work) *Nordiskt Socialt Arbete* 13,(2), 3-17.

Oltedal, Siv (In press) *Praksis i socialt arbeid. Ei studie av klientsamtaler på sosialkontor. (Praxis in Social Work. A Study of Client Conversations at Social Services Offices)* [Dissertation].

Pithouse, A. (1984) Poor visibility. Case talk and Collegial Assessment in a Social Work office. *Work and Occupation* (12) 1, 77-89.

Pithouse, A. (1987) *Social Work: The Social Organisation of an Invisible Trade*. Aldershot: Gower.

Pithouse, A. and Atkinson, P. (1988) Telling the Case: Occupational Narrative in a Social Work Office. In Coupland, N. (ed) *Styles of Discourse*. London: Croom Helm.

Puide, A. (1985) *Klienterna och socialtjänsten.(Clients and Social Services)* Stockholm: Stockholm University School of Social Work (Report on Social Work No. 26).

Ranger, Marianne (1986)*'Er det bare meg som roter sånn?' Klientsamtaler på et sosialkontor. ('Is It Only Me Who Messes Up?' Client Conversations at a Social Services Office)* Oslo: Universitetsforlaget.

Rees, S. (1976) Defining Moral Worthiness. Grounds for Intervention in Social Work. *Social Work Today* (7), 203-206.

Rees, S. (1978) *Social Work Face to Face. Clients' and Social Workers' Perceptions of the Content and Outcomes of their Meetings*. London: Edward Arnold.

Rostila, Ilmari (1994) The Treatment of Client Responsibility and Laughter in Encounters between Social Workers and Clients. In Gunnarsson, B.-L., Linell, P. and Nordberg, B. (eds.) *Text and Talk in Professional Contexts. Selected papers from the International Conference "Discourse and the professions"*. 26-29 August, 1992, Uppsala, 201-218.

Rostila, Ilmari (1995) The Relationship between a Social Worker and Client in Closing Conversations. *Text* (15), 69-102.

Rostila, Ilmari (1996) How to Start Talking about Money: Developing Clienthood in Interaction in a Social Welfare Office. *Scandinavian Journal of Social Welfare* (6),105-118.

Ryan, W. (1971) *Blaming the Victim.* New York: Pantheon Books.

SOU (1996) *Jämställd vård : olika vård på lika villkor. Huvudbetänkande av utredningen om bemötande av kvinnor och män inom hälso- och sjukvården. (Equal Care: Unequal Care on Equal Terms. Main Report on the Study of the Treatment of Women and Men within the Health Care System)* Stockholm: Fritzes.

Spector, Malcolm and Kitsuse, John (1977) *Constructing Social Problems.* Menlo Park, CA: Cummings Publishing Company.

Stjernø, Steinar (1982) *Omsorg som yrke. Arbeidsmåter og yrkesroller på socialkontoret. (Caring as a Profession. Working Methods and Professional Roles at Social Services Offices)* Oslo: Universitetsforlaget.

Todd, A. (1983) The Prescription of Contraception: Negotiations between Doctors and Patients. *Discourse Processes* 171-201.

van Dijk, Teun, A. (1985) *Handbook of Discourse Analysis. Vol. 3: Discourse and dialogue.* London: Academic Press.

Waitzkin, Harold (1991) *The Politics of Medical Encounters. How Patients and Doctors Deal with Social Problems.* New Haven: Yale University Press.

West, Candice (1984) When the Doctor is a 'Lady': Power, Status and Gender in Physician-Patient Encounters. *Symbolic Interaction* (7), 1, 87-106.

West, C. and Zimmerman, D. (1985) Gender, Language and Discourse. In *Handbook of Discourse* Vol. 4. London: Academic Press.

West, C. and Zimmerman, D. (1987) Doing gender. *Gender and Society* (1), 2, 125-151.

Zimmerman, D. (1966) *Paper Work and People Work. A Study of a Public Assistance Agency.* University of California, Los Angeles [Unpublished doctoral dissertation].

Zimmerman, D. H. and West, C. (1975) Sex Roles, Interruptions and Silence in Conversation. In Thorne, Barrie and Henley, Nancy (eds.) *Language and Sex. Difference and Dominance.* Rowley: Newbury House.

Åström, Karsten (1988) *Socialtjänstlagstiftningen i politik och förvaltning. En studie av parallella normbildningsprocesser. (Social Services Legislation in Policy and Administration. A study of parallel norm formation processes)* Lund: Lund University Press [dissertation].

# 2 Negotiating Meanings in and Through Interactional Positions in Professional Helping Work

ARJA JOKINEN, KIRSI JUHILA AND EERO SUONINEN

*Professional helping work is embedded in the conversational encounters taking place between clients and professionals.* This means that if we are to understand this process, we must begin with an analysis of how language is used in these encounters. In keeping with the premises of the constructionist approach, our point of departure is that language use is not just a tool that people use for reporting on events, incidents, attitudes and opinions located outside the speech itself. Language use in the interaction situation is in itself an activity with its own "here and now" logic. In order to explore this "here and now" logic in face-to-face interaction, we need to focus our attention both on the kind of social reality participants jointly produce in a given situation and on the ways they accomplish this (Miller & Holstein 1991, 178; Maynard 1989, 143-144).

Initially we approach and define the professional interaction situation as *negotiation*. The concept of negotiation is appropriate in two senses: first of all, it describes the arbitrary (re)negotiable nature of meanings constructing social reality and secondly, it highlights the involvement of all participants in the interaction situation in the process of producing meanings (Firth 1995, 10-11; Gergen & Kaye 1994; Linell & Fredin 1995, 302, 314-315; Shotter 1993, 26-28). Because meanings are produced in a chain of interaction, we have to study how these interpretations take shape in the interaction process. This means that turns of talk in a negotiation must be examined in relation to one another. As links in the chain of interaction, each turn of talk is related to what earlier has been said or not said. Also, each turn creates the basis for *what* follows in the chain. In investigating these processes, it is useful to make use of different levels of analyses.

## Dimensions of Analysis

The following figure describes the levels of analysis we have chosen to use in our examination of professional helping work:

**Institutional Context**
who is negotiating and where

**NEGOTIATION**

**Interactional**
**Positions**
how does the
negotiation proceed

**Meanings**

what is constructed
during the negotiation

### Figure 1  Dimensions of Analysis of Professional Helping Work

Placing the concept of negotiation in the middle of the triangle illustrates our belief that the dimensions concerned (i.e. the three corners in our triangle) are not isolated from each other in situations of professional interaction but rather are interwoven with one another. From an analytical point, however, it is useful to make this distinction because it facilitates locating the specific emphases of empirical analyses at different points in time. On the other hand, the place of negotiation in the centre of the figure also highlights the fact that we regard *all* dimensions as negotiable rather than as fixed and determined in advance.

Among professionals and clients, negotiation takes place in an *institutional context*. The official tasks of the organisation, its declared goals and the work cultures that have grown up within the organisation, are tightly intertwined in all negotiations. The institutional context serves as a frame for the activities of the participants involved. This frame both promotes and works against certain practices of conversation. Many investigators of talk at various worksites see the interaction situation in institutional contexts primarily as a resource, rather than determinant, of speech (Drew & Heritage 1992; Marlaire & Maynard 1993; Maynard 1989). From this perspective, the negotiation situation is viewed as the *site* where interpretations of the institutional possibilities and institutional limitations ultimately take shape.

In conversations between professionals and clients, different *meanings* are constructed having to do with the clients' problems as well as with the needs of intervention and change. Problems, as viewed from our research perspective, are not something the participants to the negotiation bring along with them. Instead, problems take shape within the negotiation situation.[1] In the words of Marlaire and Maynard (1993, 192): "Whether talk provides for the visibility of a trouble, whether a trouble becomes a problem, whether a problem gets 'labeled' and obtains proper attention from professionals, all involve the contingencies of participants' organising practises in actual talk and interaction". The labelling of a problem in a particular way makes available a certain battery of alternative solutions and excludes others. Definitions and concrete measures go hand in hand (cf. Miller & Holstein 1991, 186; Holstein & Miller 1993, 158).

The successful production of meanings in conversation requires responsive and sensitive co-operation between the professional and the client. We describe this co-operation with the concept of *interactional positions*. For example, when one or the other party to the interaction takes up the position of asker, it is a reasonable proper choice for the other party to take up the position of replier; or when one takes up the position of information deliverer, the logical choice for the other is to assume the position of listener (Peräkylä & Silverman 1991). Similarly, if one adopts the position of "troubles teller", the other party to the conversation can adopt the position of emotional listener (Jefferson & Lee 1992). In these and related ways, the meanings produced in a conversation are always anchored to such *combinations of interactional positions*.[2] This also draws attention to how it may be possible to create and pursue many different kinds of highly flexible relations of co-operation between professional and client within the same institutional context.

**Interactional Positions and Meaning Construction: Two Cases**

In this chapter, we have chosen two excerpts from encounters between professionals and clients that *differ from each other as widely as possible*. Our analysis is inductive in the sense that we set out from the details of interaction and only later link up our interpretation with the institutional context and other background data. In doing this we lean upon the idea of "anthropological strangeness" where the strategy, in the early stages of the analysis, is to try to bracket out all preconceptions of the matter at hand. The first excerpt is from an encounter between a team of professional helpers and a client family; and the second from an encounter between a professional and client.

*The Power of Passive Listening*

Our first excerpt is drawn from a longer episode that began with a discussion of different temperaments within the family. Assisted by the mother of the client family, one of the professionals has described the father's temperament as calm and collected and has added humorously that "his excitement threshold is pretty high". The next episode begins with a situation where one of the professionals repeats a question, formerly presented in a humorous manner, in a collected, matter-of-fact sort of way.[3] F denotes the father of the client family, M the mother, and P1 through P6 the professionals present (P1 through P4 are males, P5 and P6 are females). We focus in this analysis on the communication between the father and the professionals because that constitutes the main focus of the conversation.

*Excerpt 1 Is the Excitement Threshold Too High?*

```
1    P2:  Does all this also apply to your mutual
2         relationship that ((changes to cool matter-
3         of-fact tone)) one is (1) that you Ronald are
4         more placid and nothing can make you lose your
5         temper while you've got more of a temperament and
6         .hhh may need=
7    F:   =Well you can quite easily get
8         me to lose my [temper
9    M:   [yes]
10   F:   if it (.) °if it erm°
11   M:   [>Let's say that I can get him into a temper but
```

```
12         but it's not< heh.
13   F:    [( ) it's not like I'd consciously wanted to
14         like .hhh
15   M:    [it's like
16   F:    [constrain myself by saying that I must not
17 a       get into a temper now.
18   P3:   Yhm
19   P2:   Yeah
20 b F:    So it's not like this.
21         ((Quiet mumbling by professionals))
22   M:    [It's like more the sword of the word
23   F:    [That I do like express my feelings
24         if I've got something to say like .hhh
25 c       pretty clearly I'd say (.)
26   P2:   Mmm
27   F:    And it's usually been like this with us that (.)
28         we haven't had bad rows but we do
29         talk a lot and make clear our vie- views
30         on things .hhh and it's usually like [like
           ((some unclear overlapping utterances omitted))
35   F:    That we respect each others' (.) opinions and
36 d       in the way that (.)
37   P2:   Mmm
38   F:    I wouldn't say that we have any (.) special
39 e       problems ºI don'tº
40   P2:   ºWell whenº=
41   F:    =You have to have your opinions and er[:
42   P2:   [We erm
43         earlier were wondering about this thing
44         that how on earth (astonishment) have you
45         managed to find (.) such a good (.) harmony
46         and (.) I: <still> wonder how (.)
```

On first inspection, it may seem that very little is happening in this conversation. The professional is simply inquiring whether the description of the father as placid is an accurate one, and the father expresses his disagreement in the form of a rather long monologue. However, it is very interesting that the father does not finish his description with the clear statement at beginning that "you can quite easily get me to lose my temper", but he sets out to elaborate, adjust or explain his first version:

1    you can quite easily get me to lose my temper (lines 7-8)
2    I don't constrain myself by saying that I must not get into a temper (13-17)
3    it's not like this (20)
4    I express my feelings pretty clearly (23-25)
5    we haven't had bad rows but we do make clear our views (28-30)
6    we respect each others' opinions (35)
7    I wouldn't say we have any special problems (38-39)
8    you have to have your opinions (41)

Each of the seven reformulations that follow the first version add new elements or some emphasis to the ongoing deliberation. They reflect a simultaneous presence of *two dimensions of meanings*, i.e. the dimension stressing individual emotional expression (even negative expressions; formulations 1, 2, 4, end of 5 and 8), and the dimension stressing harmony and understanding within the family (beginning of 5, 6 and 7). The "but" in formulation 5 indicates that not only we as researchers but the father, too, make a distinction between these two dimensions.

Some of the father's versions are quite independent and would not seem to require any complementary versions; so it would be *quite reasonable that someone else would pick up the conversation* at these points. We have indicated the last lines of these "complete" versions with letters **a** through **e**. The conclusions **a**, **b** and **e** are clear cases in the sense that they are both logical points of conclusion and they end with a falling intonation or with a quieter volume of speech. Points **c** and **d** end with pauses and are to a certain extent similar to **a**, **b** and **e**.

*Each of these five turns is followed by a response from at least one other participant in the situation, but in most cases that response is rather weak or passive.* The response after **a** is an unstressed "yhm" and "yeah", after **b** quiet mumbling by the professionals, after **c** and **d** "mmm" and after **e** a quiet beginning, "well when".

The only response that represents a floor taking is the last one, i.e. "well when". The other responses are clearly cases of minimal response. In general they could be interpreted as conversational continuers. In some situations they could be taken to indicate approval and support for what has been said above. In this situation, however, where (1) we do not have a narrative turn of speech, where (2) earlier turns constitute logical entities, and where (3) the speaker concludes with a falling intonation, the minimal or passive response (in its extreme form a silence) can be interpreted to indicate that the professionals have not considered the versions offered as being sufficient or very successful. In this light, it is quite understandable that the father of the client family takes the minimum response seriously: as a request to reconsider. The fact that the father offers new formulations complies with the expectations created by the professionals' passive response.

The term we suggest for this passive response is a *dubious move*, by which we want to highlight the interactional power contained in the feedback but which is very hard to detect. This type of feedback tends to produce a positional combination between professional and client, which may be described as *sceptic versus version improver*. The effect of doubt, which creates the expectation of an improved version, can thus be produced not only by verbal description (by speaking frankly)[4] but also by passive feedback (conveying the message indirectly). *The specific power of this kind of passive listening lies in it assigning the formulation of the new version(s) to the client, even when the impetus for revision initially comes from the professional.*

### The Power of Encouraging Talk

Our second excerpt consists of two parts and involves a female professional (P) and a male client (C). The conversation revolves around a topic that was raised by the professional: the relationship between the client and his wife. The dialogue in the second part (starting from line 21) takes place one and a half weeks after part one.

*Excerpt 2  So Things are Looking Up Again?*

**Part One:**

1 **a**  P:   *It's just that you said over the phone that you'd*
2          *been doing fine for a whole week at home*
3      C:   ᵒMmᵒ
4 **b**  P:   *So (.) you talked things over and >I mean how did it*
              *start<?*
5      C:   I don't know I just went home heh
6 **c**  P:   *But I mean normally when you've gone home you*
7          *haven't said anything to each other*
8      C:   Now we've just been fighting
9          (1)
10 **d** P:   *But if that helps to clear the if you if you can*

11          *sh- shout about these things*
12    C:    She doesn't shout (.) she's usually quiet heh.
13          it's me who gets (.) angry.
14 **e** P:    ºYeahº ^*well perhaps you have to get angry to*
15          *get her to speak*
16          (2)
17    C:    Yeah I'll make (.) her talk again heh.
18 **f** P:    *So you feel things are [looking up again at home*
19    C:    [ºYeah thisº
20    P:    *Yeah*

## Part Two:

((the professional presents the following opening turn after the client has said he has cleaned the house together with his wife))

21 **g** P:    ^*But like that sounds like that you've never*
22          *said anything that you've done something together*
23          *so (.) don't you feel at all that you've made*
24          *progress in sorting out your relationship*
25          (1)
26    C:    No heh.heh.heh.
27          (1)
28    C:    It can just last a few moments
29 **h** P:    *Well of course it can last just a few moments (.)*
30          *but I think you haven't had very many moments*
31    C:    Well at least during the past couple of months
32    P:    Yes
33          (1)
34 **i** P:    *So that (.) you've now got a job and you've cleaned*
35          *the house together=at least your wife gets you out*
36          *to work (.) at least that's a beginning*
37    C:    Especially as I was alone at home the first of May
38    P:    *You were?*
39    C:    Yeah
40    P:    *Aha (.) I was just going to ask you about May*
41          *the first*
42    C:    It was fine heh.heh. except that the television
43          was pathetic

44   P:   $^{o}Mm^{o}$ *(.) where was your wife and the kid=*
45   C:   I don't know and I haven't asked (sniff)
46        (1)
47 j P:   *That's unbelievable ^but (.) but that I mean that*
48        *at least you were able to stay at home*

The first impression of this conversation is that the professional has numerous interpretations of the client's relationship and of how this has developed and should be developing. The formulations and reformulations produced by the professional unfold into the following chain of versions:

a.   You said that you'd been doing fine for a whole week
b.   You talked things over, how did it start?
c.   Normally you haven't said anything to each other
d.   Shouting can clear the air
e.   Getting angry may get the wife to speak
f.   It seems that things <u>again</u> are looking up at home
g.   It sounds like you've made progress?
h.   There haven't been many good moments
i.   You've been doing things together which is a sign of a better start
j.   In spite of everything you were able to stay at home

As was the case in the first excerpt, each formulation presented in this excerpt adds a new dimension to the negotiation; the only difference is that the specifications are now made by the professional - not by the client. In the professional's formulations, speaking as well as doing things together seem to emerge as the chief criteria of a healthy relationship (points **a** through **i**). Yet, the professional's final formulation **j**, drawing attention to coping alone at home, has virtually the opposite meaning. The common element all these formulations share is that they indicate in one way or another that things are improving.

In trying to understand how the evolution of meanings may be understood as part of the process of interaction, we can begin by looking at the client's turns of talk and then proceed to examine the professional's actions in the negotiation situation.

*There is a clear and systematic reluctance by the client to accept and join the professional's "it's-all-going-to-be-all right" interpretations.* His first device of obstruction is to offer only minimum response (line 3) in a situation where the professional is trying to coax him into producing a positive description of the family's situation. Secondly, he belittles the professional's interpretation by "justs"(lines 5, 8 and 28). The third device he applies is to reject the professional's interpretation (lines 12-13 and 26). And finally, he presents information that undermines these interpretations made by the professional (lines 37 and 45).

It is fascinating that the professional persists in producing positive interpretations in these exchanges even though the client's responses contain ample elements in favour of an opposite conclusion. This raises the question: *what sort of devices does the professional apply in order to persevere with positive interpretations, despite resistance on the part of the client?* We have categorised the devices employed by the professional into four groups:

1    Summaries of progress in the relationship between the client and his wife (**a**, beginning of **b**, beginning of **g**, **i**)
2    Questions (end of **b**, **f**, end of **g**)
3    Relativization of the belittling or negative interpretation by the client (**c**, **d**, **e**, **h**)
4    Exchanging dimension of meanings (**j**).

The professional does not appear to apply these devices at random: each seems to have its own place in the course of interaction. All *summaries and questions* contain some positive interpretation, and their functions seem to be to encourage the client to agree with these interpretations as well as to follow up the (positive) description in his own words. On both occasions when the professional raises the theme of couple relationship, she uses these very devices. Here, her summaries and questions are closed; interpretations are already given. For instance, in point **b** the professional first presents her summary of the fact that the client has succeeded in talking with the wife. Then, leaning on this summary, she follows up with the question as to how the speaking actually started.

The professional applies the device of *relativization of a negative interpretation* in situations where the client (with one minor exception, line 19) does not yield to the temptation of the summaries and questions but instead belittles or even rejects the interpretations of progress. He does this with his responses beginning with "but", "yeah" and "well...but". In applying the revitalisation device, the professional either opens up a positive perspective on the negative description presented by the client, or moderates it by means of a past-present contrast. From line 8 up to line 15, there unfolds a series in which the client's negative descriptions alternate with the professional's positive descriptions. The professional translates "fighting" into "shouting which cleans the air" (point **d**) and the one-sided "getting angry" into "getting into a temper" which might encourage the wife to talk (point **e**). At point **h**, the client's interpretation of the relationship improving only "momentarily" is turned round through a past-present comparison. The professional points out here, and also at point **c**, that there <u>earlier</u> were even fewer such moments.

The professional uses the last device on the list, i.e. *exchanging meaning dimensions*, at the very end of this excerpt (point **j**). This is a last-resort device in the sense that the professional refrains from applying it until all other means have failed. In order to understand this device, we need to trace the conversation back to line 34. Here the professional submits a three-item list presenting a positive summary of the client's relationship with his wife, which is described as a small beginning for a major change (lines 34-36). However, the client does not respond directly to this interpretation but introduces the "news" that he spent the May First holiday on his own (line 37). This seems to derail the professional for a moment. She takes a timeout by redirecting the focus from being alone and then reverts circuitously to the question of what sort of holiday the client had had (lines 40-41). The professional's response to the client's reply that everything went well (lines 42-43) is a quiet minimum response. Then, she reverts to the subject of family and relationships, presenting a direct question about where the wife and child had been on May First, thus marking being alone as a non-preferred action (line 44).[5] The client's response <u>that he</u> does not know nor has he even asked the wife (line 45) further undermines the interpretation that the relationship is improving.

We now arrive at the point appearing to be the watershed for the professional. Following a short pause, she expresses her disbelief by saying "that's unbelievable", which she then cuts short with an abrupt "but" (line 47). Then, she formulates a positive interpretation of the situation: "but at least you were able to stay at home" (line 47). *The family and couple relationship dimension is thus replaced by an individualistic dimension. However, the encouragement is still there.* So in the end, it seems that this continuation by encouragement, at least in the short term, is more important than adherence to the encouraging meaning dimension. In other words, the professional seems to be oriented to the so-called recourse-centred way of conversation, which constructs the interactional context in ways preventing the client from producing "problem" or "trouble talk" about his situation.

For the devices applied by the professional in her interpretations of positive development, we propose the term *encouraging moves*. These moves we understand as being construed in relation and response to the client's *obstructionist moves*. The positional combination taking shape in the interaction situation can thus be described as an *encourager-obstructionist* pair.

At first glance this combination may appear to be asymmetrical and while this interpretation is a plausible one, the encourager - obstructionist positioning we propose has another interactional rationale. As we see it, *obstructionist moves fuel encouraging moves and vice versa.*[6] The conversation is not asynchronic in the sense that it does not involve breaks, i.e. the turns in the negotiation flow easily from the alternating incentives.

**Discussion**

As stated and illustrated graphically with the figure at the beginning of this chapter, institutional context serves as a frame for the activities of negotiation between professionals and clients. So in reviewing what we have thus far done, it is important to contextualize from where we have drawn our exemplars. Our first excerpt is from a family therapy training session. In this clinical training program, the therapist team consists of one teacher-therapist and five students already working as psychologists, psychiatrists and social workers but who participate here as part of advanced career training. The family in this excerpt has been instructed to apply for therapy because their 12-year-old son is unusually quiet in the company of strange adults. Some of the teachers at the boy's school have felt that the situation has become quite problematic. The excerpt presented here comes from a videotaped record of a total of six therapy sessions with the boy and his family. The excerpt is taken from the fourth session with the family and involves their face-to-face interaction with the therapist responsible for the interview and the team of therapists who previously followed the discussions via a video monitor.

The second excerpt is from the field of social work. The setting is provided by an interview arranged by the probation and after-care office, an agency whose responsibilities include the supervision of parolees. The client in our excerpt is on parole and is required to visit his parole officer regularly. The client's situation is reviewed during these visits.[7]

Our argument is that the interactional positions and the dimensions of meanings we found are not deducible in any simple and straightforward manner from their institutional contexts. What we attempt here is to study *whether institutional conditions are realised in negotiations and if so, in what way is this being accomplished.* In family therapy the main problem is expected to lie within the family and hence family relationships are at the focal point of professional helping work. Against this background it is hardly surprising that the father commits himself to a serious deliberation of his own place and behaviour in the family. The responses of the therapists involved indicate that their expectations and strategies are attached to this very same issue.

In the social work negotiation, on the other hand, the couple relationship and the family do not intrinsically belong to the centre of attention but rather are constructed in the client's life as coping resources. In the negotiations where those resources are located and identified, the 'family problem' and its treatment occupy a secondary position. This makes understandable the professional's move from a *familial* meaning dimension to an *individualistic* one.

In our analysis we have concretised two different positional combinations: sceptic versus version improver as well as encourager versus obstructionist. However, it would be misleading to argue from this extremely limited database that there prevails in family therapy a problem-centred orientation and in social work a resource-centred one. Focusing on two excerpts of conversation differing from each other as far as possible conceals the fact that data from both institutional contexts reveal episodes of interaction that are problem-centred and solution-centred. Further, it seems highly likely that many other types of positional combinations are also construed in professional helping work: something which, incidentally, represents a major challenge for future research). These combinations may also vary and cover longer or shorter periods of time even within the same encounters. At present, it does not seem so important to discover how prevalent certain combinations are in a certain institution. Of much greater importance is a more general identification of the different combinations of positions in professional helping work. These have to be made visible so that it will be possible to address the question of how meanings are formulated in these varied combinations.

For instance, in our material it *initially might appear that the client* in the sceptic versus improver combination is the chief promoter of meanings in version forms; whereas in the encourager versus obstructionist combination it would seem that the professional is the primary producer of interpretations. However, as analyses of interaction *become* more detailed and focus on other levels, the situation begins to appear in a somewhat different light. That is, under the pressure of dubious moves, the client *continually* is forced to improve on his initial interpretation and eventually arrives at one he might never have constructed without the professional's minimal responses. The requirements set upon the client seem to rise continually during the conversation, as the client makes what appear to be independent choices about which the therapists remain doubtful as long as the client "himself" finds the right dimension of meaning. In the encouraging professional - obstructionist client setting, the situation is reversed. During the course of the conversation, the professional produces new interpretations on the basis of the obstructionist *client's* responses. At the same time, the professional is continually lowering the achievement level set for the client. The contribution of the obstructionist client is thus quite crucial to the formulation of meanings. *The party who speaks most is not necessary at the helm.*

In both encounters, however, there is clearly in evidence a professional competence that if any device (such as a question) fails to produce what the professional would regard as an adequate response, there is still a second battery of devices that he or she can resort to. And if these fail to produce the desired response, there exists a third, possibly even a *fourth*, battery to use. Perhaps it is *impossible to have a conversation* that creates something without some form of persuasion.

In order to understand the welfare state apparatus we need to understand the micro-level communication between the professionals and their clients. Our initiating of analysis aiming at this kind of understanding suggests that persuasion is an inevitable part of the professional helping work encounters, even if the conversation looks like client centred in a sense that she/he speaks much or is praised. The most relevant question to be studied is not then if there is some kind of power relation present in the encounters, but *how* power works in micro practices and what kinds of consequences or visions *this* creates for the client.

## Notes

1    Research has been funded by the Finnish Academy. Our approach to the issue of problems owes a great deal to the constructionist research tradition (Kitsuse & Spector 1973; Spector & Kitsuse 1987; Holstein & Miller 1993; Miller & Holstein 1991), particularly to the line of inquiry concerned with face-to-face interaction (cf. Marlaire & Maynard 1993). According to the constructionist tradition the focus of attention is on processes through which the participants interpret different circumstances and behaviours as social problems and how they categorize these problems (Schneider 1985). Professional helping work is one important arena where such processes of interpretative categorisation takes place.
2    Peräkylä and Silverman (1991) use the more general concept of "format" instead of positional combination. Jefferson and Lee (1992), for their part, are concerned in their

analysis with just one particular format, i.e. "troubles telling". The reason why we have chosen to use the term "combination of positions" is that we want to underscore the fact that there are always two parties involved in these formats and that the understanding and consent of both *are* crucially important.

3   Transcription symbols used:

| (.) | short pause of less than half a second |
|---|---|
| (2) | duration of pause in seconds |
| [ ] | beginning and ending of overlapping speech |
| . | falling intonation |
| ^ | rising intonation |
| °quiet° | quiet voice |
| <u>underline</u> | loud voice or some form of stress |
| > < | quicker pace |
| < > | slower pace |
| .hhh | audible breathing in |
| fin- | hyphen at the end of word indicates unfinished word |
| e: | colon after vowel indicates stretching out of vowel |
| heh | laughter |
| ( ) | empty parentheses indicate that transcriber was unable to hear what was said |
| (( )) | comments by transcriber are in double parentheses |

4   This is the case, for example, on line 42 where the professional interrupts the father and makes the emphatic point that he is surprised the couple can live in harmony in the first place. In a certain situation this might be read as praise, but in this particular context it is hard to interpret it as anything else than a dubious move, as meaning: I very much doubt the accuracy or truthfulness of your description. The other professionals seal this interpretation later on by critical questions (not shown in the excerpt).

5   That is, at this point the professional could have continued encouragement of the client by saying something like, "that's nice that you had a good time".

6   The encouragement that appears in this material consists to a large extent of praise. In cultural terms the most preferred response is not necessarily acceptance; modest denial may in many situations be regarded as more proper. As the proverb goes, "Self-praise is no recommendation".

7   The first material was collected by Jarl Wahlström, who has analysed the material in his doctoral dissertation (Wahlström 1992). The second excerpt is from the material collected by Juha Kääriäinen for his doctoral dissertation (1994), although eventually he never used the material in this work.

# Bibliography

Drew, Paul and Heritage, John (1992) Analyzing Talk at Work: an Introduction. In Drew, Paul and Heritage, John (eds.) *Talk at Work. Interaction in Institutional Settings.* Cambridge: Cambridge University Press.

Firth, Alan (1995) Introduction and Overview. In Firth, Alan (ed) *The Discourse of Negotiation. Studies of Language in the Workplace.* Oxford: Pergamon.

Gergen, Kenneth J. and Kaye, John (1994) Beyond Narrative in the Negotiation of Therapeutic Meaning, in McNamee, Sheila and Gergen, Kenneth J. (eds.) *Therapy as Social Construction*. London: Sage.

Holstein, James A. and Miller, Gale (1993) Social Constructionism and Social Problems Work. In Miller, Gale and Holstein, James A. (eds.) *Reconsidering Social Constructionism. Debates in Social Problems Theory*. New York: Aldine de Gruyter.

Jefferson, Gail and Lee, John (1992) The Rejection of Advice: Managing the Problematic Convergence of a "Trouble-telling" and a "Service Encounter". In Drew, Paul and Heritage, John (eds.) *Talk at Work. Interaction in Institutional Settings.* Cambridge: Cambridge University Press.

Kitsuse, John and Spector, Malcolm (1973) Towards a Sociology of Social Problems. *Social Problems* (20), 404-419.

Kääriäinen, Juha (1994) *Seikkailijasta Pummiksi. Tutkimus rikosurasta ja sosiaalisesta kontrollista.* Helsinki: Vankeinhoidon koulutuskeskuksen julkaisuja 1/1994.

Linell, Per and Fredin, Erik (1995) Negotiating Terms in Social Office Talk. In Firth, Alan (ed) *The Discourse of Negotiation. Studies of Language in the Workplace.* Oxford: Pergamon, pp.299-318.

Marlaire, Courtney and Maynard, Douglas (1993) Social Problems and the Organization of Talk and Interaction. In Miller, Gale and Holstein, James A. (eds.) *Reconsidering Social Constructionism. Debates in Social Problems Theory*. New York: Aldine de Gruyter.

Maynard, Douglas (1989) On the Ethnography and Analysis of Discourse in Institutional Settings. In Holstein, James A. and Miller, Gale (eds.) *Perspectives on Social Problems*. Greenwich: Jai Press.

Miller, Gale and Holstein, James A. (1991) Social Problems Work in Street-Level Bureaucracies: Rhetoric and Organizational Process. In Miller, Gale (ed) *Studies in Organizational Sociology*. Greenwich: Jai Press.

Peräkylä, Anssi and Silverman, David (1991) Rethinking Speech-exchange Systems: Communication Formats in AIDS Counselling. *Sociology* 25(4), 627-651.

Schneider, Joseph W. (1985) Social Problems Theory. The Constructionist View, *Annual Review of Sociology* (11), 209-229.

Shotter, John (1993*) Conversational Realities. Constructing Life through Language.* London: Sage Publication.

Spector, Malcolm and Kitsuse, John I. (1987) *Constructing Social Problems*. New York: Aldine de Gruyter.

Wahlström, Jarl (1992*) Merkitysten muodostuminen ja muuttuminen perheterapeuttisessa keskustelussa: Diskurssianalyyttinen tutkimus.* Jyväskylä studies in education, psychology and social research, 94.

# Part II
# Talking With and About Children and Parents at the Workplaces of the Welfare State

In the next two chapters, we are provided with accounts drawn from child welfare work in the Nordic welfare state systems. Of all the contributions to this book, these are the two most ethnographic. Both Forsberg and Vagli approach this area in roles as field workers and their accounts provide us with thick descriptions of scenes and talk from child welfare work they have witnessed. While Vagli's account, more than Forsberg's, is more heavily flavoured by her impressions as a reflective field worker, both demonstrate how ethnographic reporting can function to complement and contextualise conversational materials from welfare work settings.

Of all areas of welfare state operations, working with parents and children in child welfare contexts is perhaps the most problematic both for professionals and clients. In the first place, this involves interventions by the state into the family: the one sphere of everyday life regarded as most private. Moreover, invasions of family spheres by state professionals may lead to removal of children from their home. This fact - involving how state power is presented and exercised - may be a crucial factor in creating the problematic nature of child welfare in the Nordic systems. Child welfare laws in Finland and Scandinavia require that social workers act to insure the child's well being. Consequently, welfare professionals are obligated to function as experts to investigate and assess questions involving the health and safety of children in their families. Yet, in so doing, social workers possessing this kind of power approach families in the roles of friendly visitors. Thus the very real power of the state invested in social workers often presents itself in a benign wrapping. In meetings with social workers, families in the Nordic countries, as elsewhere, know that their children may be taken from them if they refuse to talk at length about the details of their lives. This power issue, the role contradictions it generates for social workers and other problematic areas of child welfare work in the Nordic countries reveal themselves, as Forsberg and Valgi show, in the talks social workers carry on among themselves as well as with children and their parents.

# 3 Involvement, Attendance and Participation of Children in Child Protection

HANNELE FORSBERG

## Introduction

Throughout the 1990s, childcare policy in many European countries has come under the influence of the discourse of the child's perspective: one emphasising children's rights, own viewpoints and competencies. This has challenged the self-evidence of the family as the only and natural context of children's lives, the power of parents over children and has advocated the need for expansion of children's legal, moral and participation rights in child protection. However, there are many signs suggesting that the older discourse, which emphasises the importance of the family and parents for children, still has strong roots in child protection. Rhetorical slogans like "partnership with parents" and "supporting the family" are familiar signs of this discourse. This raises the question: How are these two different discourses used in contemporary child protection practices?

In international comparisons of family policies, the Nordic countries often are perceived as countries where children are more likely to be treated as individuals with rights of their own than in other countries (see e.g. Millar & Warman 1996, 46). In Finland the Child Welfare Act of 1983 (with some additions to the existing law in 1990 and 1993) requires that a 12-year old child's own view should be taken into account before initiating any child welfare measure. This should also applied to even younger children if they are perceived to be mature enough. The same act states that a 15-year old child has an independent right to speak when a child welfare intervention directly concerns her or his own life situation.

In this chapter, I am interested in whether there such a phenomenon as participation of children at the local level does, in fact, exist and, if so, how is it actually constructed in the context of Finnish child protection. How is the status of children as participants recognised and regulated? And how is the position of children interpreted in relation to those of parents and professionals in the interaction between child protection experts and their clients?

The data for considering these questions have been gathered by ethnographic methods, mainly by observing everyday child protection encounters in two different Finnish child protection settings: social welfare offices and family support centres.

I will begin by describing the setting, data and approach of my research. Then I will move on to examine the prevailing ways by which the participant status of children is defined in the interactions of children, parents and professionals in studied child protection encounters. The position of children is shaped by three different frames of action. The frames of children's rights, of family centred action and of peers all construct in differing ways the participant status or position of children. On the other hand, however, the implications of this different framings are mixed and ambiguous. The chapter concludes with a discussion of my findings and their implications for child protection practices.

## Setting and Data

The data for this article was gathered as part of my doctoral study concerning child and family definitions within child protection practices (Forsberg 1998). The material for the study was collected by ethnographic methods, mainly through observations carried out at three Finnish social welfare offices in 1990 and at three family support centre units in 1995. Both of these sites are institutions of the Finnish welfare system having responsibility for dealing with child protection issues.

In Finland the implementation of micro-level child protection or child welfare is primarily in the hands of municipalities (municipal child welfare boards) and social workers of municipal social welfare offices. According to the Child Welfare Act the child welfare system is obligated to take measures, if the health and/or development of a child is seriously endangered by lack of care or other conditions at home, or if the child seriously endangers his/her health or development, the extreme case being taking the child into care or providing him/her with substitute care. Social workers at Finnish welfare offices often work according to what is known as the integrated social work model. This means that, besides the child protection work, a social worker is also responsible for such matters as the treatment of alcohol abuse problems as well as assistance in financial problems. For my study, however, I have analysed only those situations involving social workers at welfare offices dealing with child protection issues.

The family support centres observed for my study are also part of the municipal child welfare system, but they are a fairly recent working method established only in a very few municipalities simultaneously with the dissolving of the system of child welfare institutions. Family support centres resemble in certain respects Swedish "hemma-hos-arbete" (e.g. Hessle 1997, 247) and some British "family-centres" (Pithouse & Lindsell 1996, 474). The family support centres studied try to provide solutions to psycho-social problems of families with children in community care. Most of the clients are referred to these centres by social workers at local social welfare offices. The work is motivated by the view according to which the family (the biological family) is seen as being of utmost importance to the development of a child, even in cases when the capability of the parents to take care of their children is considered inadequate. The expressed aim of family support centres is to work in a solution-oriented and family-centred way. The centres focus on helping families make use of their own resources.

Even though family support centres and social welfare offices operate from the same legislative base and deal with similar child protection problems, there are important differences between them. Social workers at social welfare offices (who have an academic education) are higher in the professional hierarchy of the child protection system than the staff members of the family support centres. The staff members of the family support centres often have a less advanced educational training, though this is not always the case. Besides their basic professional education, all staff members of family support centres have been received several years training in solution focused family work.

Social workers at social welfare offices have more legal responsibilities with correspondingly more legal power in child protection cases than do staff members of the family support centres. They have as well more demanding caseloads than do workers at these centres. But, what is important, after being established family support centres constructed themselves as something different, as an alternative to the child protection work traditionally done by social workers at social welfare offices. In a way, this was a challenge to my comparative setting.

The data analysed for this article are drawn from observations of child protection encounters where children were physically present. The ages of the children present in these encounters range from babies to 17 year-old adolescents. In half of the observed encounters (N=30) at family support centres, there were no children present. In social welfare offices, only one forth of the observed encounters (N=37) contained children. In these encounters where children were not present, child protection issues were dealt with parents - mostly mothers - which is consistent with what researchers found in child protection institutional settings in Denmark and Sweden (Egelund 1998; Hollander 1998).

**Ethnography of Institutional Discourse**

For the purpose of studying social interaction, video- and/or audiotaped data is typically perceived as the most advantageous in analytic sense. While data gathered by means of ethnographic observation, together with interviews, is often placed on the bottom of the hierarchy of different data types in this sense (see e.g. Maynard 1989). Lately some researchers have criticised lately this commonly held view as restrictive. For example Gale Miller (1994) points out that ethnographic strategies have their own value in studying social interaction. There are situations where video- or audiotaping is for one reason or another difficult or impossible. However, when this is the case it is possible for theoretically informed observers to produce data which can be analysed even from a micro-analytic standpoint. Swedish speaking Finnish Harriet Strandell's (1994) research "Sociala mötesplatser för barn - Aktivitetsprofiler och förhandlingskulturer på daghem", which deals with interaction of children in day care centres, is an excellent example of a detail study of social interaction based on ethnographic observation. Gale Miller mentions James Holstein's (1993) study on involuntary commitment hearings as an example of this kind (Miller 1994, 287).

Gale Miller (1994) also points out how more detailed CA- or DA-type micro-analytic techniques can be extended by combining them with broader ethnographic strategies and techniques. This makes it possible to go beyond defining the data as talk. Ethnographic strategies namely make it possible to observe issues like space and gestures. It can be said that ethnographers' longer term and more varied experiences in social settings offer richer and more diverse data for analysing social interaction (Miller 1994). Observation and more detailed DA- or CA-type strategies are different, but rather than competing with each other they could be seen to enrich each other (see also Pösö & Juhila 1999).

My analysis in this article is based mainly on observed interactions between children, parents and child protection experts. When this is the case, it is clear that highly detailed analysis of interaction is impossible. My notes based on observed interaction try to be "near verbatim" notes written mainly in the observed encounters. I will present selected examples of interaction in my data, but my whole analysis does not derive from them. The focus of ethnographic analysis is broader containing among other things non-verbal observations on space and gestures, and in my case here also before and afterwards discussions of child protection encounters with child protection experts and their interviews.

I analyse child protection work as embedded in institutional discourses. By institutional discourses I mean the usual interpretative and interactional activities used by considered setting members (Miller 1994, 282-284). The focus of my analysis is in the ways in which child protection workers in interaction with their clients use resources available to organise their activities and assign meanings to the position of children in relation to the parents and the professionals. Participant status of the children is thus analysed through interpretation of professionals' interaction (mainly talk) with their clients and understood from a dynamic perspective (Aronsson 1991).

The approach blends aspects of situation sensitiveness with the cross-situational aspects of the work. In other words, the analysis focuses on the cross-situational frames of action associated with the presentation of the child in situation-specific episodes of participants. In so doing, the analysis focuses on an important issue in the ethnography of institutional discourse: namely, the ways in which setting members simultaneously construct social settings and enter into the institutional discourses. In this way, the emphasis in understanding an institution as not primarily an abstract, structural and territorial entity, but rather an entity involving the interpretative and interactional practises of participants (Miller 1994).

Child protection workers direct the activities within settings such as asking questions clients are expected to answer, issuing directives to which clients have to respond, or otherwise acting in ways requiring clients to take account of their actions. Clients are part of the interaction and they may maintain the prevailing power relations by responding in organisationally approved ways or by resisting to do so (Miller 1994, 284-286).

## Three Dominant Frames of the Interaction

Including children at child protection meetings is not self-evident. Inviting them to professional encounters means better possibilities to children bring their interests to the problem-solving process. On the basis of my data, there can be distinguished three different shared frames of action (compare Goffman 1974[1]) according to which child protection workers suggest children to be present at these meetings. At social welfare offices the *legally* informed *frame of children's rights* is used as a motive by professionals to invite children to the client meetings. In the family support centres, on the other hand, the therapeutically informed *family-centred frame* of action is invoked to suggest that the whole family, including children, should be present when handling with child protection issues. In addition, both social welfare offices and family support centres make use of a frame I have characterised as using the ideas of *children's peer culture* as a resource to expect children's presence. These three frames construct different participant status for children and position them differently in relation to their parents and the professionals. How are these frames locally 'put together' in practical encounters forms the focus of my research concerns. Let me begin with the frame of children's rights.

### Children's Rights

The frame of children's rights used in social welfare offices implies legally based actions such as hearings with children, assessing children's interests and views and even advocating children's needs against those of parents if deemed necessary. This frame becomes relevant in situations involving children's placement in substitute care or children's choosing of where to live when parents divorce. In other words, when the child's family breaks up for different reasons the child becomes an individual subject in a legal sense. In my data, the ages of the children met by the frame of children's rights vary from 10 to 17 years.

The following extract is one example of an encounter where the frame of children's rights becomes topical. It is a meeting in which the views of children are heard because their parents are divorcing. These kinds of meetings are not automatically considered as child protection meetings. However, according to the social worker at this meeting, there are child protection aspects within it.

A divorcing couple is visiting social welfare office with their two daughters to make a contract of guardianship and visiting rights.[2] Anna (A), the older of the daughters is about 15 years old and Lotta (L), her sister, is 10 years old. In the beginning of the meeting the parents' views of guardian and visiting rights has been discussed. Then the social worker starts to examine the children's views. The father suggests that the girls should discuss the matter without parents' presence. The social worker agrees and the parents leave the room where the girls then stay alone with the social worker (S1):

1    S1 (to the younger girl Lotta): How have you had it at your mother's?
2    L: (not intelligible)
3    S1: Would you like to meet your father more often than we suggested?
4    L: (doesn't answer, starts crying)
5    S1 (turns to Anna): Was it a very difficult thing that this came up
6    (refers to Anna's arrest for intoxication, which was taken up while
7    the parents were present).
8    A: I guess not.
9    S1: Did it come up unexpected?
10   A: No.
11   S1: How did you feel?
12   A: I don't really give a damn about anything.
13   S1: Did you, when you heard about your parents' divorce, feel that
14   everything was going to pieces? (The social worker lowers her voice
15   and I can't make out what she says, the girl also answers very quietly
16   so that I can't hear; they are saying something about Anna's use of
17   alcohol.)
18   S1: Did you feel bad about us taking up the matter a while ago?
19   A: Not really.
20   S1: Do you have plans for what to do after the tenth grade?
21   A: No.
22   S1: If I'd ask, would you like to move back to your dad?
23   A: No. We just fight all the time.
24   (S1 changes the subject and starts to talk about the children's interests
25   and hobbies; they talk in a low voice, and I can't really make out what
26   they are saying.)
27   S1 (still to Anna): Is it difficult for you to talk to your parents about
28   your own affairs?
29   A: I don't know. Sometimes it is, sometimes it isn't.
30   S1: Has this situation made it harder to talk?

31    A: Yeah.
32    S1: Well, but it is still so that, as you don't have a father any more in
33    your reconstituted family or incomplete family - or, it isn't actually
34    quite so, he is very much part of your life - but you don't have him
35    living with you, so you will be a very important person in your family
36    as a support for your mother and as a big sister.
37    S1: (Turns to the younger girl, Lotta:) Have you felt very bad about
38    this situation?
39    L: Oh yeah.
40    S1: It was still very brave of you to come. It is after all so that adults,
41    in other words, your parents make this agreement and are responsible
42    for it. You have just been heard in the matter. Let's hope that you will
43    like living in your new home by yourselves, the three of you.

The discussion with children ends here and the parents are called in to sign the agreement.

The extract is one example of how the position of children as participants is constructed in the interaction with the parents and professionals by the use of the frame of children's rights. As a result children are (physically) "individualised" for a moment from their parents. They are heard by the social worker without the parents' presence.

As an answer to the questions the social worker has addressed to Lotta, she cries or is silent (lines 1-4), which is a typical way of acting for younger children in studied professional encounters. Without wondering aloud why Lotta is crying, the social worker moves on to discuss with Anna about her arrest for intoxication (line 5). By her questions the social worker apparently interpret this as a symptom of Anna's parents' divorce. In this way, she places the child and her problems belonging to the context of the family. The social worker goes on with her questions, which can be interpreted as aiming at forming a picture of the relationship of Anna and her father. Anna answers by describing the relationship as quarrelsome. This type of questioning by the social worker seems aimed at constructing the divorce of their parents as troublesome for the children. Thus, Anna's problematic behaviour is placed again and again in the context of the family. In the end of the encounter the social worker raises Anna to a position as "more adult" as a consequence of the father's moving. By defining Anna as a support for the mother and for the younger sister, the social worker attempts to construct a more responsible position for the older daughter in reformulating family relations. The younger daughter remains in her place as a child of the family and is commended by the social worker for her bravery in coming to the office. The meeting with the children ends with the statement by the social worker that the adults bear the responsibility for the divorce and its consequences. In the context of their participant rights, the sole responsibility of the children in these kinds of situations is to express their views. This task is that which activates the relationship of child protection experts and children. What is the relationship between them in the meeting?

In the situation the social worker fills in a certain form, to gain the view of the children as the law says. However, the encounter can be interpreted as adult-centred. The meeting with children happens within a certain timetable, in a formal office, which is furnished primarily for bureaucratic purposes. The interaction between children and the expert is organised through talk. As is typical in most institutional encounters, the professional asks questions and the child clients are supposed to answer to the questions. The older girl is better in verbalising her views. In this sense she achieves a more competent participation status in the meeting. The younger girl has difficulties in acting like that. For Lotta, discussing with an adult social worker about her feelings seems to be much more difficult. Crying, silence and mumbling are her ways of acting in this situation.

At times both the social worker and the children speak in very low voices. Periodically it is difficult to hear their words even though their talking is taking place in a very small room where the observer sits close to them. Speaking in a very low voice could be interpreted to signal a respectful attitude on the part of social worker to the children, or the sensitiveness and frightening of the situation for both of the participants.

After this encounter, the social worker talks to the observer about the situation. She reports finding it difficult to meet children. As she sees its, it is the parents - not the children - who are responsible for the situation, because of their decision to divorce. The social worker feels this is a moral conflict: she is aware of the legal participation rights of the children, but sees the parents as having primary responsibility for the situation.

In the data, there are however other social workers who seem able to meet with and listen to children in a much more "natural" ways without dramatic overtones. Yet, in all cases where children were included in social welfare office encounters within the frame of their legal rights emphasising the child as an individual subject, it was common for social workers to emphasise parents as having primary responsibility. Meetings were usually constructed as adult-centred and children were most often heard in the presence of their parents. Only rarely do children visit social welfare offices on their own or meet with professionals when their parents are absent. In the data there is only one occasion when a child - or more precisely, a young man - meets alone with a social worker. His situation is special. He is 17-years old and lives alone. He does so with the support of the social workers who report that he was abandoned by his parents.

In actual practice, the data show that the frame of children's rights is quite marginal in comparison to the far more typical mode of action where child protection issues are dealt with the parents without children being present. It seems therefore that children are only viewed as individuals and given more responsible participant status when parenthood for some reason is called into the question and/or when parents are not able to take responsibility of their children. In the encounters observed at the social work offices, it seem that children are dichotomised with respect to how they are constructed as participant subjects. They are viewed either as a difficult client group with whom the social workers lack methods and resources to work with or perceived as a natural client group with whom the professionals can manage.

**Family Centred Frame of Action**

In family support centres the motive to invite children to client meetings can be explained by the frame of therapy. This is unlike the frame of law in use at social welfare offices. This difference provides one indicator of the contrasts between the institutional foci of child protection work in these two settings. In social welfare offices, this focus is more legally informed than the therapeutic one informing work at family support centres. Central to this frame are ideas of systemic family therapy emphasising that the whole family should participate in treatment if one family member has problems. Here, children are perceived as crucial participants in the encounters. Consequently, since even very small children are supposed to participate to encounters at family support centre, the age range of child participants at these meetings is much more varied than at social welfare offices.

Compared to the frame of children's individual rights, the family centred frame of action emphasises that it is not useful for child protection workers to have a direct contact to the children when their parents are absent. But as earlier noted, the presence of parents is commonplace in practice at social offices carried out in the name of children's legal rights. This raises several questions. Does the participant status of children differ when work is carried out in a family centred frame of action? In practice, what kind of participation of children does this frame guarantee?

The following extract is an attempt to concretise the implications of the family centred frame for the participant status of the child in relation to parents and experts at client meetings.

Mother (M), her 13-year-old son Kalle (K), and his 7-year old brother Teemu (T) are meeting together with a male staff member (S1) at a family support centre.

1  S1: (to mother) What do you most of all expect of this meeting?
2  M: That we could, all of us together, make things better for Kalle by
3  talking.
4  S1: (still to mother) What do you expect for yourself?
5  M: I don't know, I'm not so important. Most of all I want, hope that I
6  wouldn't have to be afraid that the police would call.
7  S1: Kalle, why did you think it was useful to come here?
8  K: (yawns) I don't know. I just came.
9  S1: Teemu, why did you think it would be of some use to come here?
10 T: (not clear)
11 S1: What about your father, have you talked about him?
12 M: Kalle said that he didn't want his dad here.
13 S1: I'd still be interested in talking about the father and about Hanna
14 (the daughter who is older than the boys and planning to move out
15 from the home). Could we pretend that each of you would be Hanna
16 and you'd take turns and answered the way you'd think Hanna would
17 respond when I ask her something. Shall we start with you (mother)?
18 (Talks to the mother:) What do you think, Hanna, how are things in
19 your family at the moment.
20 M: (as Hanna) I think that Kalle breaks up our family harmony with his
21 comings and goings.

The round about Hanna's role continues. Following it, the expert expresses his wish that Hanna should be asked to come the next time. Then he turns the discussion to reflecting the meaning of the father, who lives elsewhere, in the life of the family.

The expert first direct his question to the mother. The mother's answer constructs the responsibility of the problems at hand collectively for all persons present. The expert however tries to find out if the mother or the boys have some individual needs and expectations. Even the individual perspectives of family members who are not present in the meeting are taken account through the role play activity led by the expert. Providing space for the individual family members' perspectives seems to be an important principle of the expert's action. The types of questions posed by the expert differ from those asked by the social worker in the previous example. He asks open questions aimed at eliciting the subjectivity of the clients. The idea is that when the question does not guide the answer too much, the client will have more space to present his/her own views.

At first glance, the equal space for all family members' personal views seems to be an important principle of the family centred-orientation of the example. But, as this extract shows, there are some indications that there are differences between the participant status of children and adults. These differences can be read more explicitly through much of the observational data. First, the expert directs his questions primarily to the mother. This can be interpreted as assigning authority to the parent, the head of the family. Secondly, when the expert asks about the role of the absent father in the life of the family, it is the mother who answers in the name of Kalle. The expert accepts this without checking whether this, too, is Kalle's point of view. Thirdly, when the expert asks the children questions, they answer if they can or are willing to or have the courage to respond. The questions directed to Kalle are framed by a certain professional knowledge. This reflects the orientation of solution focused therapy where the main task of therapeutic work is to find constructive and positive answers to the problems at hand. However, the responses by the children to the expert's queries do not easily lend themselves to this kind of work. Both boys answer lackadaisically and the younger one soon falls quite silent. Their behaviour vis-à-vis the adult expert is reminiscent of that of the children in the social welfare offices extract. This similarity suggests that we could interpret the behaviour of these children as telling us about the power of adults over children.

One thing is clear. The point of departure for the family centred frame is that the child whose problem behaviour is in the background for the meeting is not primarily perceived as an individual with problems. Instead, the child and his problems are considered as family problems. More explicitly than in social welfare offices the responsibility for solving the problem lies in principle on the shoulders of the whole family. Most often, however, it is the parents who seem to be the primary clients, just like in social welfare offices. The status of children as participants in family-centred work seems to be dependent on both of adult parents and adult experts.

The participant position of small children in encounters framed by the family centred orientation is worthy of further consideration. One way of doing this is found in the following extract. Here, an attempt will be made to describe how the meeting would appear if it was seen only in terms of those speech acts performed by the five-year-old boy Aleksi (A) present in the meeting together with his mother (M) and two staff members (S1) and (S2).

The mother and her son are visiting the family support centre for the first time. It is difficult to see clearly what the immediate child protection problem is at this meeting. There seem to be many problems in the family. The ex-husband is described as terrorising the family, the mother is exhausted and two boys in the family are having some behavioural problems. Most of the time at the meeting is devoted to the adults who discuss themselves. The five-year-old boy who is present gets attention four times very briefly in the course of the meeting. The first time is at the beginning of the meeting when the mother bursts into tears and the second time is quite soon after that.

(following some problem talk by the mother)

1  S1: (to mother) That (the terrorising ex-husband) has really been a
2  terrible situation from your point of view, it must have demanded a lot
3  of strength from you.
4  M: Yeah, it has, it's, it's taken a lot of energy and then the fact that,
5  well, I don't have anyone (cries, her voice breaks), sorry (blows her
6  nose).
7  S2: I didn't notice to say to you, Aleksi, that if you want to draw or look
8  at books, you can quite...
9  S1: And there might be lego toys in that basket and well other toys as
10  well, we'll look at them too and then one really important matter that I
11  forgot to say, in other words, that we have a, well, custom that we talk
12  about 45 minutes, an hour at the most.
13  M: Yeah.
14  S1: And well, after that we'll take a break, you can stay here and we'll
15  go with Sonja (S2) to that other room for example and talk about the
16  things that came to our minds, minds well during this discussion and
17  then we'll come back, and we'll tell them to you.
18  M: Okay, yes.
19  S1: Is this okay?
20  M: Yes.

21   S1: Okay, that tape recorder of the researcher confused me so that I
22   forgot to say in the beginning. (they still simultaneously talk about the
23   toys)
24   M: You can take your shoes off, Aleksi, do take your shoes off.
25   S1: It doesn't matter, he can very well have his shoes on. Nn.
26   M: Oh yes that, what was said at the family guidance clinic was that...

On lines 7-9 the experts praise the boy for playing activities and at the same time indirectly cast the boy as some kind of a "side-participant" (Cederborg 1994) while they go on talking with the mother. The mother's comment to take the shoes off (line 24) or the experts' "it doesn't matter" can be interpreted as ways of directing the boy to settle down to his play. The third time the boy, who has been busily playing with toys, gets attention is at the very end of the meeting when there has been talk about a boat trip the family has taken:

1   S2: (to Aleksi) What was most fun on the boat?
2   A: Nothing.
3   S2: Nothing?
4   A: You see I didn't get any candy at all.
5   M: No you didn't, we went straight to the cabin.
6   (they turn back to the problems at hand)

The expert remembers the presence of the child and turns to him, but with his polite words he indirectly reconstruct the marginal position of the child in the meeting (see Cederborg 1994). The final time Aleksi gets attention is at the end of the conversation when the staff members act in accordance with solution focused therapeutic guidelines. At this point, they give positive response to clients and Aleksi gets his share, too:

1   S2: We think that it was nice that you came along, Aleksi. You're a
2   resourceful boy, you found, even though we don't have very many
     toys
3   here and they are what they are, and you let us talk in peace. That was
4   really nice. You're a fine boy.

Although the expert points out to Aleksi that he is an important participant (line 1), by her words "you let us (adults) talk in peace" (line 3) she explicitly emphasises the adults' position as responsible of child protection problems. The mother of the family is the main participant of the meeting. The boy remains a side-participant in terms of discussing the problems at hand. Aleksi's drawing and playing, his shoes, and the candy he did not get remain background issues in this sense. This is a very typical position in which small children are placed in family meetings. Sometimes they are even physically removed from the setting. This happens when adult experts and/or parents interpret the topics discussed as being unsuitable for the ears of the children. For example, incest happened to be a topic like this. On some occasions, children perceived as being noisy were also removed from the encounter, because the experts indicated it was impossible for them to concentrate on discussions with parents while these children were present. This kind of action is paradoxical in relation to the ideas of family centred work. The children are supposed to participate to the child protection meetings, but then they are moved away from those meetings.

The verbal competence or willingness of children to express themselves plays an important part in the possibilities of children to participate in a way adults prefer. Some of the experts interviewed in the study explained that the children's presence in the family meetings often serves other purposes than verbal communication. This gave the experts opportunities to observe how members of the family relate to one another as well as to monitor the interactions within the whole family.

When invited to child protection meetings on the basis of the family centred frame, small children do not converse a great deal with adults. One could see this as telling us about the passive participant status of children. On the other hand, children themselves seem to be unwilling to participate by speaking. They refuse to respond, mumble or remain silent. Instead they find their own activities, like playing, drawing, sometimes disturbing adult's speaking etc. Children are also able to participate by listening to adult's speaking even though they do not comment it. In this sense, they are by no means passive participants at these meetings. Recent research by Silverman and his colleagues focused on interaction of children with adults in professional settings have shown too that children possess competence even in cases where they remain silent (Silverman et al. 1998).

**Peers**

In contrast to the encounters based on the frames of children's rights and family centred action, a third frame was identified as occurring at meetings observed at one of the social welfare office units and two of the family support centre units. This frame is one I characterize as the frame of peers. This frame utilises children's peer group interaction and is used with children who have experiences of same kind of problems. In this frame, in contrast to the first two, the children's participation position and relations to parents and experts are produced in a new way. Specifically, in encounters of this sort, children from different families are met as a collective without their parents' presence.

In the following extract social workers at a social welfare office are meeting some school age children, who spend time together and have caused problems in the neighbourhood. The children (C1, C2, C3 etc.) form a gang together. At the meeting's beginning, they get soft drinks. In contrast to the children in the previous examples, these children are very noisy. They laugh a lot, cough much and speak simultaneously in extremely loud voices. Throughout the meeting, the children are very unsettled. They are loyal to each other, but construct adults by their speech as "dumb" and "assholes". They change the topics of their talk quickly, while the experts try to keep conversation on certain topics, which means mainly school issues and hobbies.

1    S1: Do you smoke regularly, all of you?
2    C1: Yeah, at home!
3    S1: How about Jatta and Sini?
4    C2: We can smoke at home.
5    C4: I have stopped.
6    C5: I'll stop in the summer.
7    S1: There's one possible group decision for you, it might be worth your
8    while to think of quitting.
9    C2: Sini will probably not stop, she's such a heavy smoker.
10   S1: Have you smoked long?
11   C2: Three years.
12   S1: Even you? So small and already smoked three years?
13   C1: Small, I'm not small.
14   (Coughing, simultaneously.)
15   C4: Can we end this soon? I want to get out, there's Jasu.
16   S1: We could probably end this as well.

The experts of the extract are representatives of a certain institution, who ask children questions concerning their way of life. The responsibility of children is to answer the questions. The experts support children to stop smoking as a group. In other parts of the meeting the experts use this kind of group solidarity of children when trying to get them to keep attending school. Here, the experts do not appeal to the parents of the children but to children as a collective and in this way trying to exert pressure on them to stay in school. As rewards for this, the experts promise the children free tickets to swimming hall.

Through the episode it is possible to see how the relationship of experts and children changes when the parents are not present. The children's participation position takes another and much more explicit form. By their behaviour children break the code of typical child client, who is quite silent and unwilling to talk with the professionals.

Does speaking aloud and challenging adult authority - as children do in this example - then mean that children have gained an equal and active participant position with adults? Speaking aloud and nonsense can be viewed as an interactive possibility used by children who are not necessarily in agreement with the resolutions adults are offering them. Instead speaking "normally" is potentially morally implicative (Silverman et. al 1998, 238-239).

Faced with such groups of children, experts often appear to be insecure about their professional role. They seem afraid of noisy and non-passive somewhat aggressive children. The experts appear not to know what to do with these children nor how to behave with them in a professional way.

In the next extract from a family support centre, another frame of peers can be identified. Two staff members (S1, S2) are planning a school change for one of their child clients (Sirkku).

1    S1: And we have planned, when we think of Sirkku attending to that special
2    school, that they could meet, Elina and her, before school starts. So that
3    Sirkku would have a contact with someone from the special school already
4    before school starts.
5    S2: Are they the same age?
6    S1: Pretty much so.
7    S2: In the same grade or something?
8    S1: The same age at least. And Elina has gone through the change to the

9    special school not so long ago, just last autumn, and it was such a
      positive
10    experience. And Sirkku is very willing to meet Elina and the mother
      has
11    promised that we can arrange it.

The experts are utilising the experiences of another child (Elina) in
changing school, with the agreement of the parents in the background.

When using the frame of peers, experts talk with children, but very
often they utilise other kind of actions as well. Playing games, going to
movies or to theatre are examples of these. However, experts are unsure if
these are professional means to handle child protection issues.

## Contradictions of the Frames and Their Implications for Child Protection

As suggested in the foregoing, the dominant frames examined appear to
define and shape in different ways the participant status of children and
their relations to parents and experts. The frame of children's rights
constructs the child of a certain age as an individual legal subject with
competent participant status. One consequence of this is that the position of
parents is unclear and remains in the background when children and
professionals are taught to meet as potentially equal partners. The family
centred frame, on the other hand, makes it the whole family's responsibility
to participate in child protection meetings. In such encounters, children of
all ages and their parents are expected to participate together in the shared
work of solving problems. The third frame, concerning older children,
emphasises children's participant abilities and shared experiences. This
frame constructs their participatory status and relation to their parents and
professionals much differently than the other two frames. Children as a
group with shared interests are viewed as capable of meeting professionals
without their parents' presence. Besides encounters focused mainly on talk,
children in this frame are offered action-oriented meetings involving such
activities as painting, attending the theatre and swimming together. But, as
we have seen, in practical situations of child protection work, these frames
blend together in different and sometimes very ambiguous ways. As a
result the participant positions of children assume a number of different
forms. This means that when considered at the local level the general

notions of children as individuals with their own rights in Nordic countries becomes a much more complex issue.

One of the main reasons for these kinds of contradictions is the dominant idea of right presupposing an autonomous individual. But children are also very much dependent on others. The results of my analysis seem to point out the importance of recognising this ambiguous nature of children's position. This, in turn, means recognising that rights are not only a concern for professionals in carrying out work with clients. The rights of the child also have to be a concern for others such as family members and peers with whom children interact in their daily lives. This recognition, however, presuppose something more than a child framed in terms of autonomy and individualism. It must also be based on a view of the child as a genuine participant whose voice is heard in the situations impacting significantly on her or his life. If this goal is to be achieved, it will demand the adoption by society of a situation sensitive morality willing to accept the complicated nature of everyday life (Oakley 1994, 30). Central to this is positioning children in the proper context of their meaningful relations. But, as James and Prout (1996, 42) emphasise, this placement does not mean abandoning children as active subjects. Although ambiguous at many points, the contours of ways of emphasising children's participation and activity in these processes may be discerned in the data presented here.

My analysis of the participant status and position of children in two Finnish child protection settings is by no means an exhaustive answer to the complicated question of the position of children in relation to parents (or other significant persons) and child protection professionals. My findings here may be seen as challenging the dominant way of working with children primarily through the parents found at these agencies. Clearly, more careful research in this area is needed. As indicated earlier, such investigations have to be carried out by keeping in mind that it is the adults who nearly always are describing and analysing the position of children.

## Notes

1    The concept of frame is Goffman's vocabulary and according to him it is a constellation of meaning that informs definition and understanding of situation and events. Individuals fit their actions to this understanding and this understanding organises activities (Goffman 1974).

2    According to the 1984 Act of Child Custody and Right of Access it is possible to make a contract of custody and access by the parents endorsed by the municipal welfare authorities.

# Bibliography

Aronsson, K. (1991) Facework and Control in Multi-party Talk. A Pediatric Case Study. In Markova, I. and Foppa, K. (eds.) *Asymmetries in Dialogue*. New York: Harvester.
Cederborg, A.-C. (1994) Young Children's Participation in Family Therapy. In Cederborg, Ann-Christin (ed) *Family Therapy as Collaborative Work*. Linköping Studies in Arts and Science. Linköping: Linköping University.
Egelund, T. (1998) Mere af det samme - nye barneregler i Danmark. *Nordisk Sosialt Arbeid* 4 (18), 201-210.
Forsberg, H. (1998) *Perheen ja lapsen tähden - etnografia kahdesta lastensuojelun asiantuntijakulttuurista*. Helsinki: Lastensuojelun Keskusliitto.
Goffman, E. (1974) *Frame Analysis: A Chapter on the Organization of Experience*. Cambridge: Harvard University Press.
Hessle, S. (1997) Den sociala barnavården inför 2000-talet - några lärdomar från 1900-talet. Artikkeleita ja tutkimusraportteja. *Janus* (5) 3, 243-260.
Hollander, A. (1998) Barns rätta att komma till tals - ökat inflytande för barn eller vuxna? *Nordisk Sosialt Arbeid* 4 (18), 194-200.
James, A. and Prout, A. (1996) Strategies and Structures: Towards a New Perspective on Children's Experiences of Family Life. In Brannen, J. and O'Brien, M. (eds.) *Children in Families. Research and Policy*. London: The Falmer Press.
Juhila, K. and Pösö, T. (1999) Negotiating Constructions: Rebridging Social Work Research and Practice in the Context of Probation Work. In Jokinen, A., Juhila, K. and Pösö, T. (eds.) *Constructing Social Work Practices*. Aldershot: Ashgate.
Maynard, D. (1989) On the Ethnography and Analysis of Discourse in Institutional Settings. In Holstein, J. A. and Miller, G. (eds.) *Perspectives on Social Problems, Volume 1*. Greenwich, CT: JAI Press.
Millar, Jane and Warman, Andrea (1996) *Defining Family Obligations in Europe*. London: Family Policy Studies Centre.
Miller, G. (1994) Toward Ethnographies of Institutional Discourse. Proposal and Suggestions. *Journal of Contemporary Ethnography* (23) 3, 280-306.
Oakley, A. (1994) Women and Children First and Last: Parallels and Differences between Children's and Women's Studies. In Mayall, B. (ed) *Children's Childhoods. Observed and Experienced*. London & Washington: The Falmer Press.
Pithouse, A. and Lindsell, S. (1996) Child Protection Services: Comparison of a Referred Family Centre and a Field Social Work Service in South Wales. *Research on Social Work Practice* (6) 4, 473-491.
Silverman, D., Baker, C. and Keogh, J. (1998) The Case of the Silent Child: Advice-giving and Advice-reception in Parent-Teacher Interviews. In Huchby, I. and Moran-Ellis, J. (eds.) *Children and Social Competence: Arenas of Action*. London & Washington: The Falmer Press.
Strandell, H. (1994) *Sociala mötesplatser för barn. Aktivitetsprofiler och förhandlingskulturer på daghem*. Helsinki: Gaudeamus.

# 4 The Social Organisation of Legitimate Risk Assessments in Child Protection: A Study of Backstage Talk and Interaction in a Local Child Protection Agency in Norway[1]

ÅSE VAGLI

Any institution that is going to keep its shape needs to gain legitimacy by distinctive grounding in nature and reason: then it affords to its members a set of analogies with which to explore the world and with which to justify the naturalness and reasonableness of the instituted rules, and it can keep its identifiable continuing form.

Any institution then starts to control the memory of its members; it causes them to forget experiences incompatible with its righteous image, and it brings to their minds events which sustain the view of nature that is complementary to itself. It provides the categories of their thoughts, sets the terms for self-knowledge, and fixes identities. All of this is not enough. It must secure the social edifice by sacralizing the principles of justice.

Mary Douglas (1987, 112)

## Introduction

This is an exploration of daily life in a child protection agency of the Norwegian welfare system. By scrutinising the way child protection workers in this agency work out decisions, I try to make visible some general traits in the particular logic and the social organisation of their work. My goal here is to open an understanding and conceptualising of elements and general dimensions regulating and forming the construction of the work carried out by these representatives of the welfare state.

I will argue that the general traits of the social organisation in this agency may be seen as a set of legitimating process. The basic elements in this process have to do with establishing occupational identity protection as well as creating a bearable work situation for professionals doing work that is risky and difficult. My aim, thus, is similar to Pithouse and Atkinson (1988), when they interrogate the narratives of talk at social work agencies. Borrowing some of their words, I would say that it is in the backstage situations and in the talks between the social workers that the work is "witnessed" and assessed. It is in these encounters that work is symbolically constructed and socially organised.

What I try to do here is to make a detailed inquiry into the empirical material of the interaction between social workers in the agency and try to transform this from a "language of enactment" (Bernstein 1996) into an analytical and conceptual language: a language of description.

Local child protection agencies in Norway are administratively organised within social service departments of local municipalities. At these agencies, social workers have the responsibility for selecting cases for further processing within child protection. The process of selecting cases for child protection is started in the agency on requests from schools, parents, other official agents and private persons. Social workers in the local child protection agencies of Norway are granted wide discretion in the area of child protection. This is unlike many other countries where the courts have more of this responsibility. Even after the Child Protection Act was altered in 1993, and a new administrative body added, to make final decisions in cases where caretaking was proposed by local agencies, the local agency still decides if caretaking is to be undertaken. This situation places social workers in these agencies with perhaps one of the most powerful mandates of the welfare state: intervention into the private lives of people. Their power may thus be seen as linked to the power of interpretation and categorisation (Foucault 1994).

The empirical material in this chapter is based on an ethnographical study done during 6 months in a local child protection agency in a middle-sized Norwegian community. The study was carried out just before and after the Child Protection Act was revised in Norway in 1993. The main method was participant observation of interaction and talk between the social workers. In addition, the written texts produced in connection with decision processes were studied to inform me about the case history. This approach is motivated by an interest in the logic of practice in social work. Based on earlier research experiences (Vagli et. al 1991), I questioned the dominant perspective of child protection work in the Norwegian research tradition, framing this work as law-based, rule-regulated and scientific.[2] Studying child protection workers in their backstage arena gives access to how they themselves described their work through actions, routines, interactions and talk. This approach to the activity of child protection provides insights into the context this work operate within and the social factors influencing and producing the work. In this way it is possible to plot the discursive and social traits of the processes making up a case history or case career.

The presentation here of field material is done through an ethnographic description of the atmosphere and the talk in the agency. This is structured around my field experience and represented in the form of four scenes. The first and second scenes are representations of meetings at the agency and the life inside its walls. The aim of these scenes is to introduce several key themes. These are:

1    The typical and ritualistic traits of the daily life in the agency;
2    The contrasts between the life inside the room of a child protection agency; and
3    The material structures of the buildings and the barriers to the world outside.

The third scene is a presentation of an extract from a casual talk between two social workers. Here topics linked to a specific case are opened and the themes introduced in earlier scenes are looked upon in more detail. We follow this specific case into the fourth scene. This is an extract of a formal meeting between all members of the agency and consultants from the local child psychiatric unit. By following a case in different settings, it is possible to plot the processes, social organisation and development of the construction of the case. In the final part of the article, a number of more general and concluding lines are drawn.

## Methodological Considerations

Before presenting the material, I will briefly present some methodological considerations linked to this kind of study. This research was done in the ethnographic tradition with the researcher listening and noticing what was going on as well as talking to the members on site. Goffman (1989) describes the strength of this ethnographic approach as being linked to the researcher' position near the field of inquiry. To "get your body tuned up" to the situation, is how he puts it, and this is at the core of ethnographical work. In this manner the researcher gains access to the way events proceed and to how these are linked to the social situation. The researcher also gains a close impression of how the actors perceive the situation. To develop an analysis the researcher must work to objectify and articulate this understanding.

The ethnographic way of doing research has to recognise the personal and the imaginative aspects of the interpretation process. As Hammersley and Atkinson put it (1995, 205):

> The process of analyses is formally taking shape in analytic notes and memoranda; informally it is embodied in the ethnographer's ideas and hunches.

Clifford Geertz (1972, 10) describes ethnographic fieldwork and the process of interpretation this way:

> Doing ethnography is like trying to read a manuscript - foreign, faded, full of ellipses, incoherence, suspicious emendations, and tendentious commentaries, but written not in conventionalised graphs of sound, but in transient examples of shaped behaviour.

The main analytical lines in this chapter are based on ethnographic material, general observations and my experiences in meeting the child protection agency and the people working there. The interpretations are also inspired by elements of conversation analyses. I have found the concepts of conversation analyses to be helpful in getting close to my empirical material and to enhance my understanding of it. In the data presented here, I provide examples of general ethnographic descriptions as well as detailed extracts from talks between child protection workers. As the citations are not transcribed from a tape, the accuracy of the extracts of talk as direct representation of what is going on can be questioned. Hand written notes can never have the kind of accuracy as detailed transcripts have. But I found that while listening to formal meetings in the agency it often was quite easy to follow the interaction and to take detailed notes. The workers talked rather slowly and were often hesitant. There were also rather long breaks between the speakers. So, I would say that my notes are fairly accurate representations of the talking. However, this way of obtaining interaction data obviously limits the possibilities of doing detailed analyses of the conversations, but I have found it sufficient detailed for my purposes.

To develop an analytical distance is also an issue linked to the transformation of the "language of enactment" into the "language of description". For the ethnographer, some difficulties in this transformation involve the insights and adoption of the actor's point of view. But the problem of analytical distance and a reflective practice is not specific to the ethnographer's situation. As in other research, the objective/subjective dimensions in producing interpretations represent a key problem. But it may be said that for the ethnographer, the bodily and personally close situation in the field of inquiry, place the ethnographer in a even more complex interpretation situation than research based on more distant methods. As in other research, the balancing work necessary to develop analyses is closely linked to theoretical and literature concerns. To work with the data while alternating between reading and thinking theoretically are the main elements in this balancing activity.

A researcher has to admit the constructive nature of her work. Even if one tries to keep close to the data in a naturalistic presentation, one still ends up telling a story.[3] As Hydén (1995) has remarked, to tell a story is always to leave out another possible story. In this situation, the influence of theory and cumulative knowledge of the research traditions the researcher writes herself into is of great importance. Theory, then, may be understood as a way of orienting oneself in a detailed empirical landscape and as a linking of the interpretation to some validating elements lying in the cumulative nature of research.

Lastly, two more considerations must be mentioned. In this chapter are presented examples of the everyday life and work linked to a specific case. It must be emphasised that the situations presented must be seen as a kind of snapshot of typical traits of the daily rounds and elements of a case career. It also must be emphasised that this is a case study linked to a specific time and place. The ethical consequences of going into the private sphere of child protection workers are another important consideration to be made. This has to do with securing and respecting the worker's anonymity, but also include concerns for their privacy. In the talks presented here people are often revealing personal feelings in a very direct way. Sometimes I feel uncomfortable about using utterances and therefore have left them out. There are no specific rules concerning what to leave out, but I have used my own judgements. Taking such necessary ethical considerations involves aspects of bounded loyalty between an obligation to open up child protection to official discourse and loyalty towards the social workers. The need for insight into this kind of activity and the forces regulating it must be a prime concern. One issue to be highlighted, however, is that the aim of my work is not to moralise or criticise social workers. The prime goal here is to explore and stay close to the empirical material and to try to develop an analysis that make visible the way child protection work is constructed.

## Scene 1  Meeting a Child Protection Agency

*Walk past some shops and office buildings. Enter a brick building through an ordinary office door. See the sign:*

> *Second floor: Department for social services.*
> *The Child Protection Agency.*

*Walk up the stairs to the second floor. Meet a closed iron door. See a sign and press a bell. Hear a voice through a loudspeaker on the wall, asking: "Who is it?" Hear a buzzer sound. The door unlocks. Enter a room divided by a glass wall and a counter forming a half wall. Have to wait for someone to open other doors.*

*It is very quiet at first. Then, I hear, but do not see a woman talking to someone behind the counter on the other side of the glass. The woman cries. The calming voice of the woman on the other side of the glass. An explaining and understanding voice asking questions. Sitting, while waiting I can hear everything being said.*

*After a while a person comes to fetch me. The person smiles at me. Opens another closed door. We walk along a corridor.*

*We are inside the child protection agency.*

*It is ten o'clock in the morning. It is quiet in the room. A kind of solemn atmosphere. Three women are sitting around a little coffee table talking to one another in a kind of intimate atmosphere. The women speak quietly. They look down often while they talk. Sometimes they look up into each other's faces. They have grave and concentrated looks on their faces. A man's voice is in the background, talking quietly behind a half wall. Sitting near the coffee table, one can hear what he is saying.*

*The women around the table stand up. The talk around the coffee table continues in the room for another minute and then stops.*

*What kind of a place is this? The heavy, locked doors towards the outside and the calm and quietness inside. The suffering and helplessness in the entrance outside the room and the warm and intimate atmosphere inside the room. First sad and frightening, then comforting.*

*What is going on here? Why all this talk? What are the people doing here? What are they talking about?*

*And this quietness and solemn atmosphere inside the room. It seems as if there's something sacred going on here.*

*Listening to what they say, it seems that the people are telling stories about themselves. They are also telling stories about parents, children and other people in the village. There are no children or families to be seen here on the inside, but here are being produced images of and reflections about people outside of the room.*

## Scene 2  Airing Cases. Establishing Identities and Creating Basis for Internal Legitimate Decisions

*Tuesday at nine o'clock in the morning. It is time for the long meeting with the long name, the child protection worker group meeting.*

*Six woman and two men around a little coffee table. They are talking about Tommy. One of the female workers tells her story about Tommy. She talks about her reactions to the situation of being in charge of Tommy. She expresses her feelings of responsibility. He is at an institution, but since he has graduated from secondary school, he is coming home. But where shall he go? His parents are no good; they do not take responsibility for him. The woman talks about her frustration about the institutions. She needs support to stand up against them so that they will take responsibility. The others in the staff follow up. They are expressing support and empathy. What can be done? Shall we take a plane down to the institution and talk to them? Who will meet Tommy when he returns? What can we do to help him? Who should really be responsible for Tommy? They talk.*

*Afterwards they are talking about a father who beats his daughter. She has told her school. The father wants nothing to do with the child protection agency. He is only being firm with his daughter, he says. The workers talk - they have many questions: What can be done when the father resists having contact? How can we get into a position to help the girl? How can we get through to the father? Do we need to get help from the police? Or should one of the strong male child protection workers try to talk again to the father? Who dares to take the case?*

*Sitting there, I shiver in the cold wind of power linked with an urge to help. But the cold winds are not being commented and my uncomfortable feeling is soon forgotten. Of course, they are worried about the girl and feel responsible for her.*

*The talking goes on and on. They talk from nine o'clock to twelve o'clock. Talking about one case after the another. One day this case and that case, another day another case and still another case. New cases are coming in and being presented, told as stories. Old cases are talked about in a kind of code, using forenames of the people involved and referring to episodes and situations talked about at earlier meetings.*

*I wonder: Why are they talking so much to one another about the cases? There seldom seems to be a clear decision coming out of the talks in those meetings. The talks have a circular form, repeating themselves and stopping by floating in the air. The talks do not resemble an argumentative dialog or a discussion with the purpose of making arguments and trying out arguments. It is more like a therapeutic situation where there is one main speaker and where the others are listening and commenting upon what this person says. Inside the agency the talks create an image of intense feelings, of vulnerability, tensions, ambivalence and uncertainty. Sitting there listening, looking and noticing, I get caught up and melt into an atmosphere of intimacy and honesty, of feelings and urges to be good and help people, to take responsibility, to take personal risks and to carry a burden as outcasts in the local community. I melt into a feeling of watching brave persons sharing support and feelings. It is like being in a therapy room were people are interpreting each other reasons for actions and for hesitations.*

*It seems like there is a kind of ritual connected with showing and sharing feelings and emphatic competence. So instead of developing an argument for this or other conclusions, these talks may be seen as a way to support the worker and to help the worker create a professional acceptable identity. In this way the talks can be understood in terms of developing and legitimating the worker, rather than the case. Pithouse and Atkinson (1988) have described talk in social work as establishing a 'narrative contract' between the workers. This fits my experiences. By talking to each other, the good intentions of the workers, their emotional links and abilities to sense the problems of the clients are documented and demonstrated. By demonstrating in an implicit way to colleagues that one is a proper social worker, the workers legitimate the right to take any kind of decisions.*

*But there is something troubling me: When they are so honest and open about so many things, why do they never talk about power? Coming to the agency from the outside one feels the power linked to the material aspects of the building. The contrast between the suffering of the woman outside the glass-counter and the calm and questioning voice from the woman inside the glass reception booth enclose power. When you are outside the room or enter the room from the outside, power becomes visible as an obvious element of the agency. But the persons inside the room do not seem to be aware of the power aspects. They always seemed puzzled that people expressed fright in confrontations with them and that people from the outside did not wish to have anything to do with them if they could help it. The workers seem to see themselves as being helpless and victims of struggling and fighting with evil, not as carriers of power.*

*Yes, here, inside the agency, in the intimate, calming cage, power is not a topic of talk. But how is it possible not to feel the power built into the structure of the business of doing child protection work? Do they not see that their mandate of doing interpretations, sorting, classifications and decisions carries power?* [4]

*So why do they never talk about the power linked to the categorisation of people and the power to interfere in peoples lives? Why does it not seem to disturb these kind people that they have the power to get the police to open up the door to a house because they have heard that the father living in it beats his daughter?*

*There's a thought: Perhaps the power is talked away?*

*Perhaps one of talk's functions here is to secure personal dignity in doing dirty and illegitimate work, a way of creating a bearable identity as child-protection worker?* [5] *Here it is more necessary to make repairs linked to having all that power and thus create a collective forgetting. Yes, I think that the audience inside the room is not an audience to discuss power and problems linked to it. Inside the room, power is shut out. It seems as if it is almost forgotten. Perhaps this is one of the functions of talk, to shut out the power, because power is not compatible with professional identity and its righteous nature (e.g. Douglas 1987,112).*

## Scene 3  The Casual Presentation of a Difficult Case. Giving Voice to Ambivalence, Risk, Responsibility

Here we follow the question about the contents and functions of talk into a more detailed presentation of activities in the agency. In asking what are the functions of talk we here will look at examples where feelings are expressed and see what these expressions may lead to.

*One morning after the morning meeting two of the women workers leave the coffee table and go to their desks behind different half walls. Another woman, "C", takes some papers from the large iron cabin with many drawers. She is looking at the papers and walks slowly in the direction of an office in the end of the room. Then another woman "A" enters the room. She approaches "C" on her way to her office with the papers in her hand. Stopping a distance away from "C", "A", opens:*

*Data extract 1*

| | | |
|---|---|---|
| 1 | A: | I do not know what more to do... I do not have any worries about the boy... |
| 2 | | How far shall I go in being a police investigator? |
| 3 | C: | I have had several telephone calls and reports from people in the village. |
| 4 | | They tell things about the mother. We must follow up more of these reports. |
| 5 | | Have you talked to the mother's brother? |
| 6 | | We need help... It will be a disaster for Mikael if we are wrong. |
| 7 | A: | My opinion and the kindergarten's opinion is altogether |
| 8 | | different than the father's and the neighbour's view. |
| 9 | | But I have talked to so many now in this case. |
| 10 | | I am in such doubt. ... But I do not find anything. |
| 11 | | Everyone seems to see the problem, but I don't. But what if I am wrong? ... |
| 12 | | Perhaps someone else should take over this case? |

**One Case, Two Women. What is This Talk About?**

We see here in this talk that several general aspects about child protection work are voiced. One aspect is linked to the complexity of the situation the child protection worker finds herself in. The complexity of arriving at a decision seems as if it is nearly paralysing "A". I feel there is desperation in her voice. The burdens she is giving voice to may be seen as linked to the burden of responsibility. Her responsibility is "to find something" (line 10). This can be understood as being required to find evidence that can be accepted in a child protection decision. Her reluctance to do more investigations (line 9) may be understood as a reluctance to complicate the matter even more. It is as if she is saying: "Enough is enough, I can't take more information. It will muddle up my case". As Heino (1997, 385) notes ". . .the next evidence may force the child protection worker to take on a new perspective and make the case even more complex".

The way "A" talks in this extract, makes it seem as if she herself will have to assume personal responsibility if she is pursuing a "wrong" perspective (line 11). One might ask: What is at stake in child protection for the child protection worker? What does she fear will happen if she is wrong? Is it fear of losing face as a professional who arrives at a decision that does not hold technically in relation to the law? Or is it fear of losing face in front of "everyone" who seems to see the problem? Or is it the boy's fate she is worried about? Are the burdens linked to having worries for the boy, but not finding valid evidence, responsible for such a feeling?

She also expresses the problems of being the one having to carry out the investigation, to meet people face to face, while making inquires and to stand up against people seeing things differently than she does herself (line 7 and 8).

In support of the suspicions most troubling her, "A's" last sentence says much about her personal burden: "Perhaps someone else ought to take over the case". So it seems that her personal situation of burden may be that which troubles "A" most, not worries about the boy's situation. The question remains here: Is there anyone or anything to assume this load? Is there a solution sought to relieve her of these burdens of complexity and the overwhelming feelings of responsibility?

## And What About the Expression of Ambivalence?

"A" starts out saying firmly that she has no worries about the boy. But later in the extract she expresses doubts: "I'm in such doubt" (line 10) and "what if I'm wrong" (line 11). The clear marking of uncertainty seen here may be a way of open up for a "reserve" plan. As Heino (1997:385) suggests, an alternative interpretation must always be at hand for the child protection worker. This may be a way of legitimating the interpretation and a way of saving face. She must always be prepared for changes.

It is also interesting to note that her claim of a being in a "not worrying position" are made stronger by the contrast she points to being as a police investigator (line 1 and 2). This may be seen as a rhetorical way of creating a "contrast structure" (Smith 1978). According to White (1997), this also marks other features of the poetics of child protection. Expressions of ambivalence may also be understood as a strong indication of the burdens the child protection worker feels that her work carries. In reflecting upon "A's" way of expressing herself in this scene, I see her rhetorical competence and that the use of feelings function to strengthen her credibility. But I also hear a lot of pain and suffering. In my eyes this situation has a theatrical flair, but the feelings expressed seems real to those involved in this scene. It is as if a drama is going on here. Sitting there watching them I was overwhelmed by the intensity of the situation and of the feelings expressed. But is this reality or fiction, real feelings or theatre? Who knows? And does it matter? As I see it, the woman is responding here to a situation and constructing it in response to a hidden manuscript that she herself has not invented.[6] The expression of feelings here has a meaning for the situation in which this woman is placed.

"A" is in this extract talking to "C", who is the leader of the agency. "C" is also talking to "A". So there's something going on between them. I do not think it a mere coincidence that the two women stopped in the middle of the room and started this talk. Some of the talk may be understood as linked to their relation and the roles they occupy in the case history. So the tone of confrontation I hear between "A" and "C" may also be referring to something that has happened earlier, something outside this situation.

"C" like "A" is giving voice to a feeling of responsibility. She is saying that she has had several phone calls from people in the village urging more investigation. Perhaps her feeling of responsibility can be seen linked to a general responsibility for establishing a good reputation for the agency. Her interest appears in this way to be linked to the boy's family, the neighbours and people in the village. She also expresses strong worries for the boy (line 6): "it will be a disaster for the boy if we are wrong". In addition to putting pressure on "A", she is also in this manner giving voice to the risky position the agency finds itself in. And her conclusion is: "We need help". Thus it may be seen that "A" expresses personal responsibility, while "C" expresses a collective responsibility. "C" also may be understood as suggesting a removal of individual responsibility from the hands of "A".

Both women express the need for help. But who or what can help them out of the vulnerable position they find themselves in? What kind of solutions do they search for?

## Scene 4  Solution Sought? Identifying a Possible Rule of Non-interference with Individual Responsibility for Making Decisions

I follow the questions just noted by tracing the same case to a scene taking place three weeks later. The scene is now a formal meeting where all members of the child protection agency and consultants from a local child psychiatric unit are present. Staff from this psychiatric unit are used regularly as consultants by this agency.

*Present at the meeting were: "I" and "K", two women consultants from the child psychiatric unit; the entire staff of child protection workers in the agency and their leader.[7] The case was presented by "A", the childcare worker in charge of the case. The other woman working with the case, "B", was presented at the meeting as being a backup for "A". She was the most experienced worker in the agency and was often used in this role in difficult cases.*

*The atmosphere in the meeting had a very special flare. The consultants from the outside functioned as a kind of high priests and masters of the ceremony. They opened the meeting and were those who asked the questions. The ceremonial aspects of the situation were strengthened by the way people talked. It was as if they were talking to themselves, looking down, having long pauses and making space for their inner reflections.*

*Again, as I watched, I felt myself melting into something sacred, something very serious and difficult. It was fascinating sitting there listening. I felt like I was watching a play about life itself, about pain, but also about strength and willingness to work with the pain and to take concern for other peoples' lives. In the reflections of what are going on here I want to focus on some of these elements of feeling and constructive features of the talk. The meeting lasted for 3 hours: from 9 in the morning until 12 noon.*

*Data extract 2*

1   I:   Will you start, A?
2   A:   B and I are not worried in this case, but everybody else is. C is worried.
3   I:   What is difficult about this case?
4   A:   It's difficult with all this pressure from outside, wanting us to mean something other than we do.

| | | |
|---|---|---|
| 5 | | We have made many investigations, about several aspects, but we can't find anything. |
| 6 | | We are not worried for Mikael, but all this fuss is influencing him in a negative way, |
| 7 | | That's obvious. But is it a job for us that the adults in this family are unable to relate to |
| 8 | | one another? |
| 9 | B: | I have met Mikael four times. I can't see, with my antennae, anything to worry about. |
| 10 | | He has been in the same nursery school for almost 2 years. |
| 11 | | Their opinions are the same. They do not report anything. |

Here, in line 1, "A", repeats what she said earlier in scene 3, but now she now handles the case as a member of a team using the expression "we" instead of "I". By making a team of "B" and herself, she thus strengthens her view, makes a contrast and challenges the others to see the case differently. She also reinforces her position by saying that everyone else is worried. Her position is also made stronger by identifying "C" as one of "the everybody else" who is worried. In this way she pins the tail on the donkey, so to speak. "B" follows up "A" in presenting the child as not being at risk. Here she uses her authority as an experienced child protection worker with an ability to sense things: "I with my antennae" (line 9). In addition, "B" refers to the opinions of other professionals at the nursery school as evidence there are no grounds for worry. "B's" way of numbering the times she has met the boy is also a way of putting force into her argument. In their world it seems like having met the boy four times is an argument for knowing him, his situation and thus to possess solid evidence for their assessments of him.[8]

I also find it interesting that "A" identifies the difficulties in this case linked to the pressure from outside to mean otherwise than "we do"(line 4). In this manner she raises the topic of the social nature of the work and that the process of decision in child protection is influenced by important others. That she chooses the words "all this pressure from outside", refers to an "outside" to be understood not only as people outside the agency, but also people outside those having the case, that is, her colleagues in the agency. This aspect raises again the topic of the relation between the individual and the collective in child protection. It seems like the person in charge of the case is the one having the responsibility.

But what then is the function of the collective? As has been noted earlier in this chapter it often seems like all the talking about cases is a "one-woman show" where others function as audience. There seems to be a kind of a therapeutic quality here around the one in charge of the case. The conversation in this extract strengthens an interpretation of the talking as a ritual rather than as a discursive dialogue involving negotiations of a decision inside the agency. It seems as if "C" and the others disagreeing with "A", the caseworker in this case, have broken some kind of rule about caseworkers being in charge. This question of the individual versus the collective also features in the next extract of this talk.

Yet, prior to continuing to the remaining part of the meeting I want to look closer into the way "A" and "B" are strengthening their position. "A" presents the problem in this case as being linked to the adults in the family and their inability to relate to one another (line 7) and in this way seems to minimise the risks for the boy. Another related aspect drawn in here is that other professionals at the boy's nursery school have nothing serious to report about his way of functioning.

As noted earlier, many non-professional persons have been interviewed about their opinions of the boys' situation, but none of their views are mentioned here.

When the conversation continues we hear the other child protection workers in the agency and their opinions of the case. This is opened by "G": one of the two men present. He is the one person in the agency having the longest experience - after "B" - in child protection work.

The conversation extract 2 continues:

12  I:  Let's take a round on this. What do you others think?
13  G:  I think that Valgerd's behaviour is queer, she is psychologically unstable.
14      I'm worried for Valgerd's ability as a caretaker.
15      She has friends among the drug addicts.
16      She is together with bad characters.
17  D:  I feel extremely uncomfortable with this case.
18      Someone told me that the boy resisted going back to his mother,
19      After being looked after by others.
20      I am worried for Mikael, have been for a long time
21      I see Mikael every day when I bring my daughter to nursery school.
22      He is a sad boy.
23      The lady seems strange and conspicuously resourceful.
24      I can not put my finger on something specific, but there is something

25        Wrong here, something that gives unpleasant feelings
26        It is awful when a child is suffering without anyone being able to
          do something.

We meet here a different narration of the case. It is the same evidence
and information, but "G" and "D" tells a different story than the one told by
"A" and "B".

Again we get an illustration of the insecure traits of the work and how
the workers use feelings and intuition as a way to legitimate their
position."G" opens up by stating that he is worried about the mother's
ability to take care of the boy.

In this way he is demonstrating close feelings for the boy. He also tells
a story about the mother behaving strangely, being unstable and "immoral"
and thus strengthens the narrative that there is something wrong with her.

"D" follows up in the same manner as "G". She expresses her feelings
towards the boy in line 22: "He is a sad boy" and in line 26: "It is awful
when a child is suffering without. . .being able to do something". In line 23
the mother is described as "strange" and "conspicuously resourceful". It is
also a part of a very clever and catching rhetoric, the way she "answers"
"B's" claim about seeing the boy four times (line 9) with telling her story
of seeing the boy every day when she brings her daughter to the nursery
school. So observing the boy daily at nursery school and feeling he is a sad
boy is used as legitimate evidence. Even though she can't put her finger on
something specific (line 24), "D's" story about her own unpleasant feelings
seeing the boy everyday make it seem correct to suspect the mother and to
view the child as being in danger.

So both "G" and "D" narrate a similar story with the same kinds of
rhetorical skills. And they come to a different story than "A", who also has
been using similar kinds of rhetorical skills.

Both stories seem probable. Both stories may be followed up with a
decision. "A" and "B's" story would lead to a dismissing the case. "G" and
"D's" story would probably lead to measures for investigating the family or
perhaps a proposal for removing the boy from the mother.

Who is right? Who knows? Only the future can tell.

I also wonder: Why doesn't "A" surrender to "everyone else's opinion
in this case"? Her position of not agreeing obviously inflicts a lot of pain on
her. So how is it possible for her to keep her position of not worrying about
the boy's situation? It seems obvious that she could have chosen a total
different view of this case and still be on the safe side according to the rules
of child protection work - especially those focusing greatly on the moral

conduct and psychic balance of mothers.[9] As "A" herself put it in a later talk: there's admittedly very strong information in this case. And as we see here, she is under considerable pressure from not just the leader and the people outside, but also from other colleagues. Going through the written papers in this case, many of the "all this" as "A" refers to (line 34) appears in written form. There is among other things stories about the boy being taken into the woods in the night by his mother. Also many people talked to describe the mother as psychologically unstable, as "G" refers to in line 13. There are also several stories about the mother not taking proper care of the boy. My explanation why "A" kept her opinion, in spite of "all this", goes in the direction of seeing the impact of the social organisation of the agency and the typical traits of the work carried out there. It seems that the social organisation of the work supports the individual caseworker's responsibility for her case and positions the others as being there not to interfere with her opinion. It seems like "A" sticks to her first impression of the case and that this is based on a kind of loyalty and understanding towards the mother. It seems that "A" has too much invested into her position to alter it.

In the next extract we follow the conversation as it continued.

27  C:  A, you said, when we talked earlier: 'What if I am wrong?'
28      I want to repeat what I said then, that it is a disaster for ... the boy. If we misjudge.
29      We need help.
30  A:  It is very easy not to like the mother.
31      She is overly dramatic and very clever in an exaggerated way.
32      She lost her temper once, pushed him down. He got bruises.
33      She told the kindergarten right away about the episode....
34      But what if I am wrong?... But all this...can we use it?
35  B:  What is a worry? In child protection, as an official institution we must attach a worry
36      To a paragraph in the law.
37      Even if D is worried we must have something concrete to attach to the worry.
38      What can we investigate further? Our creativity has ended.
39      We re stuck, but we are not worried for Mikael.[10]
40      .
41  D:  I have a feeling, a very strong hunch. We had a case recently we
42      Had to dismiss. This gives me bad feelings that are very strong.
43

| | | |
|---|---|---|
| 44 | | Perhaps I can't work in child protection being like this |
| 45 | | There are many small episodes here, but we do have feelings. |
| 46 | | We are after all human beings. |
| 47 | B: | One must make a difference between getting it out and demanding that it be used. |
| 48 | | One has to have self-discipline. |
| 49 | | Can't ease my fluttering heart in a case about putting a child into care. |
| 50 | C: | Perhaps we must learn to live with our worries about children |
| 51 | B: | One must make a difference between tools for internal use and tools for external use. |
| 52 | | We can think aloud together and discuss internally. |
| 53 | | Outwards, we must come to a decision and carry through the measures |
| 54 | D: | We can also be there to help her. |
| 55 | A: | I don't feel I can justify in front of Valgerd, that more assessment about her ability |
| 56 | | To care is needed. That would be harassment of Valgerd. |
| 57 | B: | This case shows that the internal environment we work in is so important for a case. |
| 58 | | When we disagree it's difficult. |
| 59 | I: | Warning light on! If colleagues disagree on a case, one has to take it up immediately. |
| 60 | | Internal disagreement must be taken up seriously. |
| 61 | | We have to show a unified face to the outside world. |

Here we are once more introduced to more rhetoric of ambivalence and its relation to making the argument seem stronger. This can be seen when "A" shows that she admits she is afraid that she is wrong (line 34). After this 'confession', "B" gives a lecture about child protection work and what is legitimate evidence (line 35,36,37,47,48,49,51,52,53). Her speaking seems strange because it differs so much from the way the others talk. She is here paying attention in a more explicit way to the difference between inside and outside the agency. Feelings are good and legitimate on the inside, but not on the outside.

This extract relates to one of the questions I raised in the former extract about the relation between the individual caseworker and the collective. We see here that pressure is put on the ones who disagree by stating that disagreements are difficult. Several of the speakers focus here on the belief that internal disagreement in a case is dangerous. One has to ask:

Why is it so dangerous? Why is it so important to agree?

It seems to me that the agency's norms have to do with giving respect to the individual nature of responsibility and to support decisions a caseworker arrives at through therapeutic and emotional rituals. In this way, a key role of the collective in child protection may be to give support and back up the caseworker. The rule seems to be one: If you see things differently, do not broadcast it, not even to colleagues.

It appears that "A" has to follow her opinion to balance many aspects linked to the nature of child protection: She has to consider her own feelings and her own gut intuition. When the most experienced worker in the agency supports her, this gives a good reason not to give in. The relation to the mother in the case may also be an explanation of her firmness in this position. She can't defend more investigations in front of the mother, she says.

The power structure among the workers may also have something to do with the results in this case. In observing the internal interactions in the agency I was made aware of a tension linked to its leadership. In this context, the confrontation between the pair "A/B" and "C" might also be seen as linked to a more general criticism aimed at "C's" way of leading the agency. Thus internal fights for dominance, leadership, and about questions of concrete and legitimate knowledge are also issues here.

**Summing Up**

I opened this exploration into the logic of child protection work with a quotation from Mary Douglas's book *How Institutions Think*. This citation indicates the analytical perspective I have tried to pursue: an exploration of the ways a welfare institution of child protection forms its logic, constructs its realities and how the actors inhabiting this institution strive to legitimise the work. This latter aspects, I have suggested, is done by developing rules and rituals to sacralise the work as well as to protect the self-images and self respect of the case workers. In this way, these contribute to preserve the form, shape and survival of the institution.

Thus, the perspective pursued here is a structuralist one, seeing the actors as competent persons responding to the situations they find themselves in.[11] In this perspective the actors' actions are formed by the conditions of the situation and thus no consciousness or strategic impulse is linked to instituted rules and way of thinking. As Fleck puts it (1935, 41):

> The individual within the collective is never, or hardly ever, conscious of the prevailing thought style which almost always exerts an absolutely compulsive force upon his thinking, and with which it is not possible to be at variance (as quoted in Douglas 1987, 13).

The approach presented here has been one aimed at exploring the meaning of the special form of the interaction in the agency. I have seen the themes in the talk of child protection workers as indicators of the social and structural conditions forming their decisions. I also have viewed this talk as expressing efforts and strains linked to the risky situations bound up with making these extremely serious decisions. Thus, I perceive child protection as being formed by forces from internal as well as external contexts. These forces meet inside the child protection agency and are manifested in the interaction and talk between the workers in the agency.

The special features of the field shown in the interactions inside the agency demonstrate a work that entails several vulnerabilities. The vulnerabilities displayed in the talks reflect a lack of solid knowledge as well as other kinds of knowledge demanding personal judgements. Also the lack of public esteem, perhaps following the "dirty" nature of power to interfere in private affairs, is a vulnerable trait of this work. These aspects put the social worker and the profession itself under great pressure and at risk. This makes it necessary for agencies to develop protective measures. The airing of cases, the repetitive and ritualistic forms of the massive amounts of talking and the demonstrative emotional rhetoric of agency interaction may be understood as ways developed to protect individual and professional dignity and identity. Moreover, these activities, I have tried to show, represent ways of coping with vulnerabilities. As I have tried to demonstrate, it seems like the "dirtiness" of the work are "talked away" inside the agency. Thus by talking and narrating the case, the social workers show to themselves and their colleagues the urge to be helpful and good - characteristics that Margolin (1997) has described as a typical social worker traits.

In this perspective, the talking is a kind of legitimisation of the worker's right to take the decision she finds to be a correct one as well as a way to demonstrate that she is a proper social worker. The talk documents her good intentions, her emotional ties to clients as well as her abilities to sense the problems of the clients. So, one major function of agency talk may be to create images of the work as clean and good and thus produce a collective forgetting of the more troublesome aspects of power and illegitimate decisions.

This situation of power linked with an urge to help positions child protection work in a kind of schizophrenic or contradictory situation. This has been documented also in the work of Sunnesson (1981,1983) and Margolin (1997). The contradictory situation may account for the feelings of strain and guilt social workers report experiencing. Recently, when 484 child protection workers from different child protection agencies in Norway were asked about personal strains in their work, nearly two-thirds reported feeling some or considerable strain linked to general opinions of child protection work. About half of the respondents reported experiences of having bad consciences about their work (Veland 1996). Other researchers (Claezon 1987; Håkkansson & Stavne 1983; Killèn 1981) have also found similar difficulties in child protection work.

Concrete consequences of these vulnerabilities may be seen at several levels in the decision making process. One aspect is the consumption of time. Child protection workers use immense amounts of time and effort to carry out their mandate. In the case presented here it seemed to me that a combination of exhaustion and the pressures of time worked to force the workers to bring the case to a conclusion.

Other consequence of these vulnerabilities may be seen in the lack of consistency in the treatment of similar cases (Vagli et al. 1991; Packman, Randall & Jacques 1986). This is evidenced as well in other research findings showing great variance among the work carried out by different child protection agencies (Kristofersen & Slettebø 1992, 1996).

As we have seen, there may have been several legitimate outcomes of the case construction process in the agency. This directs attention to the social factors influencing how cases are constructed in child protection work. The ethnographic perspective developed here visualises the complexity of the work and shows that social workers are put into a complex tapestry of processes. A central question raised by this is: Is it the best we can do to leave the protection of children to professionals behind closed doors?

## Notes

1    I will thank Basil Bernstein, Mike Seltzer and Hannele Forsberg for comments, suggestions and corrections in the process of writing this chapter.

2    White (1997, 19) makes a similar comment about the dominant perspective in child protection research in Great Britain: "Many commentaries on current practice have failed to examine the rich details of the everyday. They have paid little attention to the 'thinking as usual' (Atkinson 1995). Thus their work has tended to imply that dominant forms of practice have, in some way, been imposed, either directly, by the Government, or the judiciary....In short, in failing to examine the hurly-burly of institutional discourse, they have tended to edit out the productive and reproductive capacity of agents."

3    Hammersley (1992) has discussed the tension in ethnographical studies between a naturalistic approach as a justification of authenticity and an obvious constructivistic nature of the tradition.

4    As Egelund (1997, 257) says with reference to Foucault: "The practice of power is spun into the constructing discourse, and the discourse carry the practice of power. It is this differentiating process that are the centre and basis for the disciplining power."

5    Hughes (1951) describes "dirty work" and its consequences.

6    I refer here in an indirect way to Bourdieu & Wacquant (1993). On page 28 in the Norwegian edition of this book Bourdieu's constructivistic approach, linked to a structuralistic tradition, is described in the following way: "Even if...the social agents are constructing the social reality, individually, but also collectively, you must take care not to forget, as some interactionist and ethnomethodologists do, that the social agents do not construct the categories they use in this construction work."

7    The participants were: female caseworker in this case - A; female caseworker 2 in this case - B; the female leader - C; female worker - D; female worker - E; female worker - F; male worker - G; male worker - H; consultants - I and K; Valgerd - a fictitious name for the mother in this case; and Mikael - a fictitious name for the boy in this case.

8    Egelund (1997) found out that child protection workers very often do not visit the family about whom they are making decisions.

9    As has been shown by many investigations in child protection cases, the decisions are often legitimated by means of reference to moral judgements of the mother's behavior (Dingwall, Eekelaar & Murray 1983; Egelund 1997; Hydén 1995; Clifford & Lichwach 1996).

10    The dot in between lines indicates that something is omitted from the original conversations. Several dots on the same line indicate hesitation.

11    Karl Mannheim says: "Both motives and actions very often originate not from within, but from the situation in which the individuals find themselves." The citation is from Freidson (1988, 85) who uses it to head the chapter he calls: The Organisation of Professional Performance.

# Bibliography

Atkinson, Paul (1995) *Medical Talk and Medical Work*, London: Sage.

Bernstein, Basil (1996) *Pedagogy, Symbolic Control and Identity: Theory, Research, Critique*. London: Taylor & Francis.

Bourdieu, P. and Wacquant, L. (1993) *Den kritiske ettertanke. Grunnlag for samfunnsanalyse.* Oslo: Det Norske Samlaget.

Claezon, Ingrid and Larsson, Siv Britt (1985) *Det svåra valet*. Stockholm: Liber Forlag.

Dingwall, Robert, Eekelaar, John and & Murray,Topsy (1983) *The Protection of Children.* *State Intervention and Family Life.* Oxford: Basil Blackwell.

Douglas, Mary (1987) *How Institutions Think.* London: Routledge & Kegan Paul.

Egelund, Tine (1997) *Beskyttelse av barndommen. Socialforvaltningers risikovurdering og indgrep* København: Hans Reitzels Forlag.

Fleck, Ludwik (1935) *The Genesis and Development of a Scientific Fact.* (1979 translation) Chicago: University of Chicago Press.

Foucault, Michel (1994) *The Birth of the Clinic.* New York: Vintage Books.

Freidson, Eliot (1970, 1988) *Profession of Medicine. A study of the Sociology of Applied Knowledge.* Chicago:University of Chicago Press.

Geertz, Clifford (1972) *The Interpretation of Cultures.* London: Hutchinson.

Goffman, E. (1989) On Fieldwork. *Journal of Contemporary Ethnography* (18), 123-132.

Hammersley, M. (1992) *What's Wrong with Ethnography?* New York and London: Routledge.

Hammersley, M. and Atkinson, P. (1995) *Ethnography. Principles in Practice.* (2nd edition) London and New York: Routledge.

Heino, Tarja (1997) *Obscure Areas of Clienthood in Child Protection. The Construction of a Child Protection Client by Social Workers.* Stakes, National Research and Development Centre for Welfare and Health. Research Studies 77: Helsinki.

Hughes, Everett C. (1951) Work and the Self. In Rohrer, J. and Sherif, M. (eds.) *Social Psychology at the Crossroads.* New York: Harper.

Hydén, Lars-Christer (1995) Det sociala misslyckandet som berättelse. Att återställa den moraliska ordningen. *Socialvetenskaplig tidsskrift* (3).

Håkansson, Håkan & Stavne, K. (1983) *Jag känner mig så himla osäker.* Stockholm: Skeab Forlag.

Killen Heap, Kari (1981) *Barnemishandling. Behandlerens dilemma.* Oslo: Tanum-Norli.

Kristofersen, L. and Slettebø, T. (1992) *Til barnets beste. Regionale variasjoner i barnevernstiltak.* NIBR-rapport: 6. Oslo: Norsk Institutt for By-og Regionforskning.

Kristofersen, Lars B. (1996) Regionale variasjoner i barneverns - Norge 1990-1993. *Norges Barnevern* (2).

Lichtwarck, Willy and Clifford, Graham (1996) *Samarbeid i barnevernet : ideologi, endring og konflikt.* Oslo: Tano.

Margolin, L. (1997) *Under the Cover of Kindness. The Invention of Social Work.* Charlottesville: University Press of Virginia.

Pithouse, Andrew and Atkinson, Paul (1988) Telling the Case: Occupational Narrative in a Social Work Office. In Couplan, N. (ed) *Styles of Discourse.* London: Beckenham.

Smith, Dorothy E. (1978) K Is Mentally Ill: The Anatomy of Factual Account. *Sociology,* (12), 23-53.

Sunesson, Sune (1981) *När man inte lyckast. Om hinder, vanmakt och oförmåga i socialt arbete.* Stockholm: Almquist & Wiksell Förlag.

Sunesson, Sune (1983) Socialhjälp - makt och altruism. *Nordisk Socialt Arbeid* (3), 52-62.

Vagli, Åse et al. (1991) *Atferdsproblemer og tiltak for barn og unge. En undersøkelse fra Finnmark.* NIBR-rapport:1. Oslo: Norsk Institutt for By-og Regionforskning.

Veland, Jarmund (1996) *Er det greit å være barnevernsarbeider i dag?* Paper. Nordisk symposium om sosialt arbeid. Trondheim, Norway. 21-23 August 1996.

White, Susan (1997) *Examining the Artfulness of Risk-Talk.* Paper. Conference on Constructing Social Work Practices. Tampere, Finland. 13-15 August 1997.

# Part III
# Talking About Unemployment, Activation and Career Training in the Welfare State

Work has held a time-honoured place in the ideologies of the Social Democratic political parties of Finland and Scandinavia. Therefore, a key area of policy planning and implementation in the Nordic welfare systems long has been one directed toward providing full employment for everyone. This ideal of jobs for all able bodied, together with the "work ethic" and the view that unemployment is an evil to be eradicated, have played a central role in labour-market and related programs of Denmark, Finland, Norway and Sweden. Given these strong ideological anchors and the massive compilations of data measuring such programs at the macro-level in Nordic societies, it is surprising how little is known about how unemployment benefits as well as work related initiatives of various sorts are effectuated at street-level by welfare professionals.

Thus, the following two chapters provide us with much needed data about these little-explored areas. In the first selection from Denmark, Olesen presents a minutely detailed picture of the interactional dynamics and results of public encounters between employment officials and unemployed persons. Using a blend of quantitative and qualitative methods, his account is unique in that it provides space for the users of these welfare programs to voice their assessments of service delivery. In the second selection from Finland, Vehviläinen - a former career counsellor - returns to familiar grounds to focus specifically on how counselling practitioners deal with problems presented to them by their adult student clients. Marshalling an array of conversation analytic date, she presents us with a rich account of how these relative newcomers to the professional ranks of the NWS operate in their dealings with troubling issues presented by their clients. The differences and similarities between her account and that presented by Olesen provide a comparative perspective for examining how work, joblessness, careers and related issues of importance are dealt with in public encounters at the micro-level of the NWS.

# 5 Discourses of Activation at Danish Employment Offices

SØREN PETER OLESEN

This chapter is about public encounters between unemployed persons and employment officials at Danish employment offices. The purpose is to give a summary of some of the findings in a detailed comparative study of 32 action plan talks and to demonstrate the combination of research methods used.

The *first section* introduces the study of encounters at employment offices between unemployed members of unemployment insurance funds and employment officials, implementing the activation goals in the Danish labour market reform from 1994 through talks about individual action plans. The *second section* summarises selected results from the study. The *third section* combines quantitative and qualitative methods and considers some of the methodological problems in studying talk-in-interaction in institutional settings. Finally the *fourth section* briefly presents conclusions from this study and perspectives in the study of public encounters more generally, including a few perspectives concerning professional counselling making a difference.

## Section 1 Introduction

*Activation and the Balancing of Individual Wishes and Labour Market Demands*

During the last decade a change has been taking place in Danish social and labour market policy (Labour Market Studies: Denmark 1996). As in several other countries, activation and integration have increasingly become overall catchwords (Boje 1992). The change has been manifest in the policy towards members as well as non-members of unemployment insurance funds. This study, however, focuses exclusively on members of unemployment insurance funds and encounters at employment offices.

More broadly speaking a rearrangement of the welfare setting is going on (Pierson 1991; Rothstein 1994). Activation policies put more emphasis on the individual as regards flexibility and availability than the kinds of demands seen in the labour market policy of the previous decades.

In 1994 a thorough reform of Danish labour market policy took place. This resulted in a decentralisation and new strategic instruments in Danish labour market policy. Prominent among these were individual plans of action and talks about the elaboration of such plans aimed at employment through counselling and guidance, job-seeking, training or education. Individual action-plans were to be produced through a process of information and counselling, including one or a number of talks of the duration of about half an hour. During this process the purpose according to the new laws was to obtain a balancing of the wishes and qualifications of the unemployed individual on the one hand and on the other the needs and demands on the labour market. This may be considered a crossroads of policy rationality (Larsen et al. 1996) and the interactional order (Goffman 1983). The question raised by this was: Is it possible to reconcile individual wishes with state and market demands through talk-in-interaction in public encounters - and what happens if one tries?

Since the reform in 1994, the elaboration of individual action plans has been a right for the unemployed after 6 months of unemployment (originally 3 months during the first reform years). The elaboration of the plans takes place through conversations and other kinds of contact between the unemployed person and employment officials. This indicates that the encounters and specifically the face-to-face interactions between unemployed and officials may be crucial as regards the final delivery and the eventual reception of strategically important parts of welfare state unemployment policy.

However, public encounters and the relationships between citizens/users/clients and officials effectuating welfare state policy is so far a neglected research field, especially in the Danish setting (Koch & Eskelinen 1997) specifically regarding relations between individuals and social welfare authorities. Thus, evaluations of the labour market reform to date have focused primarily on the regional (meso-) level or have been of a generalising statistical character (e.g. *Undersøgelse af arbejds-markedsreformen* 1995; Winter et al. 1995; Haahr & Winter 1996; Larsen et al. 1996; Langager 1997; Bjerregård Bach 1997).

Internationally, attempts at establishing the public encounters as a research field were launched in the 1980s but still are of a provisional character (Bleiklie 1996). Nevertheless, public encounters are taking place to an increasing extent, not least in the Nordic welfare systems, characterised as they are by increasing numbers of public employees producing and delivering service to citizens/users/clients.

As an illustration of this, the number of action plan interviews at Danish employment offices was 214,061 in 1994, 291,809 in 1995 and 262,164 in 1996. On the average, well over 2 interviews are held per action plan. The total number of individual interviews at employment offices was 627,814 in 1996, at a level of about 150,000 more than prior to the labour market reform (Arbejdsmarkedsstyrelsen 1995, 46; 1996, 75; 1997, 59).

The increasing number of public encounters places new demands on public employees. Traditional civil servant roles change considerably, and officials become vested not only with legal powers but also with wider discretion. Hansen (1995, 36) emphasises the need for a new ethics able to structure the autonomy and discretion that civil servants increasingly have obtained in the implementation of public policy.

Research in public encounters is not in itself going to lead to such a new ethics, but research could be of practical importance and consequence in the evaluation and development of guidance- and counselling strategies and methods. New demands are also placed on citizens/users/clients, as contact with the welfare state system increasingly become a matter of negotiating terms and adapting measures, rather than making a matter of a "take it or leave it" offer. Traditional bureaucratic routines are no longer adequate. An increasing number of public encounters means new forms of linkages and ruptures between individual and society or, rather, between the micro-, meso- and macro-level of society (Mouzelis 1995), thus leading to new demands on social theory and on social research methods.

Most research in welfare state and social work problems has been on a macro- or meso-level and/or has focused on alienation and clientification rather than involvement and participation of the citizens/users/clients (Koch & Eskelinen 1997, 84). Social work is here understood as a broad concept. In a Nordic setting, social work includes the concept of public encounter and therefore encompasses the counselling and guidance of unemployed people. While the tendency towards alienation and clientification should not be neglected, there is a clear and strong need also to focus on integration, involvement and participation in the implementation of social and labour market policy as well as on other factors leading to implementation of welfare state policy (Rothstein 1994). This is also the case here. Moreover, a number of arguments point in that direction: The policy-intentions, as mentioned, are centred on involvement of the unemployed individual in elaborating the activation measures. Evaluation and development of practice and work-methods point to or require focusing on opportunities and conditions of involvement rather than solely on alienation and clientification. Finally, specific aspects of the Nordic welfare states and Nordic political culture regarding popular participation might be emphasised (Klausen & Selle 1995; Rasborg 1997).


## Section 2  Selected Results

In Denmark in the past two years an ongoing study of public encounters at employment offices has been conducted (Olesen 1997). A theoretical frame of reference has been developed, as well as methods and techniques of processing and analysing quantitative as well as qualitative data about the micro-processes of policy-implementation in the public encounter.

The provisional results of this study - still in progress - suggest, for instance, that a specific discourse structure, a case work model, on average seems to prevail across rather different types of encounters, but also that systematic differences occur between different categories of talks.

Unsatisfactory conversations, for instance, are more unequal as regards linguistic dominance and more routinised than satisfactory conversations. This is especially so from the point of view of the unemployed individual and the interactional order as well as from the point of view of labour market rationality. Further, the results suggest that face happens to be more protected in satisfactory than in unsatisfactory con-versations. Also, the results demonstrate that there are big differences between the encounters depending upon the type of official and the type of unemployed person involved.

### 2.1  Theoretical Framework and Key Concepts

From the viewpoint of policy implementation a public encounter can be defined as face-to-face interaction between two persons. In this case the one part is a representative of a public authority, here the employment office, vested with legal powers, discretion and the obligation to deliver public service. The other part is a citizen/user/client seeking public service, here an unemployed person (Grunow 1978; Lipsky 1980; Goodsell 1981). A somewhat similar way of looking at the encounter might be to apply the classic sociological concept of gatekeeping (Erickson & Schutz 1982).

From the interactional point of view this kind of public encounter is a matter of talk at work. This refers to talk-in-interaction as "the principal means through which lay persons pursue various practical goals and the central medium through which the daily working activities of many professionals and organisational representatives are conducted" (Drew & Heritage 1992, 3). According to Goffman (1967, 1983), structural traits are reproduced in the interaction process. However, there is also the possibility of softening and loosening structural traits if face is preserved. Goffman (1983, 8) mentions processing encounters in this connection. The experience of action plan talks as being satisfactory/unsatisfactory and the occurrence of professional counselling and guidance measures is assumed to be one of the decisive aspects as regards the possibility of softening/-loosening structural traits.

The theoretical construction of the encounter in this study is thus one in which the face-to-face interaction process between an unemployed person and an employment official is viewed as the merging of two separate processes. The starting points of these processes lie far beyond the encounter itself. On the one hand a policy implementation process, ending in the application of counselling/guidance-strategy and method, and on the other hand, a service-seeking process (Winter 1981, 1985, 1994a, 1994b; Lindh 1994; Lovén 1995; Arbejdsmarkedsorienteret vejledning 1995; Bleiklie 1996).

The policy implementation process rests on the assumption of some sort of linearity between policy-decisions and the delivery of service by some kind of hierarchical organisation passes on, finally, through the application of counselling and guidance methods. However, this linearity may be complicated or impeded by deprecating mechanisms at different levels, even and maybe especially among the street-level officials (Lipsky 1980). Officials may further apply different styles (Kagan 1994). The service-seeking process may be complicated or impeded as well: the service-seeking person must overcome a number of barriers or thresholds in order to get the service he/she is entitled to (Jacobsen 1982). To some people, however, service seeking is the wrong word. They may consider the service as irrelevant, or they may feel it is a kind of "offer you can't refuse". In other words, citizens/users/clients have different public identities, based on their actual political, economic and social rights as well as on their previous experiences with public services (Hetzler 1994).

Thus, the interaction in the encounter is determined in a complicated way by the situation, the dispositions of the parties and by their positions as well (Mouzelis 1995). It is obvious that in some respects the encounter is very far from an equal relationship. The actors often have very different points of departure (e.g. Willis 1981).

It is also obvious, however, that the question of who dominates the encounter, as well as whether and how face is preserved, is an empirical matter in the single encounter. It is not unequivocally predetermined by the dispositions or the positions of the parties involved (although they are important). It is a question as well of the course of the interaction (Drew & Heritage 1992, 53).

The figure below illustrates how the implementation and service-seeking processes are assumed to be merging or overlapping with the interaction process:

| Policy Implementation Process | Interaction Process | Service Seeking Process |
|---|---|---|
| The national social and labour market policy as adapted at regional and local levels. | The public encounter between unemployed persons and welfare state officials. | The living conditions, culture and experiences of education, employment and unemployment among unemployed persons. |

──────────▶ Official ◀──────▶ Unemployed ◀──────────

**Figure 1   The Theoretical Perspectives as Regards the Public Encounter**

Turner (1987, 168) warns against a premature linking of micro- and macro-perspectives. One might argue, however, that the development in labour market relations and in social and labour market policy requires concepts and theories, which establish vertical connections between different structural levels. Mouzelis (1995, 156) proposes such vertical linking of different levels in theoretical as well as empirical research, calling for the construction of concepts that break down the barriers and strengthen the bridges between them.

*2.2 The Problem*

The overall problem of this study of 32 encounters in the implementation of labour market policy refers to the intentions of the 1994 Danish labour market reform of balancing individual and labour market considerations in encounters/talks at employment offices about elaboration of individual plans of action.

With this outset the main theme of the study was constructed as follows. What is going on in the encounters, and what are the conditions - as regards linguistic dominance, attendance to interests, preservation of face and professional guidance methods - of balancing individual and labour market considerations in talks about individual plans of action?

The selected results in this section focus on linguistic dominance, measured by the distribution of speaking time and the distribution of initiatives and responses in two categories of talks (satisfactory versus unsatisfactory) and further on 4 types of officials, related to the same two categories. Based on interviews with the unemployed persons immediately after the encounters had taken place, the 32 encounters studied were divided into 2 fairly distinct clusters of 17 satisfactory and 15 unsatisfactory encounters from the point of view of the service-seeking individuals. The reasons given by the unemployed persons for their perception of the talks they had participated in as being satisfactory/unsatisfactory is of interest in itself, but of special relevance from a labour market policy point of view as well as from the point of view of the interaction order.

Satisfactory talks - from the point of view of the unemployed - were characterised by experiencing receiving not only information about rights, duties and possibilities in the labour market system but also a general outlook and clarification as regards starting up or getting further with something. Thereby satisfactory talks functioned as a planning tool for the unemployed individual. Finally, according to the unemployed persons themselves, satisfactory talks were interactionally characterised by contact, presence, interest, support, empathy and encouragement exhibited by employment officials. This was evidenced in officials who showed they were well prepared, who asked relevant questions and demonstrated role security/authority on behalf of their clients.

Unsatisfactory talks, regardless of giving demanded information, were characterised by not bringing clarification but rather by dealing with halfway solutions or indifferent offers, which were not believed to increase the chances of getting employment and to which the parties had low expectations. Unsatisfactory talks, therefore, were not assumed to be of any use or being worth anything. They constituted an unavoidable evil or were at best redundant. Further, they were characterised by the unemployed and also the official party as appearing to be indifferent, uncaring, non-engaged, inattentive regarding the human aspects of the talk and, finally, by both parties being unprepared.

One way of elucidating the balancing of individual and labour market considerations during the action plan talks is through the description and analysis of similarities and differences between the two categories of encounters mentioned, using linguistic data and analyses of language use.

## 2.3 The Design and the Data Structure

The overall methodological design of the study and of the discussion in this paper as well is thus comparative (Ragin 1987, 1994; Yin 1989). Quantitative as well as qualitative techniques and analyses are applied in a comparative design with the purpose, among others, of finding and analysing interactional similarities and differences between satisfactory and unsatisfactory encounters.

The data were structured along the assumed line of the policy implementation process (Winter 1994). A preliminary study of selected encounters was conducted in 1994 (Olesen 1997a). The intentions and the passing of the labour market reform of 1994 were covered by documents. The labour market reform implied a decentralisation to the regional level. Documents and interviews with leaders at various levels in each of the two regions included in the study were collected. These focused specifically on the intentions and implementations of the labour market reform. At the local level, 4 employment offices, two in each of the two regions, were involved. Interviews with office-leaders were collected before the encounters took place. After each round of 4 encounters, the 8 staff members were interviewed about their perception of the labour market reform, the action-plan talks and their strategy and use of counselling and guidance methods in the talks. During this period, office observations were made. Finally, and most importantly, the talks in the 32 encounters were observed and tape-recorded. Immediately after the encounters had taken place, the unemployed persons were interviewed about their perception of the encounter, the talk and the action-plan as such, following a loosely structured, not standardised, interview-guide. The data-collection took place during the months January to May 1996.

**The Structure of the Data:**

| | |
|---|---|
| National level: The 1994 labour market reform | Documents |
| Regional level: Regional policy, 2 regions | Documents, interviews |
| Office level: 4 offices, 2 in each region | Interviews |
| "Street-level": 8 officials, 2 at each office | Observations, interviews |
| Encounter-level: 32 talks, 4 with each official | Tape-recordings, observations, interviews, documents |

Talks between the 8 officials and the 32 unemployed persons took about half an hour on the average. They contained 4848 turns. The sound was transformed to CD-ROM and handled with *Kit* (a software program developed in 1995 by C.V. Skov at the Psychology Department of Aarhus University). Information about the following variables of each of the turns was stored in a database (Microsoft Access): starting and finishing times; turn-taking; number of backchannellings; initiative-response aspects; instrumental aspects; expressive aspects. As regards the text, no transcription was made, while analyses were made directly on the sound, but catchwords concerning the content and the course of each turn were taken down in a text space in the posts of the database.

*2.4 Satisfactory Versus Unsatisfactory Talks: Analysis and Results*

*2.4.1   The Distribution of Speaking Time*   On average the speaking time (including pauses in turns, but excluding pauses in the encounters) in the 32 talks was 27.2 min., the unemployed having 10.7 min. or 39.5 % and the employment officials having 16.4 min. or 60.5 % of the time.

The satisfactory talks were somewhat longer than the unsatisfactory, the average length being 31.9 min. and 25.6 min., but with a relatively high dispersion in both categories. For instance the 3 shortest of the unsatisfactory talks lasted about 8, 13 and 17 min. respectively. In these cases the duration of the talks might be seen as one of the traits making them unsatisfactory. The shortest of the satisfactory talks, however, were not much longer (about 12 and 16 min. respectively), and one of these (16 min.) was indeed the most positively commented talk in the data material. Further, in the satisfactory as well as the unsatisfactory talks, all of the unemployed said they had been able to speak and say what they wanted; and only one mentioned specifically that this had been too short a talk (13 min.). Thus, this analysis does not solve any riddle about how long time action-plan-talks or other kinds of public encounters take or ought to take. In addition, for good reasons, individual action-plans and action-plan-talks were not considered as standardised implementation measures (Rapport 1992,57).

As regards the distribution of the average speaking time it was a little more unequal in the unsatisfactory than in the satisfactory talks: 37.2 % and 63.8 % vs. 41.5 and 57.5 %. The fact that even the satisfactory talks appeared to be rather unequal as regards speaking time might be considered surprising. The parties may have had some preconceptions of talk in institutional settings. None of the unemployed, however, complained about the employment officials talking too much, not even in the talk with the most unequal distribution of speaking time (where the employment official had 80.1 % of the speaking time). In a few cases, on the contrary, the unemployed persons mentioned that they themselves had perhaps talked excessively.

Looking specifically at the speaking time of the unemployed person as the product of the length of a talk and the quota of the total speaking time in the talk leads to a more plain connection between speaking time and satisfaction. On average the unemployed in the unsatisfactory talks had a speaking time of about 8 min., whereas it was about 12½ min. in the satisfactory talks. In 8 of the 15 unsatisfactory talks the unemployed had less than 8 min. while this was the case in only 4 of the 17 satisfactory talks. However, this should not be considered a simple causal relationship. Rather, the tendency towards unequal distribution of the speaking time is just one aspect of the unsatisfactory talks. The subject of speaking time is also treated below in connection with the analysis of 4 types of employment officials (paragraph 7.2).

*2.4.2 Turn-taking* As much as 85.9 % of the 4848 passages in the talks were smooth, 11.1 % with overlap and only 1.7 % was interruptions. Thus the talks may be broadly characterised as overall well ordered, presumably reflecting their institutional character. There was a little less smooth turn-taking (that is, without overlap or interruptions) by the unemployed while officials were somewhat more correct and less spontaneous than the unemployed. Interruptions and overlap as marginal phenomena in the talks occurred more frequently in the satisfactory than in the unsatisfactory talks. These were assumed to be indications of intensity in the interaction rather than of tensions and conflicts.

*2.4.3 Number of Backchannellings* Backchannellings are manifestations of attention from the listener to the speaker (Berg Sørensen 1988a, 1988b). Interactionally backchannellings are an important part of the constitution of mutually focused attention. The tapes catch only the vocal backchannellings some of which even may have been lost. Various connections may occur between the level of backchannellings and satisfaction. For instance (a) if a party in a talk is unsatisfied it may cause a low level of backchannellings. However, (b) if a party at a talk is exposed to a low level of backchannellings it may cause interaction appearing to be unsatisfactory unless other factors indicate attention and empathy. The 32 talks contain several examples of these mechanisms. Both unemployed and employment officials, however, gave on the average 1.2 backchannellings per turn and there were only small differences between the average level of backchannellings in satisfactory and unsatisfactory talks. There was, however, a tendency towards slightly higher feedback-level from the employment official in the satisfactory (1.3 backchannellings per turn) compared to the unsatisfactory talks (1.1 backchannellings per turn).

*2.4.4 Three Phases in the Talks* The talks were divided into *3 phases, each containing 1/3 of the turns* in the talk. One tendency appearing was where unemployed persons gave few backchannellings in the first third of the turns. This then increased to a higher level in the middle and last third of the turns. On the other hand, there was a tendency by employment officials to give many backchannellings in the first third of the turns. This then decreased to a lower level in the middle and the last third of the turns. On the average the number of audible backchannellings per turn from employment officials dropped from 1.4 over 1.2 to 0.9, while the number of backchannellings per turn from the unemployed increased from 0.7 over 1.3 to 1.6 in the 3 phases of the talks respectively.

The pattern appearing in these results may be interpreted as reflecting a casework model of the talks rather than a dialogue with mutual negotiation and balancing of the interests of the parties. Towards the end of the talks, it was the officials who had the largest share of the speaking time in summing up, proposing or "making" decisions. The unemployed, on the contrary, tended to have a reduced role as an audience, giving approval through backchannellings and short turns. Behind this lay lie a wide spectrum of consent and / or resistance, both overt and covert.

The total speaking time of 14.5 hours / 867.6 minutes was distributed over the 3 phases as follows: 237.9 min. in the first phase, 311.7 min. in the second and 318.1 in the third. On the average, speaking time was 7.4 / 9.7 / 9.9 minutes per talk in the 3 phases respectively. In other words, there was a tendency towards longer turns at the end of the talks than at the beginning. Behind this, however, there were great systematic differences in the distribution of speaking time between the two parties in the talks. Of the total speaking time, the unemployed had 342.8 min. or about 40 %, as mentioned above, while the officials had 524.8 min. or about 60 %. Distributed over the 3 phases the unemployed had 125.8 / 120.2 / 96.8 minutes or on the average per talk 3.9 / 3.8 / 3.0 minutes, and the officials had 112.1 / 191.5 / 221.2 minutes or on the average per talk 3.5 / 6.0 / 6.9 minutes.

Thus, starting with a little less speaking time than the unemployed in the first phase, the officials on the average had over 50 % more speaking time in the second phase and over 100 % more speaking time in the last phase than the unemployed. The systematic differences, described here, were somewhat more outspoken in the first region than in the second. In the first region the officials thus had the longest speaking time in all 3 phases, and in the third phase almost 3 times the speaking time of the unemployed.

Behind these results lies a discourse structure reflecting a role shift during the talks. The talks began with the officials having the role of asking questions and the unemployed answering. The talks finished with the officials having the role of telling about activation offers and the consequences of this for unemployed person, while the unemployed had the role of listening, asking a few questions and confirming the agreements and decisions made and the conclusions developed by the official. A partly similar pattern was found in a 1982 study of student counselling (Erickson & Schutz 1982, 22). It might be questioned, however, whether this discourse structure is able to advance the intended balancing of individual and labour market considerations, including a genuine negotiation of the interests of the parties.

*2.4.5  Initiative-response Analysis  Initiative-response analysis* (Lineal & Gustavsson 1987) was from the beginning of this study thought of as a main point in the design and approach. This approach constitutes another way of illustrating linguistic dominance than the distribution of speaking time.

Initiative-response analysis may as well be applied to a quantitative, a qualitative and, as in this case, a predominantly comparative methodological design. Per Linell and Lennart Gustavsson developed it at Linköping University in Sweden. It was used in Denmark by Torben Berg Sørensen (1989, 1995) and in Sweden by Erik Fredín (1993) in analyses of talks at social welfare offices. Linell and Gustavsson (1987) depart from an ideal type concept of a classical dialogue, where each turn is related to the previous as well as the following turn, replying to what was said and adding something new to the interaction. Each turn is thus considered a move in a language game. The analysis makes a distinction between aspects of turns pointing to the following turn, initiatives, and aspects pointing backward to the previous turn, responses. As an ideal type the classical dialogue is constructed as a conceptual and analytical tool, not as a normative ideal. It may have some relation to existing values about how the interaction ought to be in this case, for instance values and norms about reciprocity, co-operation and balancing of individual and labour market considerations in action-plan-talks.

Linell and Gustavsson developed an elaborate set of 18 turn-categories. In this study, however, it was possible to divide the turns into three categories:

1   *Minimal responses* (turns pointing only backwards in the dialogue, responding to the previous turn without adding something new to the dialogue); coding value 2.
2   *Extended responses* with limited initiative (turns pointing backwards as well as forwards in the dialogue, but without demanding a response from the counterpart; coding value 3.
3   Extended responses with *strong initiative* (responding to the previous turn, adding something new to the dialogue and at the same time demanding a reply from the counterpart); coding value 3.

The action-plan-talks were relatively well ordered talks in institutional settings: these were, for instance, characterised by few misunderstandings, few leaps in topic and a relatively clear purpose. The limitation to 3 categories of turns led to very few difficulties or doubts during the coding of the turns. The distance from a purely classical dialogue is probably less than in many other dialogues, including everyday talks, although a number of monologue-like turns appeared especially from the official party in the talks.

The turns were given the values 2, 3 and 4 respectively, leading to comparability with other studies using initiative-response analysis, including Linell and Gustavsson's results. They also, but not frequently, use the values 1, 5 and 6. Although this scale as a starting point was constructed as an ordinal scale Linell and Gustavsson in practice applied it as an interval scale, thereby giving way to the calculation of the average turn strength, initiative-response-coefficient or IR-coefficient, in a talk or at one of the parties in a talk. Likewise the difference between the average turn strength of the parties, *IR-difference*, may be calculated. Friends, for example, will often use many extended responses with limited initiative in their mutual communication and have an equal distribution of turn categories. This will, as an illustration of the initiative-response analysis, lead to IR-coefficients around 3.0 and IR-differences close to zero. Contrary to this, an inquiry or examination will often consist of mainly strong initiatives from the one party and mainly minimal responses from the other, thus leading to an IR-difference close to 2.0. Institutional talks typically appear with IR-differences from just under 0.5 and upwards. In the pilot study (Olesen 1997a) the average IR-difference in 10 1994-action-plan-talks was 0.61, and in this study it was 0.62. Berg Sørensen (1995) by way of comparison showed an average IR-difference of 0.43 in talks at Danish social welfare offices, whereas Fredín (1993) found an average of 0.66 in talks at Swedish social welfare offices. This indicates a relative stability and reliability in the initiative-response-analysis of linguistic dominance. Thus, the IR-coefficients and IR-differences are assessed as rendering fair estimates of linguistic dominance in different categories of talks as well as in the single talk. Further these quantitative estimates are considered to be reasonable points of departure for comparative as well as qualitative analyses when combined with different other quantitative and qualitative estimates. It could, for instance, be the distribution of speaking time or provisions for the preservation of face / the use of different strategies of politeness (Brown & Levinson 1987). The use of different approaches and different types of data framed by an overall comparative design forms a case of methodical triangulation (Hoffmeyer-Zlotnik 1992).

*The Distribution of Turns in 32 Action-plan-talks According to Holder of the Turn and Turn-category*

| Turn-category (coding value): | (2) | (3) | (4) | (Total in %) |
|---|---|---|---|---|
| Holder of the turn: | | | | |
| (Unemployed) | 25.3 | 63.0 | 11.6 | 99.9 |
| (Official) | 6.0 | 45.6 | 48.4 | 100.0 |
| (Total) | 15.6 | 54.2 | 30.1 | 99.9 |

Well over half of the turns in the 32 talks were of the category extended responses with limited initiative, coded with the value 3; their quota of the total amount of turns is viewed as a measure of *coherence* in the talks. A high degree of coherence in a talk means that the interaction is well functioning and mutual (Linell & Gustavsson 1987, 202). This corresponds to an overall image from the observations of the talks as being well ordered and well functioning. On the other hand the different positions and roles of the parties was reflected in the fact that 25.3 % of the turns of the unemployed were minimal responses whereas this was the case with just 6.0 % of the officials' turns. And whereas just over one tenth of the turns of the unemployed were extended responses with strong initiatives, this was the case with almost half of the officials' turns.

*The Distribution of Turns in 17 Satisfactory Action-plan-talks According to Holder of the Turn and Turn-category*

| Turn-category (coding value): | (2) | (3) | (4) | (Total in %) |
|---|---|---|---|---|
| Holder of the turn: | | | | |
| (Unemployed) | 22.3 | 66.0 | 11.8 | 100.1 |
| (Official) | 5.8 | 50.0 | 44.1 | 99.9 |
| (Total) | 14.0 | 57.9 | 28.1 | 100.0 |

*The Distribution of Turns in 15 Unsatisfactory Action-plan-talks According to Holder of the Turn and Turn-category*

| Turn-category (coding value): | (2) | (3) | (4) | (Total in %) |
|---|---|---|---|---|
| Holder of the turn: | | | | |
| (Unemployed) | 30.4 | 58.5 | 11.1 | 100.0 |
| (Official) | 6.0 | 38.1 | 55.9 | 100.0 |
| (Total) | 18.1 | 48.3 | 33.6 | 100.0 |

Comparing the satisfactory and the unsatisfactory talks, it was extended responses with limited initiative that caused coherence. Coded with the value 3, they constituted an obviously smaller quota of the turns in the unsatisfactory than in the satisfactory talks. The difference was most obvious when splitting the results according to holder of the turn. The unemployed had a much weaker footing in the unsatisfactory than in the satisfactory talks with just below one third minimal responses, coded as 2, whereas well beyond half of the officials' turns were responses with strong initiative, coded as 4. Compared to this the corresponding figures in the satisfactory talks were 22.3 % and 44.1 %.

The linguistic dominance of the official party in the talks was thus considerably more outspoken in the unsatisfactory than in the satisfactory talks. The average IR-difference, as an expression of the difference between the average strength of the turns of each of the parties, gives a condensed measure of this linguistic dominance. It was 0.62 as an average in the 32 talks as a whole but 0.51 and 0.76 in the satisfactory and the unsatisfactory talks respectively.

The provisional conclusion concerning linguistic dominance and satisfaction in the action-plan talks is thus an obvious connection although not necessarily one involving causality. Although the unemployed said they had been able to get in words during the talks, there was an outspoken lack of linguistic balance in the talks, and this deficiency was especially outspoken in the unsatisfactory part of the talks. From the point of view of the intentions of balancing of individual and labour market considerations in the individual action-plans, this could be considered a serious shortcoming. Taken together with the unequal distribution of speaking time, this amounts to the conclusion that linguistic dominance formed an important trait or symptom in the action-plan-talks.

*2.4.6 Four Types of Staff Members and Satisfactory / Unsatisfactory Talks*
The following focuses on the relation between the officials' way of handling the talks and specifically their counselling strategies and methodical consciousness on the one hand and satisfaction on the other. In the first sections of the chapter, the focus was on the talks as such, each talk being conceived as a case of an encounter between the welfare state and an unemployed person. The focus here is on the style of the official part in the encounter, each employment official being a case of public service delivery or street-level bureaucracy in action (Lipsky 1980). Talking about style in connection with the employment officials as producers of public service is an application of the conception of *regulatory enforcement style* (Kagan 1994).

Of course, one might have focused on categories of talks, departing from types or categories of unemployed. Proceeding along that line could, for example, lead to the demonstration of how young people rather than old, women rather than men and skilled or educated people rather than unskilled or uneducated find participation in talks about their employment situation satisfactory.

With the 8 employment officials in the study as a point of departure, however, and based on observations and their statements in the interviews, *4 types or styles of employment officials* were identified. Taken in their pure form these types or styles are, of course, constructions, with 4 of the officials being close to these types, while the other 4 officials seemed to represent a mix of these types or maybe even other types. The 4 types identified were:

A   The careful and thorough artisan
B   The confronting and "no illusions" placement officer
C   The routinising administrator
D   The strategically and methodically conscious professional.

Before comparing selected aspects of the 4 x 4 encounters of A, B, C and D it must be emphasised that in this comparison "other things are not being equal". Especially, if the profile or style of the employment official is considered the independent variable and the satisfaction of the unemployed the dependent variable, it has to be admitted that it is not possible to control for the influence of other variables. For instance the 4 talks with A, the careful and thorough artisan, were cases of unemployed with limited unemployment experience, while the 4 talks with B, the confronting and "no illusions" placement officer, were cases of unemployed with long-time unemployment experience. As regards the talks with C and D both categories were represented. Another kind of reservation is related to the institutional setting. Among the 4 types of officials mentioned, 3 of the 4 offices in the study are represented, each having among others its own specific culture, perception of the action-plan-effort and surroundings (the labour market in the area, etc.). These reservations given, the talks of A, B, C and D are compared in the table below. The comparison touches speaking time, distribution of turns, initiative-response measures, satisfaction at the unemployed party, involvement of the unemployed party in the work on the computer-screen and finally preservation/protection of face or politeness strategy used.

*Selected Characteristics of 4 Clusters of Talks: A, B, C and D*

|  | (A) | (B) | (C) | (D) |
|---|---|---|---|---|
| Speaking Time: | | | | |
| Total speaking time (min.) | 39.5 | 25.3 | 15.8 | 30.8 |
| Quota, unemployed (min.) | 13.9 | 7.2 | 5.6 | 14.9 |
| Quota, unemployed (%) | 35.1 | 28.5 | 35.4 | 48.5 |
| | | | | |
| Distribution of Turns (total): | | | | |
| Minimal responses (%) | 15.5 | 22.7 | 22.3 | 11.7 |
| Responses with initiative (%) | 53.3 | 45.0 | 46.6 | 68.5 |
| Responses with strong initiative (%) | 30.9 | 32.3 | 31.1 | 19.8 |
| | | | | |
| Total (%) | 99.7 | 100.0 | 100.0 | 100.0 |
| | | | | |
| Distribution of Turns (officials): | | | | |
| Minimal responses (%) | 2.9 | 7.9 | 4.1 | 8.2 |
| Responses with initiative (%) | 44.9 | 43.6 | 35.0 | 62.5 |
| Responses with strong initiative (%) | 52.2 | 48.5 | 60.9 | 29.3 |
| | | | | |
| Total (%) | 100.0 | 100.0 | 100.0 | 100.0 |
| | | | | |
| Initiative-response-measures: | | | | |
| Av. IR-coefficients, unemployed | 2.82 | 2.69 | 2.77 | 2.95 |
| Av. IR-coeff., officials | 3.49 | 3.48 | 3.55 | 3.21 |
| IR-difference | 0.67 | 0.79 | 0.78 | 0.26 |
| | | | | |
| Number of Satisfactory Talks: | 4 | 0 | 2 | 4 |
| | | | | |
| Involvement of the Unemployed in Computer-Screen Work: | + | - | - | + |
| | | | | |
| Preservation of Face: | + | - | +/- | + |

The artisan (A) had the longest talks on average, the routinising administrator (C) the shortest, but as the methodically conscious professional (D) "gave" the unemployed almost half of the speaking time, they had the longest speaking time, about 15 minutes, in her talks.

Looking at the distribution of turns, the variation was rather small between the three first types. D breaks away from the others with regard to the quota of extended responses with limited initiative, which amounts to over 2/3 of D's turns and, on average, less than half of the turns of the others, with A, the artisan, being closest to D, the professional. The difference was also marked, looking solely at the turns of the officials. In the talks of A, B and C the quota of extended responses with limited initiative, causing coherence in a talk, accounted for 35 % to 45 % of the officials' turns. However, in the talks of D they accounted for as much as 63 % of the officials' turns. Further the extended responses with strong initiative accounted on average under 30 % of D's turns but between 52 % and 61 % of A's, B's and C's turns.

All the talks with the confronting and "no illusions" placement officer were experienced as unsatisfactory as were 2 of 4 talks with the routinising administrator. On the other hand, all talks with the careful and thorough artisan and with the strategically and methodically conscious professional were experienced as satisfactory.

The unemployed were involved in work on the computer-screen in the talks with A and D, but not in the talks with B and C. As regards preservation and protection of face, it was A and D again that differed from B and C. In the talks with A and D there was pervasive concern and consideration as regards the situation of the unemployed. This was accompanied by frequent expressions of support as well as regard for the face of the counterpart in the interaction. These traits were rare, exceptional or absent in the talks with B and C.

As mentioned above it was not possible to interpret the illustrated connections as unequivocally caused by differences between the officials or by the type of official in case. The simple reason for this was that it was not possible to control for other variables. A comparison of the talks with the confronting and "no illusions" placement officer could illustrate this. One of the talks was especially different from the others. In this talk (No. 14, extract 1.a below) the unemployed had about 14 min. out of a total speaking time of about 40 min., which was only slightly more than the average quota for the unemployed party. 58.9 % of the total number of turns were extended responses with limited initiative and 25.8 % were responses with strong initiative. What was especially different, however, was that the IR-difference was slightly negative, which means that the turns of the unemployed in this talk were a little stronger than the turns of the official. The distribution of B's turns in this talk resembles the average distribution in D's talks. The unemployed in this talk was, however, very discontent with the talk. This applied to the form, the course as well as the substance of the talk, but she was, as she said herself, "not afraid of him" (B). She was steering the talk and backed out as regards offers, which she could not or would not accept. At the same time, however, she was in a very difficult position with very few employment opportunities and, further, a rather limited period with unemployment benefits remaining. Finally, her primary wishes as regards activation were met with a refusal. Taken together, this was absolutely unsatisfactory for her, and neither she nor the official was capable of making the action-plan-talk a constructive interaction. Instead it appeared as a fight. The particular circumstances in this talk means that the characterisation of B as confronting is confirmed in so far as the linguistic dominance in the remaining 3 talks with B appears as more prominent without the figures from this particular talk.

These comments throw some light on different aspects of the interplay and/or the fights between the unemployed and employment officials, co-operating or struggling face-to-face about what should become public labour market policy in their case (cf. Lipsky 1980).

Finishing this paragraph, I shall mention some of the factors outside the interaction order, which also might play decisive roles. The development on the labour market, regional policies, office-cultures, the style with which the officials enforce the policy, resources and technology, the background and living conditions of the unemployed (age, gender, education, ethnicity).

Among these external factors, as earlier noted, are the questions of class and age. Thus if an unemployed person is middle-aged, male, and has an unskilled working class background where verbal capacity and education is limited has to be considered as important in assessing whether talks are designated as being satisfactory or unsatisfactory.

### Section 3  Combining Quantitative and Qualitative Analysis

Section 2 presented some of the answers to the questions about what is going on in the action plan talk, and how language, power and counselling conditions the balancing of individual and labour market considerations in action plan talks.

The aim of this section is to demonstrate through selected exemplification, how quantitative and qualitative analyses can support each other and lead to more reliable and valid interpretations of what is going on in public encounters/institutional interaction where specific policy goals are pursued. Using different approaches, two sets of rather short extracts from the 32 tape-recorded action plan talks are analysed: each set containing one situation characterised by co-operation as well as one situation characterised by conflict or struggle between the parties at the talk.

## 3.1 The First Set of Talks

The first set contains the following 2 sequences (in an unsophisticated transcription, the numbers referring to the turn number in the database) of 4 and 8 turns respectively, demonstrating a clearly conflicting as well as a clearly co-operative situation.

### Extract 1.a from conversation 14

2009    Official: And it - err that is right, that is right. And you did it so to speak, mostly under what one calls, well then it is possible to see the end of - err, unemployment insurance....And if then - err we return to the question of "what then"? And I then ask you, well then what is it then, that you would prefer; if there was a free choice from all the options, what would (the name of the unemployed in full) then do?

2010    Unemployed: Yes, then I would like to, I would like to work at a nursing home, or as a kindergarten assistant. Yes, or with, it doesn't matter, anyway it could also be in an after-school institution. But it should, it should not be under those conditions there. It should be something, that is to say something I myself, that is something I am paid for. Not, not upon those principles there.

2011    Official: But that is to say, you have got to find a regular job upon normal conditions. And there, there I am only able to say that if we are talking about a permanent job, whether we are talking about a nursing home, or we are talking about an assistant in a children's institution, then you must go and apply for the jobs and apply for them when they are there.

2012    Unemployed: Do you know what. I am going to tell you a thing, the half year I was up in B (a nursing home), there I applied for, I don't know how many - err assistant jobs round about in the different institutions, and I have been rejected each time, and I know very well, why I receive rejections. It is because they want those young girls. They don't want the middle aged...but I can't do anything else than give it a try.

*Extract 1.b  from conversation 29*

4166    Official: Well then, you are quite clearly available within that area there.

4167    Unemployed: Yes, but I know that.

4168    Official: We have discussed that, and it is like a matter between you and your unemployment insurance fund then. It is quite all right. Err - should we concentrate us a little more again upon that about education?

4169    Unemployed: Yes.

4170    Official: I think, that I hear you saying, I thought so even last time, we talked, that you really have concentrated a deal, what it is, that you want to. You are missing only the last step in relation to saying it is just this here. You want to have something together with some colleagues. You would like to find something outdoors. You would like to have something with working hours that fit into the kids at home.

4171    Unemployed: Yes, I am very demanding.

4172    Official: I don't really think so. You list some sensible things, which fit into your life, don't you. But you should take the next step and examine the educations which you have such a little bit of a vague idea about. And there is the possibility that either you contact the schools - the address is in this - and talk with their tutors; and from that try to find out, if this is anything for you. There is also the possibility of asking the tutors, if you could come one day and follow the teaching, for example, sort of feel the temperature, what it is like. Well, at the Technical Schools it will be that, not that typical anymore, but still, often be the case, that there will be a deal younger than you are, those you will go together with...

4173    Unemployed: Yes, but it doesn't matter. It doesn't mean that much.

Looking at the first set of extracts we find a sharp confrontation in the first extract (1a) and a very co-operative situation in the second (1b). The 4 turns in (1a) contains the following steps:

2009    Official: Concluding description of the situation of the unemployed, followed by a hypothetical question about what she would like to do if there were no constraints.

2010    Unemployed: The seemingly open-minded question from the official is accepted by the unemployed in her turn, the first part of which represents her thinking out loud what she would prefer most. 2009 thus shape turn 2010. In the middle of 2010, however, a change occurs: the unemployed qualifies her wishes; she wants the occupations mentioned as ordinary jobs only, not as activation measures (job-training), financed by the labour market authorities. Listening to the voices on the tapes, the turns 2009-2010 appear as obviously relaxed although the latter part of 2010 shows a shift to a more distinct or even tense tone. This shift contributes to shaping the reply from the official in 2011. Where does this shift come from? It is not sufficiently explained by the immediate context of the previous turns. Later in the talk, however, the unemployed tells about her experiences so far with having lower status as a job-training person than the ordinary employed, thus giving one illustration of how structural traits of the context in a broader sense are in play, situated in the turn-by-turn interaction.

2011 Official: If the she wants an ordinary job, the official retorts, she has to seek and apply for them when they are vacant (what she probably knows very well), implying that no vacant ordinary jobs in this field are at the disposal of the employment office. He is thus threatening her face and in a way loosing his own on behalf of the employment office. Listening to the sound from the tapes, again, the tone in 2011 is becoming tense and sharp as the confrontation is unfolding, for the present so to speak ending in "massive retaliation" from the unemployed in the last turn of the extract:

2012 Unemployed: This kind of counselling seems to be no good and of no use to her.

Thus a CA-like or CA-inspired step-by-step analysis of this extract shows, as described in more generalising terms in paragraph 2.4.6 above, how the official B performed a confronting "no illusions" style, and how the unemployed in talk 14 was fighting back. As she mentioned herself in the interview immediately after the talk, she "was not afraid" of him.

Conversation analysis has been developed as a qualitative step-by-step analysis of the management of social institutions in interaction: (1) Interaction is context-shaped: turns address to preceding turns, specifically the preceding turn. (2) Interaction shapes or renews the context: a turn project the next turns, specifically the immediately following turn. (3) Interaction is based on the understanding of prior action at a multiplicity of levels. It is a matter of mutual understanding. Heritage calls it an "architecture of intersubjectivity" (Heritage 1997, 162). However, it seems easier to demonstrate through conversation analysis, how interaction is shaped by as well as shapes and renews context, than to demonstrate how and why this "architecture" or understanding of prior action is brought into play and functions. Heritage, using the image of a wind tunnel, notes how the shaping of the opening remark, as demonstrated in an extract, has been developed through experience. This in a way could be considered an implicitly quantitative approach. In the extract from talk 14 my argument would be that the qualitative aspects give life to the more quantitative analysis in section 2. And the analysis in section 2 might be considered some kind of construction/architecture, which is most helpful in distinguishing the prior action and even helpful in the interpretation of it.

The turns in extract 1.a, clearly, were shaped by and shaping the proceeding and the following turns respectively. Context was shaped and context was renewed. But what happened was more than that. The styles of the official and the unemployed were at hand before these turns were taken, although it was reproduced in the turns. Their past experiences were present somehow and to some degree. This was obvious even in the other talks with B.

It was obvious as well according to what the unemployed said in the interview after the talk with B. Even the positions as official and unemployed respectively, including experiences with earlier activation measures and moreover their general background, "were there" before the talk and were reproduced in the talk.

Contrary to extract 1a, 1b contains a sequence of co-operative turns. Instead of following the single acts performed in this sequence like in the analysis of extract 1a, I want to focus on 2 of the official's turns, 4170 and 4172, both involving the performance of more or less conscious methodical counselling measures. In 4170 the official was reflecting earlier and actual statements from the unemployed. In 4172, the official after a continuation of the line from 4170 proposed the unemployed to collect further information. This was characterised by the unemployed later in the talk as "home-work". This proposal was done in order to facilitate a decision about what kind of education, she should choose as the main point in her activation plan. These interventions were performed in a way that made them acceptable to the unemployed party at the talk, which she indirectly showed in the turns 4171 and 4173. Thus clearly, aspects of the turns in this extract were shaped by and shaping the immediate context.

The unemployed, who had positive experiences of talking with this official, entered the talk in a co-operative mood, while the official may be characterised by the execution of empathetic (as well as authoritative) counselling. Finally there was a reference to structural traits and some of these were reproduced through the reference for instance to the obligation to be available in case of vacant jobs. However, the extract also demonstrates the possible initiation of social change and of balancing of individual and labour market considerations, through co-operation between the parties at the talk, in other words the possible softening or loosening of (some of) the structural traits making social change possible (Goffman 1983, 8).

Thus extracts 1.a and 1.b illustrates among others the role of fighting and struggling as well as the role of co-operation and of methodical counselling measures in the balancing of individual wishes and qualification with labour market demands. The analysis has indicated that what matters in this connection is absence of linguistic dominance, attendance to individual considerations as well as labour market rationality and, finally, professional counselling method.

## 3.2 The Second Set of Talks

The extracts 2.a and 2.b are from talks 17 and 18, both of which were with the official C, the routinising administrator (see paragraph 2.4.6. above). Both talks were even with long-term unemployed women, a dental technician in the late thirties (17) and an office worker in her early fifties (18). They were members of the same unemployment insurance fund for salaried workers and officials.

The talks had many points of resemblance: same physical setting, same official, almost the same length and almost the same general initiative-response characteristics. There were, however, a few remarkable quantitative differences between the talks: The speaking time of the unemployed was 8:37 min. in 17 compared to 6:05 min. in 18. Especially in the last part of the talks the unemployed party's share of the speaking time was considerably lower in 18 than in 17. Further, the level of back-channellings differed, especially as regards backchannellings in the turns of the unemployed. Again the difference occurred mostly in the last parts of the talks. The level of backchannellings in the turns of the unemployed was increasing in 17 and decreasing in 18, indicating C being a more actively listening and empathetic official in 17 (specifically in the last phase of the talk) than in 18.

## The Following Summarises Selected Quantitative Aspects of Talks 17 and 18:

| Talk | 17 | 18 |
|---|---|---|
| Total speaking time | 21:59 | 21:01 |
| Speaking time of the unemployed | 8:37 | 6:05 |
| Speaking time of the unemployed (%, phase: 1/2/3) | 45.3 / 40.0 / 33.6 | 45.1 / 26.8 / 20.4 |
| Smooth turntakings / all turntakings | 122 / 147 | 59 / 84 |
| Backchannellings in the turns of the unemployed (phase: 1/2/3) | 0.8 / 0.7 / 1.2 | 1.6 / 1.5 / 0.6 |
| Backchannellings in the turns of C (phase: 1/2/3) | 1.2 / 1.6 / 1.2 | 0.6 / 1.3 / 1.4 |
| Coherence in the turns of the unemployed | 67.1 | 64.3 |
| Coherence, in the turns of C | 32.4 | 33.3 |
| IR-coefficient in the turns of the unemployed | 2.78 | 2.83 |
| IR-coefficient in the turns of C | 3.64 | 3.67 |
| IR-difference | 0.85 | 0.83 |
| Support in the turns of the unemployed | 1 | 3 |
| Resistance in the turns of the unemployed | 7 | 9 |
| Protection of face | + | - |
| Counselling, authority | + | + |
| Counselling, empathy | (+) | - |

In 17 the unemployed expressed her wish in a straightforward way (turn 2401) through the statement that she wanted a continuation of a computer course which she had attended earlier. In 18, on the contrary, the unemployed formulated her wish in a humble way, hat in hand, and using the weakening subjunctive mood.

Thus, qualitatively, despite the resemblance mentioned, the two cases were quite different. Looking closer at the extracts 2.a and 2.b they appear, respectively, as a case of break down of the administrative routines of C and as a case of compliance to these routines.

*Extract 2.a from conversation 17*

2507 Official: Well, now you get the plan just in - err. Could we not agree that, that as soon as you know anything, then if you now get some information, that there are some job training possibilities for instance, that then you contact me?

2508 Unemployed: Yes, I will do that.

2509 Official: If you then, if you then by any chance hear anything, before that ETB course there starts, and before it ends and so on.

2510 Unemployed: I will at least know something before the 17th of June then. Because well then, if I come upon this here (the course that the individual action-plan is about) - that I will because NN (one of the teachers) has himself sent it to me. So well, I have talked to them, and, and I am going to get over there and demonstrate a database, that is over there (at the educational centre), for a customer, so.

2511 Official: Really. Where are you going to show it?

2512 Unemployed: It is over at X (the educational centre). It is that, I have made. Well, it is just a provisional one.

2513 Official: Really. While you went there?

2514 Unemployed: Yes, there I made then a - err database for a customer. And they don't know how it works. Because they - err, they bring teachers in from outside. It was so namely, he (the teacher) has written to me, if I would come over.

2515 Official: Then, that was a bit - what kind of a customer was it, you have had there?

2516 Unemployed: It is - err Y (a vacation centre). They are going to have the whole of their, their rental of - they have then both halls and - err, and - err, and several meeting rooms and all that sort of thing, and a communal hall and all that sort of thing, so it. So, she wanted it in the ETB, instead of she sitting with her A4 paper sheet system there.

2517    Official: Well then, but it sounds then a little bit exiting. What, where were you then in practice? Was it...?

2518    Unemployed: It was, I was, was then in practice there. Where I got the database raised. Then she should come over and see, when it was finished. That is why, I would like to continue with the loose ends, because there are some other here (shows in the course catalogue) some other database systems.

2519    Official: But are you going to talk to them there then?

2520    Unemployed: Yes, because I shall then out there the first of - err, first of May.

2521    Official: OK. But then we can agree that, because - err, or rather - err yes. It will of cause be to be mixing things a little together. But there is something with that - err, or it <u>is</u> such that, that AF (the Danish employment authorities) - that is, generally seen, in the county, they have bought that course from the AMU-centre, rubbish, educational centre, so - err, so you could sort of just say, that it, that you are ready to start upon it.

2522    Unemployed: Yes, yes well but that sounds good.

Extract 2.a is from the very last part of 17. The sequence came after the agreement about what should be the content of the individual action plan. Negotiating the action plan in this case of the unemployed dental technician, C had checked her expectations and possibilities. Her plan was to get qualified to what was awaited to become the future implementation of computer technology in the area of dental treatment. After careful research and deliberation, the wishes of the unemployed were accepted as the content of the activation plan. Extract 2.a appeared shortly after this conclusion and while the plan was printed, almost as an informal continuation of the action-plan-interview.

In turn 2510, however, C may have got the impression through the information given by the unemployed that she had much more resources than previously assumed, that she, so to speak, represented an investment value. At least in turns 2511, 2513, 2515, 2517 and 2519, C returned to the interview format of questions-answers which ordinarily characterised the opening parts of the action plan interviews. Also, while listening to the answers of the unemployed, C gave an increasing number of backchannellings (2512: 2; 2514: 3; 2516: 5; 2517: 7). He was thereby practising an active listening quite unusual for the closing of a talk, and thus increasingly showing appreciation and giving the unemployed credit.

Moreover the turns of the unemployed became longer in this final part of the talk, contrary to the average pattern of the 32 talks analysed.

Finally in turn 2521, C left to the unemployed herself to put the action plan into operation in connection with her participation in a meeting at the educational centre in question. This break down in the administrative routines of C constituted an exception from the rule established in the construction of C as representing a routinising and administratively oriented type of official.

Concluding, rather than leading to different representations, the quantitative and qualitative analyses have in this case helped each other forward. The results have confirmed each other in the accentuation of the functioning, as well as the limits, of the administrative routines of C, encountering an unemployed with more qualifications and a rather stronger character than assumed at the outset.

*Extract 2.b from conversation 18*

2594　Unemployed: Well, children's clothes, I think, there are a few; children's clothes, I think, have a good sale.

2595　Official: But how much do you expect, that you can, that you can produce, if one can say, and how much do you expect, you can sell, well then just roughly? Well, that's then what we, we need to look at. How, how much does it end up in regarding employment, the plans, you then have?

2596　Unemployed: Well, it should certainly be, such that one can get 8 hours a, a day and then live off it...

2597　Official: Well that's that, then, I would like you to, to come with an estimate over, how do you imagine that it could be that?

2598　Unemployed: Yes...(barely audible)

2599　Official: What do you say to that?

2600　Unemployed: Well, I would like to make a budget, try to find out what eventually, if one can sell anything to shops... But how accurate it can be, something like that, that's - err...

2601　Official: No, well, one could say that...it could be...well, T (a firm) doesn't know either, how many - err fish they should fillet. They can't know, how many - err they can sell to happy Norwegians, that are willing to eat paper fish from Denmark, well they don't know that exactly - err. But I think that if, if we are to go in for that, or go into a grant for something at the Crafts-school, and then, well, even for your own sake then, I was nearly about to say, then it is important that you sort of make some practical thinking, about what kind of opportunities that one could say would be certainties. That you went around and tried to work out, which retail channels there could be, eventually, and which shops one could sell to? That is, having a feeling for, what can, can be of any use? Because it is clear, that if it can that, well then, we are so to say with you then, we, we won't then take a stand according to whether we think, that that which, that which one wants to produce, that - err, whether we like it or not. Well that, it concerns, it is a matter of (Unemployed-input: Whether one can live off it) whether one can live off it.

2602    Unemployed: Yes. Well then I will try to do that.

2603    Official: But could we agree on that, then, that we do not make an action plan today then, but - we agree that we meet again in, shall we say 2 weeks or something like that...And so unto then, or before rather, then you have examined, which retail opportunities there eventually could be, having worked out a simple budget over, what, what you expect to be able to produce and also preferably...

2604    Unemployed: Yes, it will most likely be that, which is going to be the most difficult, but it remains my problem of course.

2605    Official: Yes. But also preferably, well what, what is it, what are the economic perspectives in it and so on, OK? Then, you have to, also, in relation to that with the activation period. Because as I have said several times, there we have to make sure, that you are kept going all the time, and that will to a certain extent be - err, that will then be such a silly brake in a way, if you, or when you have started something for yourself. Because if it is not on full-time, then you will run into, that we all the time have to make an offer, and it could just be - then you are forced to sew your clothes at other times, one could say... Well could it be that, we agree on, that you are going to examine that?

2606    Unemployed: Yes (very low).

2607    Official: Find out, which opportunities there are for retailing. Make a brief budget, a business plan. And then we can start out with that next time - can we agree on that?

2608    Unemployed: Let's do that. Yes.

Unlike talk 17, the case in talk 18 represented a matter of compliance to the administrative routines. The extract 2.b from talk 18 was characterised by long turns on behalf of C and very short turns from the unemployed. Most of them were even in a very low voice, sometimes (for instance 2606) so weak that one might question, whether the unemployed in fact took the turn or just signalled her acceptance of the agreement through backchannellings to C.

The unemployed in 18 represented a low investment value from the point of view of labour market policy. Her wishes were to take a sewing course at a school for needlework and try to make a living out of making and selling children's clothes, a project, however, which she probably did not really believe in, even herself.

Neither C believed in the course she applied for leading to employment or an occupation she would be able to live off. In spite of this, the administrative procedures and routines were upheld in a bold on face way and with only a few weakening traits, e.g. a slight indication of stammer. The unemployed had no alternative to compliance.

Concluding, as in the case of 17, rather than leading to different representations, the quantitative and qualitative analyses have helped each other forward and confirmed each other in the accentuation of the functioning, as well as the limits, of the administrative routines of C.

In the case of 18, C is encountering an unemployed with fewer resources and a weak or even humble attitude, resulting more or less inevitably in compliance. Methodologically, the development and existence of bureaucratic routines potentially being at odds with the life-world experiences of clients, users, citizens in contact with bureaucratic organisations is thus shown to have a quantitative as well as a qualitative dimension.

Even inside one specific talk in interaction there are several quantitative dimensions, e.g. the distribution of speaking time and backchannellings as developed above. Conversation analysis often gives examples of something considered typical or predominant, such as, question-answer sequences. Further context in the form of structures, expectations or dispositions and even positions, are incorporated in the analysis to the extent that they are locally constructed or reproduced. The question often is, however, how can we know of it. One way through is the combination of quantitative and qualitative analyses. Local construction or reproduction of structural traits does not exclude quantification as part of the analysis or as a way leading to demarcations of the typical.

## Section 4  Conclusions and Perspectives in the Study of Public Encounters Between Unemployed and Employment Officials

The results have shown thus far that the 32 public encounters studied can be divided respectively into two categories of unsatisfactory/satisfactory talks. Further, it has been shown that on average the talks followed a particular discourse structure. As regards backchannellings and speaking time there was an outspoken systematic difference between the first, the second and the third part of the turns. The role of the unemployed developed from giving information, responding to questions, at the beginning of the talks to listening to the official in the end. On the contrary, the role of the officials developed from asking questions at the beginning to the telling of possibilities in the activation-system and drawing con-clusions/making decisions in the end. The question remains, however, whether this discourse structure left room for balancing the interests and considerations of the parties in the encounters, and thus for giving a genuine opportunity to negotiate and elaborate individual action-plans as some kind of an agreement or social contract.

Generally, the study has led to the assessment that a symmetric and mutual interaction or the absence of dominance, the preservation of ones own face as well as the face of the interactional counterpart, and finally, the use of elements of professional counselling measures were constituting important local conditions of making satisfactory action-plan-talks. If these conditions were met the balancing of individual and labour market considerations appeared to be likely. In that sense, the study has shown empirically as well as it has been argued theoretically, that professional counselling methods in public encounters are making a difference. In this respect, it might be asserted, the study has affirmed some of the core values in Nordic social and labour market policy: Universal benefits plus the treatment of the citizen/user/client as an individual human being in his/her own rights.

The results also have demonstrated that the action-plan-talks were rather well ordered, with the vast majority of turntakings being smooth. However, although not being a matter of unequivocal causality, the unsatisfactory talks were shorter and more unequal than satisfactory talks regarding speaking time as well as regarding initiatives and responses.

Differences of style or type on behalf of the employment officials seemed to be of big importance regarding satisfaction with the talks on behalf of the unemployed, although this was not a matter of unequivocal causal inference either.

As far as methodology is concerned the experience of using quantitative and qualitative methods has shown that this is not necessarily a matter of either/or. Rather, quantitative and qualitative analyses may supplement each other, leading to a better and deeper representation of the phenomena concerned.

## Bibliography

Arbejdsmarkedsstyrelsen (1995) *Arbejdsmarkedsorienteret vejledning - strategiske indsatsområder for AF's vejledning.* København: Arbejdsmarkedsstyrelsen.

Arbejdsmarkedsstyrelsen (1995-98) *Årsberetninger for 1994-97.* København: Arbejdsmarkedsstyrelsen.

Arbejdsministeriet & Finansministeriet (1996) *Arbejdsmarkedspolitikken under forandring.* København: Arbejdsministeriet & Finansministeriet.

*Beretning om arbejdsformidlingens virksomhed og forholdet til arbejdsløshedskasserne. Beretning fra rigsrevisor fremsendt til Folketinget i henhold til § 18, stk. 1, i lov om revisionen af statens regnskaber m.m.* (1997) København.

Berg Sørensen, Torben (1995) *Den sociale samtale - mellem klienter og sagsbehandlere.* Aarhus: Forlaget Gestus.

Bjerregaard Bach, Henning et al. (1997) *Virksomhederne og arbejdsformidlingens tilbud. Evaluering af arbejdsmarkedsreformen II.* København: Socialforskningsinstituttet.

Bleiklie, Ivar (1996) *Service Regimes in Public Welfare Administration. Case Studies of Street-level Bureaucrats as Decision Makers.* Bergen: Department of Administration and Organization Theory, University of Bergen.

Boje, Thomas P. (1992) Welfare State Systems and Labour Market Stratification. In Amoroso, Bruno and Jespersen, Jesper (eds.) *Welfare Society in Transition.* Roskilde: Department of Economics and Planning, Roskilde University.

Brown, Penelope and Levinson, Stephen C. (1978; 1987) *Politeness: Some Universals in Language Usage.* Cambridge: Cambridge University Press.

Drew, Paul and Heritage, John (1992) *Talk at Work. Interaction in Institutional Settings.* Cambridge, New York, Melbourne: Cambridge University Press.

Erickson, Frederick and Schultz, Jeffrey (1982) *The Counselor as Gatekeeper. Social Interaction in Interviews.* New York: Academic Press.

Fredín, Erik (1993) *Dialogen i socialt arbete. En studie av socialbyråsamtal i ljuset av modern dialogteori.* Linköping: Universitetet i Linköping.

Goffman, Erving (1967) *Interaction Ritual. Essays on Face-to-Face Behaviour.* New York: Pantheon Books.

Goffman, Erving (1983) The Interaction Order. *American Sociological Review* (48), 1-17.

Goodsell, Richard (ed) (1981) *The Public Encounter. Where State and Citizen Meet.* Bloomington: Indiana University Press.

Grunow, Dieter (1978) *Altagskontakte mit der Verwaltung.* Frankfurt: Campus Verlag.

Haahr, Jens Henrik and Winter, Søren (1996) *Den regionale arbejdsmarkedspolitik. Planlægning mellem centralisering og decentralisering.* Aarhus: Systime.

Hansen, Kim (1995) *Embedsmandsroller og etik.* Aarhus: Forlaget PLS.

Heritage, John (1995) Conversation Analysis and Institutional Talk: Analysing Data. In Silverman, David (ed) *Qualitative Research. Theory, Method and Practice.* London: Sage.

Hetzler, Antoinette (1994) *Socialpolitik i verkligheten. De handikappada och försäkringskassan.* Lund: Bokbox Förlag.

Hoffmeyer-Zlotnik, Jürgen H.P. (ed) (1992) *Analyse verbaler Daten. Über den Umgang mit qualitativen Daten.* Opladen: Westdeutscher Verlag.

Jacobsen, Knut Dahl et al. (1982) Fordelingspolitikkens forvaltning. *Sociologi i dag* (3) 29-49.

Kagan, Robert A. (1994) Regulatory Enforcement. In Rosenblom, David H. and Schwartz, Richard D. (eds.) *Handbook of Regulation and Administrative Law.* New York: Marcel Dekker.

Koch, Anna and Eskelinen, Lena (1997) *Samspillet mellem den enkelte borger og socialforvaltningen - en analyse baseret på nordisk forskning.* København: AKF Forlaget.

*Labour Market Studies:* Denmark (1996).

Langager, Klaus (1997) *Indsatsen for de forsikrede ledige. Evaluering af arbejdsmarkeds-reformen I.* København: Socialforskningsinstituttet.

Larsen, Flemming et al. (1996*) Implementering af Regional Arbejdsmarkedspolitik - Evaluering af det regionale aktiveringssamarbejde mellem AF, a-kasser, kommuner, amter og uddannelsesinstitutioner.* Aalborg: Center for Arbejdsmarkedsforskning ved Aalborg Universitet.

Lindh, Gunnel (ed) (1994) *Femmeren. En erhvervsvejledningsmetodik.* Fredensborg: Studie og Erhverv.

Linell, Per and Gustavsson, Lennart (1987) *Initiativ och respons. Om dialogens dynamik, dominans och koherens.* Linköping: Studies in Communication 15. Universitetet i Linköping.

Lipsky, Michael (1980) *Street-Level Bureaucracy. Dilemmas of the Individual in Public Services.* New York: Russell Sage Foundation.

Lovén, Anders (1995*) Vejledning i nærbillede.* København: Rådet for Uddannelses- og Erhvervsvejledning.

Mouzelis, Nicos (1995) *Sociological Theory: What Went Wrong? Diagnosis and Remedies.* New York and London: Routledge.

Olesen, Søren Peter (1997a) Mødet mellem velfærdsstaten og den arbejdsløse. Den arbejdsmarkedspolitiske samtale - et eksempel på forskning i socialt arbejde. In Marthinsen, Edgar and Ekberg, Karin (eds.) *Nordisk symposium om forskning i sosialt arbeid. Et møte mellem forskning og praksis. Artikkelsamling fra et symposium i Trondheim, 21-23 August 1996.* Trondheim: Norsk Senter for Barneforskning.

Olesen, Søren Peter (1997b) En sammenligning af tilfredstillende og utilfredsstillende handlingsplansamtalermellem arbejdsløse og AF-medarbejdere. *Den Sociale Højskole i Aarhus 1957-1997: Festskrift.* Aarhus: Den Sociale Højskole.

Olesen, Søren Peter (1997c) *32 arbejdsmarkedspolitiske samtaler. Samtaleportrætter. Handlingsplansamtaler i AF-regi. 32 cases.* Aarhus: Den Sociale Højskole.

Pierson, Christopher (1991) *Beyond the Welfare State? The New Political Economy of Welfare.* Cambridge: Polity Press.

Pilegaard Jensen, Torben et al. (1991) *Indsatsen for langtidsledige - en undersøgelse af administration og effekt af arbejds- og uddannelsestilbud.* København: AKF Forlaget.

Ragin, Charles C. (1987) *The Comparative Method. Moving Beyond Qualitative and Quantitative Strategies.* Berkeley: University of California Press.

Ragin, Charles C. (1994) *Constructing Social Research. The Unity and Diversity of Method.* Thousand Oaks: Pine Forge Press.

*Rapport fra Udvalget vedrørende arbejdsmarkedets strukturproblemer* (1992) København: Zeuthenudvalget.

Rasborg, Klaus (1997) Velfærdsstaten og det revitaliserede civilsamfund. In Greve, Anni (ed) *Sociologien om velfærd - gensyn med Émile Durkheim.* Roskilde: Roskilde Universitetsforlag.

Rothstein, Bo (1994) *Vad bör staten göra? Om välfärdsstatens moraliska och politiska logik.* Stockholm: SNS Förlag.

Skov, Carl Verner (1995) *Kvalitativ Interview og Terapi Analyse. Version 1.2.* Aarhus: Psykologisk Institut, Aarhus Universitet.

*Ta' Têten i arbejdsmarkedspolitikken* (1997) København: LO.

Turner, Jonathan H. (1987) Analytical Theorizing. In Giddens, Anthony and Turner, Jonathan (eds.) *Sociological Theory Today.* Cambridge: Polity Press.

*Undersøgelse af Arbejdsmarkedsreformens administrative arbejdsgange og støttesystemer* (1995). København: Arbejdsmarkedsstyrelsen.

Willis, Paul (1981; 1977) *Fostran till lönearbete.* Göteborg: Röda Bokförlaget.

Winter, Søren (1981) *Den sociale markarbejder og de politiske mål. En analyse af faktorer, der hæmmer målrealiseringen.* Aarhus: Institut for Statskundskab, Aarhus Universitet.

Winter, Søren (1985) Iværksættelsesbarrierer. *Politica* (4), 17.

Winter, Søren (1994a) *Street Level Bureaucrats and the Implementation of Political Reforms: Welfare, Employment, and Environmental Policies* (Paper). Aarhus: Department of Political Science, Aarhus University.

Winter, Søren (1994b) *Implementering og effektivitet.* Herning: Systime.

Winter, Søren et al. (1995) *Arbejdsmarkedsreformen: Regionalisering og planlægning.* København: Arbejdsmarkedsstyrelsen.

Yin, Robert K. (1989) *Case Study Research. Design and Methods.* Newbury Park: Sage.

Yin, Robert K. (1993) *Applications of Case Study Research.* Newbury Park: Sage.

# 6 Counsellors' Responses to Students' Troubles-Talk in Counselling Encounters in Finnish Careers Guidance Training

SANNA VEHVILÄINEN

In this article, I will examine ways in which counsellors in Finnish career guidance training respond to students' "troubles-talk", i.e. descriptions of negative or problematic states of affair in counselling sessions. The ways in which troubles-recipiency is oriented to by the counsellors are analysed in relation to the institutional goals and constraints of counselling in this particular setting. The findings of this analysis contribute to the answer to the question: what constitutes counselling interaction in an adult educational setting?

Prior to the data analysis, the role of counselling in Finnish adult education is briefly discussed, as well as the approach used in this article (conversation analysis).

## What Is Counselling as an Adult Educational Interaction?

Counselling in Finland is an emerging practice within the field of adult education. It is usually viewed as a work method and a site for learning rather than a problem-driven therapeutic setting. Counselling (or sometimes supervising) is a central interest in fields such as adult pedagogy, career guidance training, tutoring of students (Nummenmaa 1992), academic teacher training (Ojanen 1998; Krokfors 1997), and nursing science (Poskiparta 1997). Adult education, especially career guidance training, has been in the forefront of the development of "learner-centred" methods (Onnismaa & Taskinen 1994; Onnismaa 1997). Counselling is viewed as one of the methods which incorporates the new notions on how adults learn and how they should be taught. Both practitioners and academics in Finland widely accept such adult educational ideas as learner-centredness, self-directed learning, experiential learning and critical reflection of learners' own experiences as the most effective and "natural" ways to learn (cf. for example, Mezirow et al. 1990). The trainer's role is no longer that of the knowledge-provider, but that of a "facilitator" and "co-constructor of meanings". Adult educators are viewed as experts on interaction and learning processes, rather than experts on areas of knowledge. Accordingly, "knowledge" is seen to exist only in terms of an individual perspective, and therefore all relevant knowledge is subjective and must be constructed and instilled by the learner herself. Recent developments in short-term therapy have influenced these humanistic conceptualisations, as well as have sociological notions of the post-modern society. The programmatic overall ideal is to challenge the traditional power relations in professional-layperson relationships. Counselling is presented as the "new" professionalism: empowering, tailored and sensitive to the individual life world and more suitable for the transitions of post-modern or late modern work life than traditional forms of training and guidance (Savickas 1993; Onnismaa & Taskinen 1994; Onnismaa 1995, 1997, 1998; Vähämöttönen & Keskinen 1994; Vähämöttönen et al. 1994).

## What Is Career Guidance Training?

Career guidance training has always based its curriculum on self-directed and experiential learning and learner-centred methods. It first emerged in the 1970s as a labour market service. The initial aim was to provide a more activating, learner-centred alternative for psychological tests and behind-the-desk career services, especially for people with special difficulties in becoming employed. Since the downturn of the Finnish economy in the early 1990s, career training has become a common choice for anyone in "transition": between jobs, making the first career choice, etc. In career guidance training, a group of students (most often adults) engage in various group and individual activities in order to draw a practical, well-prepared action plan for their future career and employment. Careers trainers (later: counsellors) who facilitate this process, have different academic backgrounds; many hold degrees in psychology, education and social sciences. Psychological testing or personality assessments are seldom used. Rather, counselling and learning processes are to be realised through the experiences and interactions that the student engages in during the course time: group work and discussions, lectures, field trips, information gathering, work practice, self-evaluation, and individual counselling.

Despite the growing interest in counselling as a way to enhance adult learning, there have been no in-depth empirical studies of how adult educationally oriented counselling is carried out as an interaction. Descriptions of counselling have been framed in metaphorical terms and have tended to describe goals and ideals rather than means to achieve them. Counsellors generally do not follow particular psychological theories or techniques. Therefore, a particular interest of my study has been to describe inductively the structures and patterns of interaction which characterise and constitute counselling in this setting, and which especially constitute it as educational interaction For these purposes, conversation analysis has been applied to a set of recorded counselling encounters.

The data for the study consist of twenty-one counselling encounters from seven counsellors from different vocational training centres located throughout Finland. All encounters are from face-to-face counselling sessions between a counsellor and a student who is taking part in a career guidance-training course. In all cases, individual counselling is one of the many working methods in the course. The counsellors recorded the sessions themselves either by video- or audio-recordings. Permission was obtained from all participants to use the material for research purposes by the author. One counsellor has recorded two sessions with four students (8 sessions), while other counsellors recorded one session with one, two or five students. When I started the study, I was still working as a counsellor, and I included two of my own sessions in the data. The length of the sessions varies from 10 minutes to two hours, with the average of about 40-50 minutes. Sessions include first, middle and final sessions. Complete transcriptions (see Appendix 1 for transcription symbols) were made of twelve encounters by myself and research assistant Monja Kataja. Other nine encounters are transcribed in parts. Working notes have been made of most of the data, also of the nontranscribed parts.

## What Is Conversation Analysis?

Conversation analysis (CA) aims at describing patterned features of interaction that the participants themselves show orientation to, both in the organisation of their own turns of talk and the treatment of turns by other participants. "Talk" refers to all means of communication which the participants use in the "public" space they create for each other moment-by-moment. The focus in the analysis is on the sequential organisation of interaction. Turns of talk emerge in real-time sequences, in which each turn's first interpretative context (for participants and analysts) is its sequential position. Thus turns are analysed in terms of the way they treat and are influenced by prior turns, the way they create possibilities of upcoming turns, and the way they contribute to ongoing actions. We expect that inasmuch counselling is treated by participants in terms of a particular institutional setting and their talk is there to carry out special tasks related to this institutional context, that they will organise their interaction in particular ways. That is, they will selectively use conversational possibilities throughout their encounter so as to co-construct "yet another instance" of this particular institutional interaction. This is the basic claim - shared by many analysts of institutional talk - on which inductive analysis is possible (Heritage 1984, 233-292; Schegloff 1991; Zimmerman & Boden 1991; Drew & Heritage 1992b; Hutchby & Wooffit 1998).

**Troubles-talk and Troubles-recipiency**

Counselling in career guidance training is not about troubles as such. There is no pre-orientation to talking about problems or "finding out what is wrong". However, troubles sometimes do arise and students are encouraged to air these troubles by bringing them into group discussions or individual counselling encounters.

There are two reasons for focusing on students' problems and their treatment. Firstly, one of the aims of counselling in career guidance training is to "give support". Since counselling is a supportive activity, if anything goes wrong for the student, this should be discussed in counselling encounters. Support, of course, can mean many things and it can be interactionally accomplished in many ways. In one sense, support can be understood as a practical activity in which it is "seen to that everything works". However, support can also refer to a particular kind of behaviour invoking a particular emotional stance between participants. "Support", in this way, could be seen as the counsellor's attitude towards the student.

It seems reasonable to expect that both these aspects are relevant. However, it is not clear what counts as a "supportive response", or "supportive environment", and therefore we need categories which would lead us to actions in conversation. Sequences in which students bring up troubles and counsellors respond to them appear to be a natural area for studying counselling as a supportive activity. Troubles-talk is a practical activity in which matters that are personally experienced as troublesome - or at least presented as such - are brought up by the troubles-teller. The recipient of these troubles then has the possibility for performing emotional and practical support through her or his responses to the troubles-telling.

Secondly, and no less importantly, troubles-talk in institutional settings offers an analytical dimension bringing out crucial, comparable aspects of expertise and professional conduct. Institutional settings are often characterised in terms of the task of troubles-telling. The layperson has a problem and talks about it, and the professional performs some work on it. The particular institutional character of these dealings with problems can be highlighted by comparing them to the ways in which troubles can be talked about in mundane settings or in other institutional settings.

Troubles-talk in ordinary conversation is a loosely ordered activity. Jefferson (1988:419) proposes that although "troubles-talk does not occur as a consecutive sequence of ordered elements", there seems to be loose "etiquette" on how troubles are talked about. This may involve particular ways of approaching the trouble as well as certain manoeuvres performed to exit the troubles-talk so as to attend again "to business as usual". Generally, there are various actions the troubles-recipient can perform. Among these are signs of affiliation and elements of "work-up", such as diagnoses, reports of relevant experiences, remedies and prognoses (Jefferson 1988, 428-431).

In institutional settings the activity of troubles-talk is rather more constrained. There is often a pre-orientation to laypersons' particular kinds of troubles being a central topic. Problems are received and interpreted using a particular inferential framework and knowledge, such as medical or therapeutic knowledge, and the orientation by professionals to particular, "workable" aspects of laypersons' troubles. Typically, institutional interactions are characterised by particular constraints on the professional's response to the layperson's troubles-talk. For instance, as Sacks has pointed out, therapists do not perform in therapy sessions personal second stories ("oh, my mother was also very critical"), which would be possible and even typical in ordinary conversations (Sacks 1995; Spring 1968; see also Arminen 1998, 179-180). Instead, they may engage the client in a sequence in which the trouble description is reformulated into a "therapeutically workable" problem through the therapist's questions and formulations (Davis 1986; Peyrot 1987; Buttny 1996).

What is particularly interesting in the present setting is the contingent nature of troubles-talk. It raises several questions. First of all, what kinds of troubles are brought up? What problems do counsellors treat as belonging or not belonging to their mandate? How do they deal with this boundary? What actions do counsellors perform as responses to troubles-tellings? These are the questions we will deal with in this chapter.

## Students' Troubles

As earlier stated, by "troubles-talk" we refer to descriptions of a negative or problematic, personally relevant state of affairs, in which the teller her/himself makes available the problematic nature of the issue at hand. This telling makes relevant a response, which acknowledges the problematic nature of the trouble-at-hand and potentially performs some "work" on it. Thus, we are looking at cases in which the talk about trouble happens by the student's initiation. The collection consists of twelve examples that cover the whole data. Troubles are brought up in the following positions: (a) presented as first topics, (b) presented as new topics later in the conversation, or (c) brought up by students in response to the counsellor's elicitation within particular activities, such as "planning next actions", "brainstorming about career directions", "reporting of past activities".

Some problems deal with the student's health - physical or mental - whereas some deal with the student's experiences of different course activities, and some with issues connected to the labour market office and bureaucracy. However, as we shall see, not all health-related problems are dealt with in the same way nor does discomfort with different activities in the course get the same treatment. And finally, not all problems are treated by the counsellor as agenda-relevant problems. Some troubles belong non-problematically to the counsellor's mandate. Issues such as work placements and contacts to employers, planning individual course activities and general "careers" areas sort under the counsellor's expertise. There are also issues that are known to fall under the jurisdiction of another institution, such as labour market office, but where the counsellor still takes an active role in dealing with the trouble. There are also cases where the counsellor indicates that the issue does not belong - for a variety of reasons - to her/his mandate, but where she/he goes ahead to deal with the trouble from this position.

In order to understand what counsellors professionally do with students' troubles, we need to examine how they respond to the troubles-tellings and what sort of tasks they take upon themselves as troubles-recipients. Before focusing on this issue, we will point out some general structural features of troubles-talk sequences.

### Elements of Counsellors' Responses

As stated, troubles-talk occurs in extended sequences. Troubles are discussed over a stretch of talk, in which the trouble is worked up towards a solution or an optimistic projection. In many cases, the counsellor asks questions before providing any response. This is a way both of allowing interactional space for the troubles-teller and for accepting the topic within the agenda. Asking a question is a way to show attention by encouraging the troubles-teller to expand on the topic, but it is also a way to influence the topical direction of this expansion. Questioning also provides the advantage of finding out more about the problem before responding to it. Some inquiries deal with the "cures" the troubles-teller has tried or inquire whether she/he has tried a particular cure. These inquiries often lead to advice. Questioning can also be used to demonstrate "counter-evidence" to the trouble. For instance, a counsellor may demonstrate that the student is misinformed or has made superficial conclusions about the trouble-at-hand.

The following elements appear in counsellors' responses to troubles-tellings:

1   Empathy: acknowledging the problem as problem, showing affiliation. In this data, this is usually done through prosodic (i.e. voice) qualities.
2   Normalising: showing that the trouble is a normal or natural state of affairs.
3   Advice: performing "work" on the named trouble by recommending a course of action that helps deal with the problem-at-hand or by referring the problem to other experts. Advice is commonly a closing-relevant component bringing the troubles-talk towards a potential solution and thus to its closing.
4   Offers for help: offering to do something on the student's behalf in order to deal with the trouble.
5   Counterstatements contradicting or countering the student's trouble-description or some aspect of it.
6   Formulations: counsellor's interpretations of the trouble, presenting her/his understanding or the student's prior talk.

Such formulations in this context are fairly rare in the data and will not be in focus in this chapter. In this respect, it seems that the present data gives a very different picture of counselling than the literature on therapeutic counselling, where problem-shaping work has a central role. In general, troubles are not treated by either participants as ones which require interpretative work prior to actually trying the solve them.

## Counsellors' Orientations to Troubles-recipiency

A main finding of this analysis is that counsellors combine several response elements to achieve responses performing different tasks. In other words, counsellors not only give advice, sympathise, normalise or offer help, but in doing these things in particular combinations and orders, they accomplish actions which carry different orientations to what is the counsellor's essential task as a troubles-recipient. Therefore, we will refer to different orientations to troubles-recipiency.

The first one of these orientations can be called the activating orientation. In four cases, the counsellor's actions require the student to become active in solving her/his problem or engage the student in further activity concerning it. The counsellor indicates that something can be done to solve the problem or deal with it more profoundly, and that the student should be the main agent of this dealing. The counsellor does act as a co-constructor of a possible solution, but maintains that it is the students' main responsibility to deal with the problem. These cases may also contain a negotiation over the nature of the problem. The second orientation is to the giving of help. In three cases, the counsellor's main orientation is to act in a direction of easing the problem. The counsellor treats the problem as serious and as one that requires her/his attention and action and does not attempt to involve the student in a greater effort to solve it.

The third orientation is what might be called off-agenda orientation. In four cases, the counsellor does not actively expand the topic - more than it is necessary to in order to find out that this is not an agenda-relevant trouble - and rather quickly begins to offer responses which approach a "solution" and thus the closing of the topic. These problems deal with issues such as health or physical appearance and are treated in the interaction as issues not affecting the course or the course-relevant topic at hand. Interestingly, the signs of affiliation, empathy and surprise which would be very typical in troubles tellings in ordinary conversations (Jefferson, 1988) are mainly found in these cases. It seems that this type of troubles may open an island of "ordinary conversation" within counselling talk.

Due to the limits of space, we will not be able to deal with the whole material here. Therefore, we will focus on the two first orientations, which seem to be relevant in terms of the institutional tasks of counselling.


## Activating the Student

In this section, we will examine cases in which the counsellor, in one way or another, treats the students' problem so that he (the two counsellors in question are both men) activates the student. The counsellor either indicates that the student can do something with the problem through her/his own actions or he activates the student in the interaction itself by engaging her in the co-construction of a solution instead of offering her his solution.

*Advice, Counterstatement and Argument: From a "Problem-to-Endure" into a "Problem-to-Work-On"*

We will now examine a case in which the counsellor's and the student's views of the problem-at-hand are misaligned. In the collection, there are two cases of this type. The sequential progress of the troubles-talk is roughly the following:

1  ST:    description of trouble
2  CO:    implication of a "cure"
3  ST:    response indicating that the implied suggestion is redundant
4  CO:    advice and counterstatement
⟶     3 and 4 follow again

The student resists the counsellor's suggestions of a "cure" by indicating that (s)he has already done everything there is to be done. The counsellor, on his part, is pursuing a point that there is more to be done on the problem. The student's definition on the problem is, thus, "problem-to-endure", whereas the counsellor is constructing it as a "problem-to-work-on". In these cases, the counsellor's advice is combined with counter-evidence. Generally, producing counter-evidence is a way to eliminate the trouble. Here it is done so as to portray the student's actions in dealing with the trouble as insufficient. In both cases, the student resists the counsellor's advice and the sequence turns into an argument.

We shall now look at the other one of the cases. In the extract below, ST brings up a trouble (his back problem) during a first encounter in a phase where he narrates his career history.

*Extract 1 "Back Problem"*

```
1  ST:             ...ei >yksinkertasesti< >tarvinnu tehä< yhtää mitää
                   armeijassa. .hhhhhh...
                   I >simply< >didn't need to do< anything in the army
                   .hhhhh
2                  mut silti mä kävin kolmesataa ko(h)lkyt päivää
                   ar:meijaa.
                   but still I was in the army for three hundred thi(h)rty
                   days.
3                  (.)
4  ST:             ja olin kunto>suus< (.) ((kuntoisuusluokka))
                   and I was ((health & fitness classification))
5 (2)-> CO:        ootsä Kelaan (0.8) Kelaan ollu yhteydessä sillä tavalla
                   et sä oisit
                   have you- (0.8) have you contacted KELA so that you
                   would've ((KELA = The National Pension Fund))
6 (2)->            (0.2) #oeö:::# niinku selvittäny (0.2) niitten mahdollisen
                   tämmösen
                   (0.2) #e:::::#h sort of cleared out (0.2) their potential erm
7  ST:             mt.hh
8 (2)-> CO:        #ö:::::: [:# [ammatillisen koulutuksen ta:: kuntoutuksen
                   [ni(--)]
                   #er:::::::[:#  [vocational training or:: rehabilitation [(--) ]
9  ST:             [ kuntou[tus
                   [rehabilita[tion
11 (3)-> ST:       [oo- ] oon mä
                   [ye- ] yes I
12 (3)->           siinä mielessä että siihe tarvitaan lääkärilt (--)s todistus.
                   have in that sense that one needs a doctor's (--)
                   certificate.
13 CO:             nii
                   yes
14 (3)-> ST:       .hhhh et mi- mitä mä en taas tolta lääkäriltä voi saad[a.
                   .hhhh whi- which I cannot get from that doct[or.
15 (4)-> CO:       [niin ☐tuolta
```

148    *Listening to the Welfare State*

<table>
<tr><td></td><td>[yes from</td></tr>
<tr><td>16 (4)-></td><td>lääkäriltä et mutta< .hhhhhh yleensä näissä- (.)<br>tilanteissa ni<br>that doctor you can't but< .hhhhh usually in these- (.)<br>situations</td></tr>
<tr><td>17 (4)-></td><td>□ihmiset hakee #aika (0.5) aika monestaki paikasta<br>many people get from quite (0.5) quite a few places</td></tr>
<tr><td>18 (4)-></td><td>ta[vallaa (varmistusta siihe). ]<br>in a [sense a confirmation (for it)]</td></tr>
<tr><td>19 (3)-> ST:</td><td>[mt.hhh Ei se mitää ]kato mä oon- mä oon niinku tyy-<br>tyytyny<br>[it doesn't matter  ] see I have I have sort of settled for</td></tr>
<tr><td>20 (3)-></td><td>tähän että okei jos mä nyt (0.2) pääsen tähän (0.6)<br>this (like) okay now if I can (0.2) get to this (0.6)</td></tr>
<tr><td>21 (3)-></td><td>□työvoimahallinnon ammatilliseen koulutuksen avulla<br>nihh. [hhhh<br>through labour market vocational training thenhh. [hhhh</td></tr>
<tr><td>22 CO:</td><td>[ni [(then)/so/yes</td></tr>
<tr><td>23 (3)-> ST:</td><td>toisaalla (.) ni mä voin tyytyy siihe et mä- (0.5) ei se<br>(0.4) oo mitää.<br>(--) (.) then I can settle for this (thing that) I- (0.5) it's<br>(0.4) nothing.</td></tr>
<tr><td>24 (3)-></td><td>.hhhh [koska selkäleikkaukset<br>.hhhh [because back operations</td></tr>
<tr><td>25 CO:</td><td>[nii<br>[yes</td></tr>
<tr><td>26 (3)-> ST:</td><td>niinku polvi leikkauk>setki on< semmosii et vaikka niit<br>tehää satamäärin<br>as well as knee opera>tions are< such that even if you<br>have hundreds of them</td></tr>
<tr><td>27 (3)-></td><td>ni ne ei välttämättä tuo yhtää sun .hhhh olotilaan<br>helpotusta.<br>done they don't necessarily give you .hhhh any relief.</td></tr>
<tr><td>28</td><td>(0.2)</td></tr>
<tr><td>29 (4)-> CO:</td><td>E:i. .hhhh mutta ne saattaa tuottaa niinku sen:-<br>No:. .hhhh but they may result in (this thing that)-</td></tr>
<tr><td>30 (4)-></td><td>jos se on diagnosoitu sellaseks että[:<br>if it has been diagnosed as such tha[:t</td></tr>
<tr><td>31 ST:</td><td>[mh-hmh</td></tr>
</table>

32 (4)-> CO:  että >sä et< pysty tavallaa siihe entisee ammattiin ni
.hhhh sitte se on joku-
that you in a way can't be in your previous occupation
.hhhh then it is a-
33 (4)->  .hhhh JOko: (0.2) se (.) hö::::: vakuutus (jolla)
työnantaji(lla)
.hhhh Either (0.2) the uh:::::: insurance (that) employers
34 (4)->  >entisillä työnantajilla< on ollu,
>prior employers< have had,
35 ST:  >mh-hm?<
36 (4)-> CO:  niin tulee (.) hoitamaan ja (0.2) korvaamaan sitte sen (.)
seuraavan
which will (.) take care of (it) and (0.2) pay the (.) next
37 (4)->  ammatillisen (.) koulutuksen. Tai sitte se on <Kela>. ...
vocational (.) training. Or then it is <Kela>. ...

CO begins to inquire into the ways in which ST has tried to tackle the problem, and ST describes his complicated history with the back. In the data shown in the extract, CO makes an inquiry which implies a "cure" (2-->, from line 5 on). ST's response treats the implied suggestion (of contacting KELA) as redundant (3-->, from line 11 on). CO provides advice (4-->, from line 15 on) which argues against ST's point, and he, on his part, again rejects CO's advice as redundant (3-->, from line 19 on). CO also continues to argue for his point (from line 25 on), which basically is to show that there is more to be done to turn ST's case into a rehabilitation-retraining case, and that he would profit from a second opinion from another doctor.

Here, the counsellor confronts the student openly and presents no signs of sympathy. He orients to the student's trouble as "unfinished business" and concentrates on putting it back on the student's agenda. The counsellor here treats both troubles as serious, consequential career-relevant issues. Likewise, in both cases, the counsellor is explicit and direct in his argument, while the student, on her/his part, is also quite confident in her/his opinion. Both the counsellor and the student portray themselves as more knowledgeable than the other.

**Withholding Solution: Co-constructing a Way Out of the Trouble**

In this section, we will look at a case in which the student's complaint about her work placement experience and her elaborate account of her motivation problems receives a combined response. This is an offer for help, a withholding of advice after an overt advice request and advice after redirecting the course of the interaction. The student is looking for a way out of the problem, and the counsellor's strategy is to withhold the response that would put him in the position of solution-provider. Instead, he engages the student in co-construction of a solution to the problem.

Prior to the extract shown below, ST has stated that she has ruled out the bakery shop as a career option. She has developed an allergic reaction and she indicates that she is not interested in that type of work. CO sympathetically indicates understanding her point, but also states he still wants to explore her experiences in the job in detail. He is following a prepared routine of questions, and he takes ST through it. Also, CO states that they can rearrange - at some future point - her placement schedules and see if she could leave the bakery job earlier than originally planned. He then returns to his routine and again engages ST in further descriptions of her time in the bakery. In answering CO's questions, ST keeps returning to her trouble description. She makes it clear she feels distressed about staying in the placement and provides several reasons for it. We shall now examine the way CO manages his response:

*Extract 2 "Bakery Shop"*

| 1 | ST: | ((talking about the shop premises)) |
| | | -- #se on niin# □todella □pieni. |
| | | -- it is so really small. |
| 2 | CO: | joo |
| | | yes |
| 3 | ST: | et (.) siellei pysty kyllä toteuttammaan- (.) et yks jos lähtöö sinne |
| | | that (.) one can't realize there- (.) so that if one person goes to the |
| 4 | | >takahuoneeseen leipomaan< ni siell ei kyllä muita oo. |
| | | >back room to bake< then others won't fit in. |
| 5 | | (0.6) |
| 6 (o)-> | CO: | tota:, mhhh voisinko mää tehä tässä jotaki sun puolestah. |

|       |       | well:, mhhh is there anything here I could do for youh. |
|-------|-------|--------------------------------------------------------|
| 7     |       | (1.6)                                                  |
| 8     | ST:   | tähä asiaa:.                                            |
|       |       | regarding this thing.                                  |
| 9     | CO:   | nii.                                                   |
|       |       | yes.                                                  |
| 10    |       | (1.0)                                                 |
| 11 (a)-> | ST: | no (0.2) ainaki >mä sanoin että< kyl mää tänä aamuna lähi ihan sillä mielellä |
|       |       | well (0.2) (at least >I said that<) I did come this morning with the intention |
| 12 (a)-> |     | että kyl mää niinku vähän nyt apua tarviisin <sulta>. |
|       |       | that I would like a little help from <you now>.       |
| 13    | CO:   | joo                                                   |
|       |       | yes                                                   |
| 14 (i)-> | ST: | tästä[:                                               |
|       |       | about[ this (thing)                                   |
| 15    | CO:   | [joo                                                  |
|       |       | [yes                                                  |
| 16 (i)-> | ST: | et jotta:: .hhhhhhh mite:nkä minä: (.) voisin sinne:- (.) >mää sanoin s- jot< tuota:: that .hhhhhhhh how could (.) I (there)- (.) >I said th-< erm:: |
| 17 (i)-> |     | (0.4) EI se oo henkilöstä eijjo kysymys               |
|       |       | (0.4 )it is not a matter of person                    |
| 18    | CO:   | joo[:.                                                |
|       |       | ye:[s.                                                |
| 19 (i)-> | ST: | [ettenkö minä hänen kans pärjäis.                     |
|       |       | [it's not that I don't get along with her.            |
| 20    | CO:   | .joo                                                  |
|       |       | .yes                                                  |
| 21(i)-> | ST:  | vaan yksistään se ett jott tuota □niin:□ (0.2) meit ei niin monta siihe mahu? |
|       |       | but simply the fact that erm (0.2) there's not enough room for all of us? |
| 22    |       | (.)                                                  |
| 23    | CO:   | joo.                                                 |
|       |       | yes.                                                |
| 24 (i)-> | ST: | ja minnoon sieltä jo ka:iken opin omasta mielestän saanu mitä minä |
|       |       | and I think I've had all the lessons that I           |

| | |
|---|---|
| 25 (i)-> | tällä hetkellä häneltä oon niinku (.) ka:ivannukkii. |
| | have wanted from her (.) at the moment. |
| 26 | (.) |
| 27 CO: | joo |
| | yes |
| 28 | (0.5) |
| 29 (i)->  ST: | ett tuota: (1.2) mitä myö tehtäs nytte sitte tälle □jatkolle□ |
| | so tha:t (1.2) what should we do now with the □continuation□ |
| 30 CO: | .joo: |
| | .ye:s |
| 31 | (0.4) |
| 32 ST: | ett ei mulla nyt oikkeen (0.8) |
| | so that I really don't (0.8) |
| 33 ST: | ei todellakkaa oo mittää inspiraatioo mennä ennää .hhhh |
| | I really haven't got any inspiration to go anymore .hhhh |
| 34 | (0.4) |
| 35 CO: | joo:hh. (.) siltähän tuo kuu:lostaa.= |
| | ye:s hh. (.) it does sound like it.= |
| 36 ST: | =mmhhm. |
| 37 QU-> CO: | tuota: (1.0) no:- (0.4) mitäs:: >onks sulla< va:ihtoehtoja mie-. |
| | well (1.0) er:m (0.4) what erm >have you got< any alternatives in mi-. |
| 38 QU-> | >onks sulla< jotaki jo takataskussa. |
| | >have you already got < something in the back pocket. |
| 39 | (0.8) |
| 40 QU-> CO: | et jos: nyt kävis[it ] (.) [(--) ] |
| | I mean if you would no[w go] and (.) [(--) ] |
| 41 ST: | [no: ] (.) [Minä] |
| | [well] (.) [I ] |
| 42 | olin tuota: mhhhhhhhh sen että minä näin minun kaveria tässä la:uantaina? |
| | was erm mhhhhhhhh (there was this that) I saw my friend Saturday? |
| 43 | (0.2) |
| 44 ST: | se Teija? (0.6) joka on sieltä >paikallislehden toimituksesta?< |
| | that Teija? (0.6) who is from the >local newspaper?< |

((omitted several lines: student provides ideas for some alternative activities))

45 ST:         va:ihtasinko sinne sitte (0.6) vai- (0.2) tuntusko tuo (0.6)

                shall I move there then (0.6) or- (0.2) how do you (0.6)

46            Varsavuoren Teijaj juttu sitte minkälaiselle

                feel about the Teija Varsavuori thing

                (("Teija Varsavuori" = ST's friend))

47            (1.2) ((CO writes notes))

48 CO:         mt.hhhh (jo[o)

                mt.hhhh (ye[s)

49 ST:         [oeshan se etteenpäin kuitennii tuota (0.6) sit(e) (--)

                [that would be some sort of progress (0.6) (then) (--)

50 CO:         □joo□

                □yes□

51            (1.2)

52 AD-> CO:    □joo□ (mää) tota- (0.6) (nyt) mietin sitä että (1.2) mt että ettäm hhhhh (2.0)

                □yes□ (I) erm- (0.6) (now) I'm thinking that (1.2) mt that that erm hhhhh (2.0)

53 AD->        siinä vois ajatella nii:n että sää tällä viikolla jo kävisit

                one could think so that already this week you would go

54 AD-> CO:    (0.4) jos sää saisit sen Teijan kiinni.

                (0.4) if you could contact that Teija.

55 ST:         mmh-hm?

56            (0.2)

57 AD-> CO:    et se ois niinku yhen päivä ju:ttu.

                so that would be a one-day thing.

58            (.)

59 AD-> CO:    ja (.) ja tietysti tuolla nyt ku: (.) mä (.) e:::h tuolla nyt on::eh on sovittu

                and(.) and of course (there) now since (.) I (.) u:::h one has::eh has agreed

60 AD->        nii jotenki tässä nyt vielä   [niinku tekis tän

                so somehow one would still [sort of finish the

61 ST:         [mhhm.

62 AD-> CO:    homman (0.4) johonki tiettyyn pisteeseen

                job (0.4) to a certain point

63 ST:         mmh-hm?

64            (0.6)

65 AD-> CO:     ja tuota (0.8) myö voijjaan ihan hyvi- hyvin jos haluat mää voin tulla

and erm (0.8) we can very wel- well if you want I can

66 AD->         □käymään siellä? tai me voijjaan vaikka soittaa tästä (.) ihan

visit there? or we can even call from here (.) (right)

67              (.)
68 ST:          mmh[hm.
69 AD-> CO:     [iha heti (.) .hhhh ja ja niinku tavallaan sumplitaan se että mitenkä (0.4)

[right away (.) .hhhh and and sort of figure it out that how (0.4)

70 AD->         että että tuota k-ku sus- sulle sinulle tuntus tällä hetkellä tärkeämmältä se että

that that erm s- since you feel its more important to you at the moment to

71 ST:          mmhhm
72 AD-> CO:     että tekisit muuta

to do something else

73 ST:          nii-i

ye-es

74 AD-> CO:     ja tuota (1.2) mt öö:: sitten (0.4) sitten tosiaan sen vois tehä

and erm (1.2) mt e::h then (0.4 )indeed one could do this thing that

75 AD->         että (.) että ottasit yhteyttä sinne (0.6) siihen (0.4) sinne ((harjoittelupaikka))

that (.) that you would contact the (0.6) the (0.4) ((a work placement))

((advice about contacting the next placement continues))

After ST has returned to the trouble-description for the fourth time, CO produces a non-itemised offer for help (o->, line 6), and ST accepts the offer (a->, lines 11-12) but does not indicate the kind of help she wants. CO has already stated that he is ready to rearrange her job practice schedule and here he seems to assume that ST wants more out of him than this reassurance. This is probably his permission to not return to workplace at all. By his non-itemised offer for help, CO provides ST a chance to identify the kind of help she needs and leads her away from problem-description towards talk about potential solutions. However, she does not overtly suggest dropping out. Instead, she initiates advice (i->, line 16->), indicating uncertainty about how to proceed with the matter, and once again summarises the reasons for thinking that her placement is no longer useful. ST explicitly admits her need for help by producing a question-shaped request for advice (line 29) which makes relevant CO's advice - or a solution to her problem - in the next turn.

CO, however, provides neither advice nor solution, but withholds it (cf. He 1994). ST's advice-initiation ends with a question "so that -- what should we do now with the continuation", and CO treats it as a description of her perspective rather than a direct question (his response is "joo", line 30). ST again describes her reluctance (32-33). CO acknowledges this with a response which indicates that she has made her point ("it does sound like it", line 35). CO then begins to elicit talk about "alternatives in the back pocket" (QU->, lines 37-38). The sequence extends into a planning sequence, in which ST provides ideas and CO evaluates them.

The advice is delivered only after ST has provided ideas for alternative activities and explicitly asked CO to evaluate them (45-46). In the advice (from line 52), CO lists ST's ideas and proposes a schedule for realising them. He thus confirms ST's plans. He also promises to help her to deal with the present placement although he also indicates dropping out right away is not appropriate (59-62). In his promise for help, CO commits to negotiation with the employer (65-69), and after this incomplete turn, refers to ST's experience as grounds for this recommendation (70, 72). Thus, CO acknowledges the seriousness of ST's trouble and commits to co-operation in dealing with ST's trouble. However, he still does not make a definite recommendation about the length of ST's stay in the bakery.

In his overall treatment of ST's troubles-talk, CO is playing for time and gathering information prior to his recommendation. Even after having explicitly put himself in a position of a potential solution-provider ("is there anything I could do for you") - he withholds his recommendation until he knows what the student has planned to do if she leaves the bakery job.

The student, on her part, is looking for a way out. She is trying to move the responsibility of solving the problem to the counsellor. Still, she seems to orient to the counsellor's reluctance to suggest dropping out from the bakery shop. Thus, she does not explicitly ask for a permission to drop out, but is only fishing for it. Counsellor, however, obviously does not want to recommend just dropping out. At the same time, he recognises the student's discomfort in the placement as "serious". His solution is to offer help but to withhold at the same time an outright solution. Instead, he engages the student in reflection about alternative activities. Thus, he preserves an opportunity to help the student without directly offering her a solution. Also, this approach provides him an opportunity to engage in negotiation with the third party concerned with the issue - namely the employer.

## Normalising and Advice in Order to Activate the Student

In normalising, the troubles-recipient states or shows that the experience the troubles-teller portrays as troublesome is, in fact, a normal or natural state of affairs (Houtkoop-Steenstra 1997; Heritage & Lindström 1998). However, stating a trouble is "normal" does not mean it is dealt with. Normalising accomplishes particular work in particular situations. In this case, it is used to build a response that maintains that the student herself should be active in dealing with her trouble.

In the following example, the counsellor normalises the student's negative emotions regarding the course "independent activity period.

*Extract 3   "I'm All Stuck"*

| 1 | CO: | #ym::::# (2.2) mi□tä □sä meinaat □tehdä nyt tässä (1.8) mt (.) |
|---|---|---|
| | | #erm::::# (2.2) what are you going to do now (1.8) mt (.) |
| 2 | ST: | mä en nyt i:han (.) tarkkaan [>sillee] tiedä< mä oon välillä mä (.) |
| | | well I (.) don't [>know] exactly< I am sometimes I'm (.) |
| 3 | CO: | [(□--□) ] |
| 4 | ST: | suunnittelen kovasti ja välillä mä on ihan (.) lukos□sa□, [.hhh]hhhhh |
| | | planning a lot and sometimes I'm all (.) stuck, [.hhh]hhhhh |
| 5 | CO: | [nii ] |
| | | [yes ] |
| 6 | CO: | se on [(.) ihan (.) #varma# ] |
| | | it is [(.) quite (.) #certain# ] |
| 7 | ST: | [et: (0.4) et niinku >sano]taa< nytki tällä viikolla nin (0.6) >mä olin< |

|   |   |   |
|---|---|---|

[(I mean) (0.4) I mean >s]ay< this week for instance (0.6) >I was<

8    tavallaa >☐vii☐me< viikolla ku mä sain tietää >et< tää menee [näin tää]
in a way >last< week when I found out >that< this will go [like this]

9 CO:    [.nffff ]

10 ST:    projektihomma nin .hhhhhhhh >mä olin< tavallaan pettyny ku mun e-
this project thing then .hhhhhhhhh >I was< in a way disappointed when I di-

11    #eimu# (1.0) tarvinnukka aamulla lähtee kaheksan #aikaa# ko☐too☐,
#I didn't# (1.0) need to leave home at eight in the morning,

12    (1.4)

13 ST:    koska [mä koin et >se on<] ihan hyvä lähtee #kotoo# kahek☐san aikaa☐.
because [I felt that >it is< ] quite good to leave home at ☐eight☐.

14 CO:    [niimpä (☐juu☐) ]
[so it ☐is☐ ]

15    (1.0)

16 CO:    #joo#
#yes#

17    (2.0)

((omitted 22 lines: ST says her work group organized itself differently than she had expected, in separate individual projects. CO assesses their division of labour as sensible and points out that the group members can join together when they present their work results. ST agrees and summarises the situation:)):

18 ST:    ... mut kuitenki että: ☐#ääää#☐ ku täs on <☐ai☐kaa> (.) niinku
... but anyway like ☐#u:::h#☐ I mean there's time (.) erm

19    [(.) eh]kä täs on: (0.4) .hhhhhhh ☐sit☐ liian paljo
[(.)may]be there's (0.4) .hhhhhhh too much

20 CO:    [mmm ]

21 ST:          ai#kaa# sille (0.4) projek□tille,
                time for the (0.4) project then
22              (0.4)
23 ST:          voi olla että toisista (on) □sitte□ liia vähä#n#
                maybe some others think (there's) too little then
24              (0.8)
25 CO:          nii se on va- (.) se varmaan vaihtelee,
                yes it's cer- (.) that certainly varies,
26 ST:          mjoo
                yes
27-->   CO:     .hhhh  mut  tota  (0.4)  □#äm::::::#  □  □tää  □on
                luonnollista (0.4) □#mm# □että□
                .hhh but erm (0.4) □#äm::::::# □ □this □is natural (0.4)
                □#mm# □that□
28              (.)□että□ välillä pysty □#työskeleen välil on lukossa ja
                tulee
                (.)□that□ sometimes one is able to #work sometimes
                one is stuck and there's
29              ylä ja alamäkiä koko ajan# [ .hhh]hhhhhhh #ja ne#
                (.)□nos se
                uphill and downhill all the time[ .hhh]hhhhhhh #and
                they# (.)well
30 ST:                                      [□joo□]
                                            [□yes□ ]
31 CO:          #oo#□ (.) se #o# oikesta iha hyväkin ettei se o vielä
                (0.4) >sillon ku< (.)
                #er#□ (.) it #is# actually quite good that it isn't yet (0.4)
                >when<
32               >sillon< tietää että niinku on tapahtumassa #jotaki ja
                □on tehny
                >then< one knows that something is happening and
                □one has done
33              □jotak[in jo] (0.4) ehkä yrittäny jota[ki ja] sitten
                mennään#
                □some[thing a]lready (0.4) maybe tried [some]thing
                and then one goes
34 ST:                [□joo□ ] [joo ]
                      [□yes□ ] [yes ]
35 CO:          (0.3)  □taas  [(alas)]  et□  #se  ei  o  jotaki#  .hhhh
                monotonis□ta□,

|  | (0.3) down [again] so that it isn't something .hhhhh |
|---|---|
|  | monoto□nous□, |
| 36 ST: | [joo ] |
|  | [yes ] |
| 37 CO: | .hhhhh >tietysti< tä:mmöset #asiat et ei# on (.) |
|  | turvallista #tulla (0.4) |
|  | .hhhhh >of course< these things that (not) that it is (.) |
|  | safe to come (0.4) |
| 38 | □niinku yhdeksäs# ja□ (.)□herätä joka #aamu#□ (0.4) |
|  | systemaattisesti |
|  | □sort of at nine and□ (.)□wake up every morning□ |
|  | (0.4) systematically |
| 39 | ni .hhthhh ne e- □#mmmm#□ sitten (0.6) □#öööö#□ |
|  | saattaa (.) puuttua |
|  | then .hhthhhh they (e-) □#mmmm#□ then (0.6) #er::# |
|  | what might be (.) |
| 40 | tällanen (1.4) □#ninku#□ (0.3) piiska #tavallaan# (0.3) |
|  | kun (.) #alkaa tää |
|  | missing is a (1.4) □#sort of a#□ (0.3) whip #in a way# |
|  | (0.3) when (.) the |
| 41 | yksilöllinen jakso# (.)□mut se on (sitte) □ (.) .hhhhhhh |
|  | □ai□ka paljon varmaan |
|  | individual work period begins (.) but that is (then) (.) |
|  | .hhhhhh pretty much |
| 42 | niinku (.) #omasta i-# (.) omassa >itsessä #kiinni#< et |
|  | □mitä: |
|  | I think (.) #up to-# (.) up to one's own self (this thing |
|  | that) |
| 43 | (1.6) |
| 44 CO: | mitä siinä/mitä sinä (1.0) minkälaisen:: (.) |
|  | aikatau□#lun# (0.4) |
|  | what one/what you (1.0) what sort o::f (.) schedule (0.4) |
| 45 ST: | nii (.) jo[o |
| 46 CO: | [millase □#ohjelman si[tte□] te□kee (että) □.hhh[h |
|  | [what kind of a programme one makes[then) so .hhh[h |
| 47 ST: | [□joo□ ] [joo:. |
|  | [□yes□ ] [ye:s. |
| 48 CO: | varmaa ehditään tästä keskus#tella# [(□--□)] |
|  | certainly we'll have time to discuss this [(□--□)] |
| 50 ST: | [mut ] se: (.) se tää (.) |

[but ] it (.) it this (.)

51        se ei o nyt ⊡ihan niin⊡kun: (0.4) täysin selvä ...
         it is not quite sort of (0.4) completely clear...

CO asks about ST's plans for the next few weeks. ST says she doesn't know and immediately proceeds to use the opportunity to complain about the way she has experienced the independent study period. She organises her trouble description through a lead-up (Jefferson 1988, 422) and a connected detailing of more concrete problems. The lead-up describes her feelings idiomatically ("locked up" = inhibited, stuck) and the following concrete complaint is presented as the reason for her feelings. In the part omitted from the transcript, ST complains about the way her workgroup organised their activities. CO, however, regards this as a sensible division of labour. Following this, ST herself summarises the situation with a compromising tone allowing for exiting the troubles-talk. She points out that persons will experience the individual study period in different ways: for some, it is too short, for others too long.

CO agrees with ST's summary, but instead of moving away from the topic, he proceeds to respond to her initial trouble-description (line 27). Although ST has presented the emotional state and concrete circumstances as connected issues, CO treats them separately. As early as in line 6, CO attempts to respond to the initial description of emotion, but ST talks on, and details, as noted earlier, more concrete problems she has experienced. When CO takes the floor to respond, he deals first with the description of emotion. He normalises ST's negative feelings in various ways (27-35). Then he provides more practical account of why it is understandable that ST feels the way she does (37-41), and finally gives advice (41-46): it is up to ST her to plan her time efficiently. CO's response not only normalises the student's negative experience as understandable and natural, but also deals with the inherent complaint in her troubles telling. Let us see how the counsellor accomplishes this.

CO uses ST's idiom ("being stuck") and states it is natural to feel like that, then adds his own idiom ("uphill and downhill") and accompanies it with a "wavy" hand gesture (27-29). Then he shifts the focus: ST's feelings are not only natural but "actually quite good" - they indicate "something is happening" and one has been properly active (31-33). Finally, he states "it is not something monotonous". The referent here is left unmentioned, but it seems that CO is talking about the way things generally go in the course. He is invoking a "standard" experience, the symptoms of which may be feelings of instability or uneasiness. Thus, he is invoking a picture of a process or activity in which one is bound to feel these things if it has been done properly. Referring to ST's experience as "not monotonous" (instead of using a positive description "it is x") is another way to portray a positive aspect of an experience of instability.

ST produces minimal responses to CO's talk, who then continues to normalise the more detailed part of ST's complaint. He points out that it is understandably more difficult for students to work without external control (35-41). (This is a common complaint when adult students encounter "self-directed learning" for the first time.) He initiates his turn with "of course" (37), indicating he is about to say something contrastive to his prior talk. Indeed, he admits that the lack of routine and control is bound to present difficulties. He then proceeds to advice (41-46), in which he contends it is "up to one's own self". The advice includes a practical reminder of the fact that since students are free to decide their own schedules, they can structure their days as tightly as they wish. It also carries the implication that the student herself is responsible of this planning. In short, the point of the counsellor's response is that the student's emotions are "normal" and even "proper" because something non-monotonous is considered valuable and also because these feelings arise from the fact that students are used to routines and control. Thus, the "cure" for the trouble is mainly an adjustment that the student has to make "in herself".

Finally, however, CO partly takes a responsibility for planning ST's activities by indicating that the participants together (line 48) can discuss the issue later. Thus, he also builds a closing-relevant turn (cf. Button 1987), but ST is not about to drop the topic yet. She initiates the next turn with: "but this - this- this is not (--) (--) clear yet" and proceeds to a more explicit complaint where she shows that she is not sure what is expected of her in terms of action.

Normalising is used here to deal with a troubles-telling carrying a potential implication that there is a problem in the course arrangements or in the instructions for the independent work period. This is normalised as the student's problem and as a part of a proper experience in the course. In a sense, the trouble is turned into a problem-to-be-endured-and-dealt-with, as opposed to a problem which would require immediate action from the counsellor's part. Here, the counsellor does promise future assistance in planning the course programme, but also shows that this kind of problem is "part of the package" rather than an issue to complain about. However, the student does not comply but continues focusing on the topic. Now she frames her talk more clearly as a complaint directed at the counsellor.

Following this, the counsellor begins clarifying some issues concerning the "independent activity" period while also giving more advice.

## Summary: Activating the Troubles-teller

All the cases analysed in this section contain an element of challenge. The counsellor is giving the student something other than (s)he seems to be looking for. In the first example, the student has portrayed his back problem as one which he cannot do much more about, but the counsellor contradicts him, showing ways he believes the matter could be pursued to the student's advantage. In the set of two, of which this example belongs, the activating challenge is presented as a criticism of the student's efforts in dealing with the problem. The message here is: you should not give up yet.

In our second example - the "bakery shop" - the student is fishing for a solution for her problem. The counsellor does not give it, but helps to co-construct a plan for a solution together with the student. And finally, in the third case, the counsellor indicates that the student's feelings of confusion are "part of the package" and that the planning of her time and activities is her own responsibility. This phenomenon - presenting the student with an activating challenge when (s)he seems to be looking for advice or a solution - also occurs in this data in connection to advice-giving. In some cases, the counsellor may withhold advice after the student's request. One aspect of this strategy is that of teaching the students self-directedness (see He 1994). This seems to be one central interactional element of counselling as a facilitation of self-directed learning. Students are shown ways in which they can become active in dealing with their troubles, and they are also made accountable for being responsible for their own problems.

The troubles in the "activating" cases are brought up by the students as their responses to the counsellor's elicitation of particular activities, such as telling of biography and reporting of recent relevant activities. These troubles, thus, are presented as connected to issues that are on the counsellor's main agenda. Also, if we look at the content of the troubles, we notice that these are issues belonging to the counsellors' official institutional mandate: the course process, planning of activities, dealing with the work placements, career planning issues. On the fact of it, this seems paradoxical since these are issues to which counsellors move the responsibility primarily to the students. Yet, in some respects, this is the essence of this professional practice. According to many interpretations, the prime mission of counselling is to enhance the growing self-directedness of the student. Thus, we may view the activating response to troubles telling as one of the counsellors' devices to achieve this objective in counselling talk.

However, as earlier noted, this is not the whole picture. In some situations, counsellors treat students' troubles in a very different manner than the one described above. This is what we shall focus on next.

## Giving Help

In this section, we shall view two cases in which the counsellor's main task as a troubles-recipient is to help the student in order to ease the problem.

*Offering to Act on Behalf of the Student*

If we return to the case of "bakery shop" (extract 2) we find that the counsellor withholds advice and solution, even when it has been overtly requested, until he has elicited information on the student's alternative plans. Thus, he engages her in the co-construction of a solution. In extract (4) below, on the other hand, the counsellor's response is to offer to deal with the student's problem on his behalf. Let us now view this example in detail:

*Extract 4 Extension of "I Didn't Get the Money"*

| i | CO: | .hhhh tota □ni□ |
| | | .hhhh well |
| ii | | (1.0) |
| iii | CO: | ö::m mui[st□ats]ä mite tota selataa. |
| | | erm do [ yo]u remember how to browse that. |
| iv | ST: | [(--) ] |
| v | | (.) |
| 1--> | ST: | mä en saanu itte (niitä) rahaa sieltä (--). |
| | | I myself didn't get (them) the money from the (--). |
| 2 | CO: | .hhhh @ai@ nii::. soitiksä □sille Erjalle. |
| | | .hhhh @oh@ ri::ght. did you call (that) Erja. |
| 3 | | (0.4) |
| 4 | ST: | mt >kyl (□mä soiti□<) (0.2) se o jossai (.) koul□utuksessa (□nytte□). |

|  |  | mt >I (□did call□<) (0.2) she's in some (.) training (□now□). |
|---|---|---|
| 5 |  | (0.4) |
| 6--> | CO: | .hhhh mä □soitan □sille kohta ni mä (.)□voin kysyy samalt □siit□. |
|  |  | .hhhh I'll call her in a minute so I (.) can ask about it at the same time. |
| 7--> |  | (.)□>tai sä voit< .hhhh [>mä oon jok-<] |
|  |  | (.) >or you can< .hhhh [>I (am (--)-< ] |
| 8 | ST: | [(-ss-u-) ] mu äiti soitti sinne eile. |
|  |  | [(--) ] my Mom called there yesterday. |
| 9 |  | (.) |
| 10 | OP: | [(--) (--). |
| 11 | OH: | [soitti vai. |
|  |  | [she did. |
| 12 | OP: | (--) (--). |
| 13 | OH: | no mitä se sano. |
|  |  | well what did (s)he say. |
| 14 | OP: | mä ittekki >□soitin sinne< (ni ne/mä) sano että (0.4) mt kyl (teiän) pitää |
|  |  | I called there myself too (so they/I) say that (0.4) mt (you) do have to |
| 15 |  | maksaa mulle ku mä saan jotai työ:: (.) (työ) (--) (korvausta) |
|  |  | pay me because I get some labour:: (.) (labour) (--) (benefit) |
| 16 |  | (-[-) |
| 17 | OH: | [TYÖmarkkina#tukee# |
|  |  | [LABOUR market benefit |
| 18 | OP: | nii sitä. |
|  |  | yes that. |
| 19 | OH: | nii-i?, |
|  |  | that's right?, |
| 20 |  | (.) |
| 21 | OP: | eikä mitää □päivärahaa. (.) jos se ois päivärahasta ni sitte ei maksettas. |
|  |  | and no daily allowance (.) if it was about daily allowance then it wouldn't |
| 22 |  | (.) koska työmarkkinatukee sillonha ne joutuu □maksaa□. |

|     |     | be paid. (.) because labour market benefit is what they |
|-----|-----|-----|
|     |     | will have to pay then. |
| 23  |     | (0.6) |
| 24  | OH: | hyvä |
|     |     | good |
| 25  | OP: | äiti soittaa sinne Kelaa vielä= =ja (0.6) |
|     |     | Mom will call Kela again= =and (0.6) |
| 26  |     | jollei nyt raha ole huomenna tilillä ni |
|     |     | if the money is not on my account tomorrow then |
| 27  |     | (2.0) ((ST makes gestures with his fists?)) |
| 28  | OP: | □mä meen itte sinne (--) (--)□ |
|     |     | □I will go there myself (--) (--)□ |

ST brings up the trouble as a new topic in the middle of another activity (looking at a computer programme). CO immediately attends to the issue as a matter that must be included in the agenda, although she moves it to a later part of the encounter (reference to the phone call, line 6). The trouble is presented as a known topic and as a final state of affairs: "I myself didn't get (them) the money from the (--)" (line 1). This announcement is presented out of blue without contextualisation. The student seems to expect the counsellor to know what money he is talking about and what it means for him not to be able to get it. Here, he is talking about his labour market benefit that he has not received despite several attempts.

CO's immediate reaction to the student's troubles-telling is "ai nii" (oh right) with a stretched and animated tone. "Ai nii" has a sense of having been reminded of something important. It is as if the counsellor remembered that this issue was to be on their agenda. Her next question (line 2) seems to follow this agenda: ST was due to call Erja (the job adviser for the course) about this problem. From all this, we can gather that the issue of the student's benefit is a topic they have discussed before.

CO does not produce signs of surprise or affiliation. The nature of the trouble seems to be clear to her and she orients to immediate action. When she finds that ST hasn't been able to contact Erja, she offers to talk to her when calling about another errand (lines 6-7). CO offers the student the chance to talk to Erja at that time. We cannot be sure what the consequences of talking to Erja would be or what are Erja's possibilities to dealt with the issue. However, it seems that the CO sees the student talking to Erja as the next relevant step in taking care of the issue.

We should note that "I can ask" does not have the sense of "emergency" which "I will ask" could have here. "I can ask" is an offer, not an indication of a necessity. Still, it is an offer for an active intervention in terms of ST's trouble and puts CO in the position of a potential advocate in ST's matter, or at least someone who can find out about it on his behalf.

CO's talk is left incomplete when ST comes in and announces that her mother has already called "there" (line 8->). After this, the conversation takes a different turn, as ST's mother and later ST himself are pictured as the advocates in the issue. ST reports that he has found out that he is entitled to particular type of labour market benefit, and he commits to pursuing the matter until it's settled. The counsellor offers some affiliative remarks and they move back to the computer.

Here, the counsellor's initial orientation to the trouble is to treat it as an issue she must attend to. Instead of indicating that this is the student's own responsibility, the counsellor sets it into the agenda and offers to take the matter up. The next case, although different in many respects, shows the same kind of orientation to the student's trouble. The counsellor treats the student's problem as one, with which she needs help, rather than one activating challenge.

*Counterstatement and Normalizing: Eliminating the Student's Main Worry*

The case we will study now represents a set of two cases. In both of them, the counsellor provides strong counterstatements in order to eliminate the aspect of the trouble which the student has put forward as her central concern (both students are women). In this case, the student brings up her trouble as the first topic, without the counsellor's elicitation. She talks at length about her anxiety and inability to "know who she is", or to select from different roles and combine them into a whole person. She is worried that she is mentally ill. The counsellor convinces her that this is not likely at all, and that her feelings are normal for a young person. Although the counsellor points out she is not an expert on these issues and recommends that the student should talk to her doctor about it, she insists that the student's troubles are not symptoms of mental illness. We shall now view the initial part of this extended sequence and focus on the way the counsellor organises her response to counter the student's concern.

ST begins to talk in the beginning of the encounter before any elicitation from the counsellor. She "pours it out" for several minutes. Her trouble description is very long and complex, and we will only paraphrase it. ST describes her problem against a norm: a person should "feel whole" and "know what she is". She names various membership categories (child, student) and characteristics (assertive-helpless) which she recognizes as partly her roles, but complains that she is totally confused and can't combine the different, often contradictory, roles into a whole person. This, she worries, is something people will notice. Because of all these factors, she has tried to find out what is wrong with her and she suspects "mild schizophrenia". She talks on, and after another reference to suspicion of mental illness, CO asks what ST's doctor thinks about it. ST replies that she hasn't told her yet, and continues to describe her problem as such a serious one that she has not dared to mention it - even to those closest to her.

ST then develops the issue: she recognises the possibility that one person can "be many" or live through several roles, but points out that this should be manageable. This, however, is something CO feels she cannot do. She then begins to formulate her problems in these terms, topicalising the "roles" rather than ST's fear of not feeling "whole". In this she pictures herself as a person who lets roles take a lead and who can "forget" she is a whole person. ST does not confirm these formulations, instead she once more offers her own formulation of the trouble:

*Extract 5 "It Is Not Schizophrenia"*

| | | |
|---|---|---|
| 1 | ST: | = >mä en tiedä< onko se skitsofreniaah mutta .hhhhhhhh (0.4) |
| | | = >I don't know< if it is schitzophrenia but .hhhhhhhh (0.4) |
| 2 | | □mut mut □mä oon ihan. |
| | | but but I am completely. |
| 3 | | (2.6) |
| 4 | | □mä: mä en tosiaankaan tiedä mikä mä oo:n. .hh .hhh |
| | | I:: I really don't know what I am. .hh .hhh |
| 5 | CO: | mutta [se ] ei vie□lä: (0.4) o |
| | | but [that ] is not (0.4) yet |
| 6 | ST: | [(#--#)] |
| 7 | CO: | skitsofreniaa välttämättä |
| | | se että sä et tiedä mitä sä |
| | | olet. |
| | | necessarily schitzophrenia (this thing that) you don't |
| | | know what you are. |
| 8 | | (0.4) |

9  CO:            >koska sä oot< ton ikänen nuori ihminen se on aika
                  harvoin että ihminen
                  >cause you're< a young person of that age it is quite
                  seldom that a person
10                niinku olis .hhhhh siitä tietoinen niin [tarkkaan=
                  sort of would be .hhhh conscious of it[so clearly=
11 ST:            [(--) =onko se ihan normaalia
                  [(--) = is it quite normal
12 CO:            ky:llä se sun ikäselle on hyvinki normaalia □että□ että
                  ihminen niinku miettii
                  it is for someone of your age actually very normal
                  □that□ that a person sort of
13                .hh □ja myöhemminkii.
                  wonders .hh and later too.
14                (0.6)
15                tulee semmosia aikoja että: että ei □niinku
                  there are times that that one sort of isn't
16                (.)□ei niinku ookkaa enää sitä mitä on ikäänku □ollu.
                  .hhh
                  (.) one sort of is not what one has been before. .hhh
17                (0.4)
18 CO:            >ja [ku ] ajattelee< että sä oot nyt ((opiskelijan ikä))
                  >and [when ] one thinks< that you're now ((student's
                  age))
19 ST:            [□□mm□]
20                (1.6)
21 CO:            ja: ja mikä sun elämänvaihe on ollu niin tavallaan
                  niinkun myös
                  and and what your phase of life has been so (it is) in a
                  way also just
22                □ihan    tähän    omaan    ikä□kauteen    liittyvää
                  □epävarmuutta estä□.
                  a normal uncertainty about one's self which has to do
                  with your own age.
23                (1.0)
24 CO:            skitsofreniaanhan    liittyy    harhakuvitelmat?    (0.4)
                  >har□ha<aistimukset
                  with schizophrenia there are delusions (0.4) delusional
                  sensations
25                (0.6)

26 CO:     joko □kuuloharhat näköharhat
           either □hearing or vision delusions
27         (1.0)
28 CO:     >onko sulla semmosia.<
           >do you have those.<
29         (1.4)
30 ST:     □.nffff□
31         (1.8)
32 ST:     e::i. (.)□ei □ei ei □k(hh)ai□ #oo#. hhh[hh .nfff
           no:: (.)□no □no no Igu(hh)ess□ I #don't#. hhh[hh .nfff
33 CO:                                                 [□mmm□
34 ST:     mut: (0.4) vaan semmosia phhhhh (2.4) mt vaan
           semmosia □pelkoja
           but (0.4) just these phhhhh (2.4) mt just these fears
35         et #mitä::# (.) siitä että #mitä mä oon# .hhhhhh
           about wha::t (.) about #what I am# .hhhhhh
36         (0.6)
37 CO:     mutta se ei o vielä skitsofreniaa,
           but that is not yet schizophrenia
38         (4.0)
39 CO:     mut(ta) >että< sä voit Marjatalta tarkemmin kysyä sitä
           mitä hän
           but (>so that<) you can ask Marjatta further about what
           she
40         .hh >ku hän on lääkäri hän tietää sen tarkemmin<,
           .hh >since she is a doctor she knows it better<,
41         (.)
42 CO:     mutta että se käsitys >mikä minulla< .hhh (.) on
           skitsofreniasta ni
           but from what >I know< .hhh about schitzophrenia
43         .hhhhhhhh nin n:n n#::# ni:#n:# >nää mitä sä oot<
           □mulle kertonu
           .hhhhhhhh then then then >these (things) what you
           have< told me
44         ei viittaa □semmoseen.=
           do not point to (such thing).=

CO first rejects ST's suspicion. She does not provide grounds for her
point, but only claims that ST does not have enough "evidence": "that is
not yet necessarily schizophrenia this thing that you don't know what you

are" (lines 30, 32). Then, she proceeds to a normalising account (34-35), where she provides grounds for her rejection of ST's suspicion: a young person seldom knows exactly who she is. This account does not contain the word "normal" but it implies that it is normal to feel as ST feels. ST formulates this in her question "is it quite normal" (36) from which CO can proceed to explicit normalising (37) and to elaborate her description of general development of young people (38-39, 41, 44-45). ST does not respond to this, and CO then provides medical counter-evidence through an inquiry about symptoms that generally are related to the mental illness ST suspects (47-60). After this, CO states she is not fully qualified to give a final opinion and recommends that ST talk to her own doctor ("Marjatta"). Then, she returns to summarise her own opinion.

CO's summary of her view and the advice about another expert are elements which bring the topic towards its potential closing. However, ST is not ready to drop the issue yet. She asks what it is that is wrong with her if not schizophrenia. CO produces another set of responses with the same elements (not shown in the extract). CO first connects ST's "bad feeling" with her depression, once more stresses that it is not schizophrenia, and repeats her recommendation to see "Marjatta". Right after this, she summarises her "diagnostic" opinion, listing the earlier counter-evidence regarding delusions, and adding a new element ("being conscious of the reality"). Then a long pause follows, during which participants seem to reflect. Then, CO again begins to normalise ST's experience, this time moving away from the generalised accounts on "young people in general" towards the experience of ST's fellow students and even her own experience. After this, ST shifts focus in her troubles-talk and the topic of schizophrenia is abandoned.

In her troubles-telling, ST has made clear that her trouble is a sort of a mental pain, which needs to be explained, and her main concern seems to be whether she is mentally ill or not. It has also become clear that ST particularly wants to tell CO and she is offering her problem to her as one that needs to be explained.

What is CO's orientation here? She cannot help ST to be rid of the anxiety itself, nor is she an expert in terms of mental illness. It is obvious that CO is not making any attempt to present ST with a challenge. CO accepts the position ST gives her, and provides her own opinion of ST's trouble. She also deals with the trouble in the terms ST has given: she begins to work with the explanation ST has given her trouble. Normalising is here used as a "counter-diagnosis" - it is an account which CO uses to reject candidate explanation. What is the status of her opinion here? After giving her opinion, she points out that a doctor would know more about the issue. However, she presents herself as someone who knows enough to be able to have an opinion, and she gives it without hesitation.

Normalising has also another function. After the two rounds of CO's counter-statements and counterevidence, there is a very long silence. After 22 seconds, CO once more begins a normalising account, this time stating that ST's feelings are similar to adolescents in general. ST remains silent and CO elaborates her normalising (7-9). ST still does not respond, and CO now points out that ST's fellow students have similar problems, and even she herself has had them in her youth.

*Extract 6 A Later Instance of "It Is Not Schizophrenia"*

| | | |
|---|---|---|
| 1 | CO: | et kyl sä realiteettitajuinen olet ollu tän kurssin □aja□, |
| | | so you certainly have been reality-conscious during this course, |
| 2 | | (22.0) |
| 3 | CO: | ja se mistä sä puhut ni on sun ikää- #□ä (.) nuorille (0.4) ihmisille |
| | | and this what you talk about is about your age- (-) (0.4) (for) young people |
| 4 | | ja: □#mm#□ (.) niinku semmoset ajatukset jo- (.) ja tunnelmat mitä sä oot |
| | | a:nd □#mm#□ (.) sort of these thoughts tha- (.) and feelings that you have |
| 5 | | kertonu on aika monilla ihan samanlaiset □mitä sulla on□. |
| | | told about are for a lot of people quite the same as □what you have□. |
| 6 | | (0.8) |
| 7 | CO: | vaikka sä: ite t- ajattelet että ne ei o □muilla. |
| | | although you yourself think others don't have them. |
| 8 | | (0.4) |
| 9 | CO: | ne vain on sun ongelmias, |
| | | they are only your problems. |
| 10 | | (0.6) |
| 11 | CO: | >mutta ku mä oon jutellu< nuorten ihmisten kans(sa) tällä kurssilla ni |
| | | >but when I've talked with< young people in this course |

| | |
|---|---|
| 12 | hyvin monilla on samanlaisia .hhhhhhhh vaikeuksia ☐oman ittensä kanssa |
| | very many of them have similar .hhhhhhhhh difficulties with themselves and |
| 13 | ja ei tiedä mitä haluaa ja (0.8) ☐ei tiedä mitä on ja h |
| | one doesn't know what one wants and (0.8) doesn't know what one is and h |
| 14 | (1.6) |
| 15 CO: | ja ihan muistan (--) itselläniki olleen ☐sun ikäsenä☐, |
| | and I remember (--) even myself having (that) at ☐your age☐, |
| 16 | (4.6) |
| 17 ST: | mmhh k(h)un pääsis vaan siitä .hhhhhh hhhh .hhh siit e->semmosesta< |
| | mmhh if on(h)ly I could get rid of this .hhhhhh hhhh .hhh this e- |
| 18 | mhhhhhhhh ☐#mm#☐ kun tuntee niinku kauheeta syyllisyyttä... |
| | >this kind of< mhhhhhhhh ☐#mm#☐ when one feels such awful guilt... |
| | ((continues to talk about her guilt)) |

The long pause has opened into a place in which the participants have not reached any conclusion. ST's response to CO's normalising account as well as to her counter-evidence has been minimal. Here CO highlights once more the picture of ST as a normal young person and likens her to her fellow students and to herself. Sharing a problem is one "standard" of comfort and support (cf. Arminen 1998). Here CO upgrades her normalising into a sharing of ST's problem. It seems the exchange has now convinced ST that she is not schizophrenic, but has yet to convince her totally of her own normality. After CO's summary, she continues to talk about her trouble from another aspect (line 17->).

This way of normalising bears a resemblance to a case which Heritage and Lindström (1996) present in their analysis the moral aspects of health visiting discourse. They examine four encounters between a health visitor and a mother who complains with a gradually growing anxiety about her lack of proper feelings towards her baby. According to Heritage and Sefi (1992, 373-376), health visitors usually respond to trouble descriptions with advice. In this case, however, the health visitor abandons the more typical "medical-technical", or "baby-expert" orientation and chooses a "befriending" orientation. In doing this, the health visitor normalises the mother's experience by first invoking general developmental explanations about the bonding between mothers and babies and then by referring to her own experiences indicates that she understands how the mother feels. She then adds that she "came out all right" despite her early "unmotherly" feelings. Like the student frightened of schizophrenia, who portrays her problems against a normative standard, the mother depicts her troubles both in terms of "normal development" and in terms of "morality" (Heritage & Lindström, 1996, 25). In her normalising response to this troubles telling, the health visitor gradually moves from general developmental issues regarding the bonding between mother and baby towards her own experience as a mother, thereby portraying a close resemblance between her own experience and that of mother (Heritage & Lindström 1996, 24-44).

Thus, normalising is a way to reassure the troubles-teller that she is neither unusual nor unnatural. In both these cases, the problem normalised is particularly threatening and difficult. As we have seen, normalising works as a way to comfort the distressed troubles-teller. Like the health visitor, the counsellor moves from general developmental terms towards disclosing her own related experiences. In doing so, she upgrades the normalising effect and brings the trouble closer towards its solution (solution in a sense of "we being able to exit the topic here and now").

It seems that the professional's personal experience, which is not typically discussed in institutional settings, becomes a possible topic in cases of an "emergency". That is, when the problem is treated by participants as very serious and the distress it generates is great. References to the professional's own experience can strengthen the effect of normalising. If the professional, being in the "helping and caring" position and possessing knowledge on "how to be a healthy, normal person", shares the problem, then it is convincingly a "normal" problem. (For a related discussion on normalising and sharing the troubles-teller's problems, see Houtkoop-Steenstra 1997, 606).

**Summary**

In this section we examined two cases in which the counsellor actively orients to the task of helping the student with the trouble. In both cases the troubles are brought up as new topics without the counsellor's elicitation. Thus, they appear from outside the counsellor's agenda and have therefore an air of an "emergency". Also, both of these troubles could be categorised as ones outside the counsellor's official mandate. However, they can be considered crucial "life situation" issues which may have a great effect on course activities and are thus legitimate topics in counselling. In fact, it seems highly probable that most counsellors would consider it very unfortunate if these kinds of problems were not brought up. Missing one's benefit or suffering serious anxiety are issues which cannot be passed with a shrug. In this sense, it is seems reasonable that these problems are not used for "lessons on self-directedness" and other activating challenges. In both cases, it is also clear that the student has already somehow tried to deal with the trouble. However, this is also how the students with the "bakery shop" and "back problem" had portrayed their troubles. By picturing one's troubles as something one has already struggled with does not guarantee immediate help. This was clearly shown in the "bakery shop" case.

Based on these cases, in order to find the reasons why the counsellors offer help instead of activating challenges, we have to appreciate their differences and also pay attention to the way in which the trouble has been introduced. In the "money" case, the student has not explicitly indicated that help from the counsellor is what he is looking for. Later, it turns out that the student and his mother have both been active and the student is committed to pursuing the matter until it is settled and he has his money on his account. The counsellor, however, treats his announcement as a reason to act. Announcement of a failure ("I didn't get the money") gives the counsellor a reason to take a position in which she offers to act on behalf of the student.

There are several reasons why the counsellor might wish to do this. This is an adolescent student, whose mother sometimes takes care of his affairs for him. The counsellor may think that the student may not get proper treatment in bureaucratic institution. Or she may doubt his ability to take care of his affairs. Or perhaps she just wants to hear the "story" first-hand from someone who knows why he didn't get the money. Also, it is possible that the counsellor thinks the best way to find out what has happened is from Erja. These are issues which best could be dealt with through interview data. Nonetheless, it seems clear that offering to act as an advocate is one possibility for counsellors, and it is probably correct to assume that this would be done with certain persons - especially with younger students. In the other case, the help the counsellor provides seems to be of the kind the student has been looking for. It is mutually shared knowledge between participants that the student has her own doctor

("Marjatta"). Despite this, she brings her trouble up with the counsellor. In fact, as her troubles-telling unfolds, we find out that she tells the counsellor before telling her doctor or other relevant potential trouble recipients. She wants especially to tell her worries to the counsellor. This makes it very difficult for the counsellor to deny expertise and refuse to comment.

The student presents a long, anxiety-filled description of her state of mind, and summaries her feelings with a reference to her suspicion of mental illness. Later, after the counsellor has countered this suspicion, she still insists that something is wrong with her. She presents as her central concern finding an explanation to her troubled state of mind, and she invites the counsellor to provide her views regarding this concern. And this is exactly what the counsellor does. She counters the student's worst suspicion and offers as well another explanation of her feelings.

We might suggest that "help" could be a relevant orientation when students bring up troubles which are treated as "serious" and which affect the course process but which do not officially belong to the counsellor's mandate. The counsellor is not the expert who can solve this problem, but the counsellor can help the student to deal with the situation. In course issues (work placements, career options, gathering information, planning one's activities), on the other hand, an activating response is the "pedagogically correct" option. This does not mean it can always be used even in course issues, but in this is what happens in our data.

## Conclusion

The activating response to students' troubles-tellings is, in a sense, a type of response orientation that could have been anticipated and even treated as a normative point of comparison for other response orientations. The activating response, after all, is connected to the adult educational description of career guidance training as a way to enhance self-directedness. One of the concrete consequences of learning to be self-directed could be that the student learns to deal with her or his own problems. However, the other orientation we examined is important as an indication that there are limits to self-directedness which the participants take into account. Not all problems are treated by counsellors as ones which can be responded to with an activating or challenging response. To put it simply, sometimes students just need help.

If we reflect on the "limit of self-directedness" based on these examples, we may ask if there is not a category of "serious" issues which one is not supposed to try to handle alone. As well as there being issues one is supposed to learn to deal with on one's own - instead of having someone giving solutions - there are also issues about which a person generally seeks help. As we have seen, counsellors, too, have to deal with this kind of issues on occasion. These problems are sometimes outside the domain of their official expertise, but it is part of their expertise to be able to deal with them in counselling talk. Both students and counsellors seem to believe it is legitimate to bring to counselling issues not strictly related to coursework.

Undoubtedly, many counsellors could recognise this dilemma as part of their daily work. They have to decide when it is best to activate and to withhold help, what types of help are unproblematic, and when to let a trouble pass as an off-agenda problem and withhold professional "work" on it. This problem is rarely discussed in concrete descriptions of counselling, but there have been some critical adult educational voices who note that the ideal of self-directness may not be a realistic one (Pasanen 1998).

We have pointed out some of the practical ways in which the activating challenge can be presented to students when they bring up their troubles. We have also shown two different cases in which the counsellor chooses another responsive orientation than the activating one, and orients instead to helping the student out. In doing this, we have pointed out one relevant interactional phenomenon which can be focused on in order to locate the "limits of self-directedness": namely, the troubles-tellings of students and the ways counsellors orient to their main task as trouble-recipients.

We could now return to the issue we raised in the beginning of the chapter. How is "support" accomplished in counselling when it comes to responding to students' troubles? We have discussed two meanings of support in counselling: counselling as an activity which secures smooth course process by attending to all kinds of problems which may occur, and counselling as a "supportive environment", which is usually understood as having an empathic, understanding attitude towards the student.

It seems troubles-talk is an effective way for the student to bring her/his issues to the agenda. Counsellors listen to the student's troubles and mostly try to perform professional work with them. As a rule, counsellors attempt to bring the trouble towards a solution within the same encounter. Even in the activating cases where the counsellor indicates the student has main responsibility for dealing with the problem and where the issue is thus moved to the student's future "agenda", the counsellor provides advice and help and thus acts as a co-constructor of the solution.

Are the counsellors creating a supportive environment? Immediate signs of surprise or sympathy, which would be typical in ordinary conversations, do not appear in the cases we studied here, but are found in some of the off-agenda cases. It seems that as professional troubles-recipients counsellors maintain the neutral footing, typical of many institutional settings (Drew & Heritage 1992, 24). This is not to say they do not "give support" but they do it in ways that are typically institutional (advice, offers for help, normalising). An exception was seen in the final exemplar where the counsellor upgrades her normalising account into an indication of sharing of the student's problem to comfort a distressed student who struggles with a serious problem.

## Appendix 1: Transcription Symbols and Principles of Translation

The transcription convention used for this paper follows the one presented in Atkinson & Heritage (1984). Some additional transcription codes are based on the conventions used in the University of Helsinki Finnish language department (see Tainio 1997). In the data extracts, the first line shows the original Finnish version and the second line the translation. An additional grammatical gloss is added when it is considered necessary. The translation is an attempt to make the original Finnish accessible both in terms of the meaning and in terms of the problems and illformedness of the talk.

| | |
|---|---|
| CO: | counsellor |
| ST: | student |
| wo[rd | point where overlapping talk starts |
| (0.8) | silence in tenth of seconds |
| (.) | micropause, silence less than 0.2 seconds |
| >word | talk quicker in tempo than surrounding talk |
| <word> | talk slower in tempo than surrounding talk |
| wo::rd | extension of a sound |
| word. | downwards intonation |
| word, | level intonation |
| word? | upwards intonation |
| word?, | slight upwards intonation |
| □word | high pitch |
| □word | low pitch |
| WORD | talk louder than the surroundings |
| □word□ | talk quieter than the surroundings |
| word | emphasis |
| word- or word< | cut-off word |
| hh | outbreath |
| .hh | inbreath |
| #word# | squeaky voice |
| £word£ | laughing voice |

| mt | smack of lips |
|---|---|
| nff | sniff |
| (word) | word in doubt |
| (--) | unclear word |
| --> | point of analyst's interest |
| ((coughs)) | transcriber's comments |

# Bibliography

Arminen, I. (1998) *Therapeutic Interaction. A Study of Mutual Help in Alcoholics Anonymous*. Helsinki: Finnish Foundation of Alcohol Studies.

Atkinson, J.M. and Heritage, J. (eds.) (1984) *Structures of Social Action. Studies in Conversation Analysis.* Cambridge: Cambridge University Press.

Boden, Deirdre and Zimmerman, Don H. (eds.) (1991) *Talk and Social Structure. Studies in Ethnomethodology and Conversation Analysis*. Cambridge: Polity Press.

Buttny, R. (1996) Clients' and Therapist's Joint Construction of the Clients' Problems. *Research on Language and Social Interaction* (29) 2, 125-153.

Button, G. (1987) Moving Out of Closings. In Button, G. and Lee, J. (eds.) *Talk and Social Organization*. Clevedon: Multilingual Matters.

Button, G. and Casey, N. (1985) Topic Nomination and Topic Pursuit. *Human Studies* (8), 3-55.

Button, G. and Lee, J. (eds.) (1987*) Talk and Social Organization*. Clevedon: Multilingual Matters.

Davis, K. (1986) The Process of Problem (Re)Formulation in Psychotherapy. *Sociology of Health and Illness* (8) 44-74.

Drew, P. and Heritage, J. (eds*.) Talk at Work. Interaction in Institutional Settings.* Cambridge: Cambridge University Press.

He, A. (1994) Withholding Academic Advice: Institutional Context and Academic Practice. *Discourse Processes* (18), 297-316.

Heritage, J. and Lindström, A. (1998) Motherhood, Medicine and Morality: Scenes from a Medical Encounter. In Bergmann, J. and Linell, P. (eds.) *Morality in Discourse*. Mahwah: Lawrence Erlbaum.

Heritage, J. and Sefi, S. (1992) Dilemmas of advice. In Drew, P. and Heritage, J. (eds.) *Talk at Work*. Cambridge: Cambridge University Press.

Heritage, John (1984) *Garfinkel and Ethnomethodology.* Cambridge: Polity Press.

Houtkoop-Steenstra, H. (1997) Being Friendly in Survey Interviews. *Journal of Pragmatics* (28) 591-623.

Hutchby, I. and Wooffit, R. (1998) *Conversation Analysis*. Cambridge: Polity Press.

Jefferson, Gail. (1988) On the Sequential Organization of Troubles Talk in Ordinary Conversation. *Social Problems* (35) 4, 418-441.

Järvinen, P., Katajisto, J., Kellberg, Anneli and Onnismaa, J. (1996) *Ohjaavan koulutuksen opetussuunnitelman laatiminen. Opetushallitus.* Helsinki: National Board of Education.

Kinnell, A-M-K. and Maynard, D. (1996) The Delivery and Receipt of Safer Sex Advice in Pretest Counselling Sessions for HIV and AIDS. *Journal of Contemporary Ethnography* (24) 4, 405-437.

Krokfors, L. (1997) *Ohjauskeskustelu. Opetusharjoittelun ohjauskeskustelun toimintamallien tarkastelua. Helsingin yliopiston opettajankoulutuslaitos, Tutkimuksia 171.* Helsinki: University of Helsinki, Department of Teacher Education.

Mezirow, J. and Associates (1990) *Fostering Critical Reflection in Adulthood. A Guide to Transformative and Emancipatory Learning.* San Francisco: Jossey-Bass.

Nummenmaa, A-R. (1992) *Näkökulmia aikuisopiskelijan ohjaukseen.* Opetushallitus. Helsinki: VAPK-kustannus.

Ojanen, S. (1998) (ed) *Tutkiva opettaja 2. Helsingin yliopiston Lahden tutkimus- ja koulutuskeskus, Oppimateriaaleja 55.* Hensinki: Helsinki University Lahti Research and Training Centre.

Onnismaa, J. (1995) Quality Evaluation in Career Orientation Studies. In Mikkonen and Räisänen (eds.) *Evaluating Labour Market Training - Outcome and Effectiveness.* Proceedings from the Seminar in Helsinki, August 1995. Labour Policy Studies 122. Ministry of Labour.

Onnismaa, J. (1997) *Ohjaavan koulutuksen laatu ja vaikuttavuus. Ohjaus- ja neuvontatyön instituutioitumisen tarkastelua.* Unpublished licenciate thesis. Hensinki: University of Helsinki, Department of Education.

Onnismaa, J. (1998) Ohjausta epävarmuuteen - ohjaus ja neuvontatyö refleksiivisessä modernissa. In Manninen, J. (1998) (ed) *Aikuiskoulutus modernin murroksessa. Näkökulmia työllistymistä edistävän koulutuksen ja ohjauksen merkityksiin ja vaikuttavuuteen.* Helsinki: University of Helsinki, Deparment of Education.

Onnismaa, J. & Taskinen, L. (1994) *Ohjaavan koulutuksen arviointia. Rajankäyntiä aikuisopetuksen, sosiaalityön, lyhytterapian ja kuntoutuksen kesken.* Opetushallitus. Helsinki: National Board of Education.

Peräkylä, A. (1995) *AIDS counselling. Institutional Interaction and Clinical Practice.* Cambridge: Cambridge University Press.

Peräkylä, A. (1997) Institutionaalinen keskustelu. In Tainio, L. (ed) *Keskustelunanalyysin perusteet.* Tampere: Vastapaino.

Peräkylä, A. and Silverman, D. (1991a) Owning Experience: Describing the Experience of Other Persons. *TEXT* (11) 3, 441-480.

Peräkylä, A. and Silverman, D. (1991b) Reinterpreting Speech-exchange Systems: Communication Formats in HIV Counselling. *Sociology* (25) 4, 627-651.

Peyrot, M. (1987) Circumspection in Psychotherapy: Structures and Strategies of Counselor-Client Interaction. *Semiotica* (65) 3-4, 249-268.

Poskiparta, M. (1997) *Terveysneuvonta, oppimaan oppimista. Videotallenteet hoitajien terveysneuvonnan ilmentäjinä ja vuorovaikutustaitojen kehittämismenetelmänä.* Jyväskylä: University of Jyväskylä, Studies in Sport, Physical Education and Health.

Sacks, H. (1995) *Lectures on Conversation.* Oxford: Basil Blackwell.

Savickas, M. (1993) Career Counseling in the Postmodern Era. *Journal of Cognitive Psychotherapy: An International Quarterly* (7) 3, 205-215.

Schegloff, Emanuel A. (1991) Reflections on Talk and Social Structure. In Boden, D. and Zimmerman D.H. (eds.) *Talk and Social Structure.* Oxford: Polity Press.

Schegloff, Emanuel A. (1992) On Talk and its Institutional Occasions. In Drew, P. and Heritage, J. (eds.) *Talk at Work.* Cambridge: Cambridge University Press.

Silverman, D., Peräkylä, A. & Bor, R. (1992a) Discussing Safer Sex in HIV Counselling: Assessing Three Communication Formats. *AIDS Care* (4) 1, 69-82.

Silverman, D., Bor, R., Miller, R. and Goldman, E. (1992b) 'Obviously the Advice Is Then to Keep to Safer Sex': Advice-giving and Advice-reception in AIDS Counselling. In Agleton et al. (eds.) *AIDS - Rights, Risks and Reasons.* London: Falmer Press.

Silverman, D. (1997) *Discourses of Counselling. HIV Counselling as Social Interaction.* London: Sage.

Tainio, L. (ed) (1997*) Keskustelunanalyysin perusteet.* Tampere: Vastapaino.

Vähämöttönen, T. and Keskinen, A. (1994) *Toimesta tuumaan. Tarjoumia toiminnalliseen ammatinvalinnanohjaukseen.* Hämeenlinna: Sosiaalikehitys.

Vähämöttönen, T., Keskinen, A. and Parrila, R. (1994) A Conceptual Framework for Developing an Activity-based Approach to Career Counselling. *International Journal for the Advancement of Counselling* (17) 19-34.

Zimmerman, D. and Boden, D. (1991) Structure-in-Action: An Introduction. In Boden, D. and Zimmerman, D. (eds.) *Talk and Social Structure. Studies in Ethnomethodology and Conversation Analysis.* Cambridge: Polity Press.

# Part IV
# Clients, Identity and Institutional Talk in the Welfare State

Though differing in a number of respects, the final three contributions to this anthology all share a major concern with the interrelations among clients, professionals and communicative work in various settings of the NWS. In the first selection, Arminen and Leppo provide us with a mosaic of life in a Finnish institution for the treatment of clients having histories of substance abuse. In combining ethnographic and conversation analytic approaches to the microlandscape of interaction in this milieu, these researchers present a Goffmanesque account of the delicate patterns of communicative work employed by staff and clients to save face, keep therapeutic agendas on track and deal with contradictions threatening vital rehabilitation goals. In addition, at a time when there is a growing interest in self-help programs, they provide here an insightful analysis of the workings of AA: the archetypal self-help organisation.

In the second selection, Hydén looks in depth at identity in the context of institutional communicative work. Though taking a large part of his point of departure in research on social worker-client interaction, Hydén also brings in the wider societal contexts of late- and postmodernity in examining institutional constructions of identity. In a free-ranging essay form, he provides a richly detailed description of the fate of self in welfare systems. In so doing, Hydén charts the forces and processes at work creating, sustaining and transforming identities among both professionals and clients.

Writing along similar lines, Rostila looks closely at conversation analytic data drawn from Finnish social welfare agencies. His concern here is with exploring the contours of communicative work taking place in these settings. In looking in particular at how money matters are dealt with at meetings between social workers and clients, Rostila shows how notions of alignment and non-alignment among conversation participants function to co-construct these public encounters in either bureaucratic or social work forms.

# 7   The Dilemma of Two Cultures in 12-Step Treatment: Professionals' Responses to Clients Who Act Against Their Best Interests

ILKKA ARMINEN AND ANNA LEPPO

## Introduction

One dilemma recurrently faced by professionals in social work and related areas is that clients may want to act against their best interests - as seen by the professionals. In professions dealing with clients suffering from addictions, this dilemma is very widespread and well known. The following account - an ethnographic and conversation analytic investigation - focuses on how one group of professionals deal with clients who publicly profess their willingness to recover from their addiction but whose commitment to the official goals of the treatment may be weak at times. The data for this study include both ethnographic field notes and video recordings of various therapy situations collected by a team of researchers at a medium-size treatment institution in Southern Finland.

This chapter aims at describing - from the point of view of treatment professionals (as revealed in the details of their talk) - which features of clients' action require intervention. In addition, this description also shows how the professionals respond to clients who express interests counter to treatment goals (as seen by the analyst). The analysis uses both ethnography and conversation analysis (CA).

Publicly, clients predominantly express their devotion to the goals of the treatment. Nevertheless, a client at times may talk, for example, in ways that can be heard as expressing positive attitudes towards substance use or as underrating the problems of substance use. In responding to this type opposing talk, the treatment professional may act in various ways. The professional may choose to let the client's opposing talk pass, to confront the client directly, or to confront contradictory views indirectly, for example, by treating them as non-serious. In examining these issues, we wish in this chapter to focus on what professionals understand as undesirable attitudes among clients and how they respond in varying ways to clients' contending talk. Our main goal here is to show some interactional consequences these various types of responses may have for clients and professionals. Although we cannot rank these response types, as they are occasioned by varying interactional events, it is possible to reflect on them in terms of their applicability to different situations. In this way, we hope to provide professionals with conceptual resources for rethinking their work.

Three sets of considerations motivate our work. The first one derives from the specific character of the kind of rehabilitation program operative in the institution we studied. The clinic serving as our research site makes use of the Minnesota model, also known as the Hazelden treatment. The Minnesota model was introduced to the Nordic countries in the late 1970s. Its increasing popularity in the 1980s was connected to privatisation and decentralisation tendencies that took place in varying degrees in different Nordic welfare systems. The Minnesota model marketed itself as an efficient alternative to publicly provided treatment services and criticised their poor treatment outcomes (Stenius 1991, 1999). The institution described here is ideologically committed to the 12-step ideology of AA (Alcoholics Anonymous), i.e., the clients' abstinence is the ultimate goal of the treatment. Alcoholism and related addictions are seen to produce in the addict a state of mind called *denial*. Denial means that the addict is unable to recognise his/her loss of control over alcohol or drug use. Furthermore, alcoholism is seen as an illness from which the alcoholic can recover only through abstinence that is best achieved by attending AA or NA (Narcotics Anonymous) meetings regularly. The goals of the treatment are thus to make the client admit the addiction and then to motivate the client to attend AA or NA in the future and thereby stay abstinent. This specific ideology makes *confrontation* a central part of the professionals' work. The treatment professionals are supposed to confront clients who are seen to be in denial (Lausvaara 1990, 67; Anderson 1981). Confrontation refers to the direct and contradictory feedback a professional gives to a client who has expressed problematic and undesirable attitudes. Confrontation aims at making the clients' view of their situation more in line with that of the professionals - and from the professional point of view, a healthier one. Given the central place of this ideology in 12-step rehabilitation programs, it is a major focus of our research.

Secondly, studies of treatment efficacy have resulted in a paradoxical finding. In the main, only minor differences have been found in the outcomes of different treatment programs when external variables, such as AA attendance, are controlled for (Institute of Medicine 1992; Project Match 1997; Longabaugh et al. 1998; Keso 1988; Koski-Jännes 1992). The fact that different types of addiction treatment seem to lead to the same result suggests that generic underlying processes have an impact on treatment results irrespective of the type of therapy chosen (Toiviainen 1997). Here we propose that this may suggest the existence of what we call the dilemma of two cultures. That is, clients at addiction treatment centres always have access to two cultures. The "dry" culture, in which intoxication is controlled or completely forbidden, is constructed and sustained by treatment agents. The "wet" culture, in which intoxication is a key source to pleasure and meaning, is embodied in the biographies of addicted persons. On the basis of our observations, we feel that much of what goes on in treatment institutions can be understood as a fight between these two cultures. This conflict, too, has been an object of our investigation.

Thirdly, our study is a methodological experiment that combines ethnographic and conversation analytic approaches. Confrontation envisaged as conflict between two cultures and as a multidimensional cultural object seemed fruitful for studying with both traditional ethnographic approaches as well as more "micro-oriented" CA methods. However, as we shall later present, the use of different approaches such as these also constitute their realities in ways that do not simply complement, but also contradict, each other's findings. At the conclusion of this chapter, we will attempt to consolidate contradictory views arising out of different research perspectives. These we will attempt to discuss in term of the merits of combinations of approaches.

## The Setting

The clinic is in Southern Finland and is owned by a non-profit organisation having a religious background. The clinic has 54 beds, of which 44 are used for inpatient treatment and 10 for various short-term courses such as courses for partners of substance abusers, follow-up courses for ex-clients, etc. The number of staff varies somewhere around 18 persons and consists in the main of the clinic director, physician, social worker, minister (priest), family therapist, psychologist, two nurses, six addiction therapists, and a varying number of counselling/surveillance workers. Members of this latter group work during nights and weekends in the role of counsellors. Generally, more than half of the staff is themselves AA members.

For new admissions to the clinic, the treatment period is 28 days long. This is preceded by an evaluation period of 2-5 days. During the evaluation each client goes through a medical examination, psychological interview, and an interview, where questionnaires are administered by the social worker, nurse and an addiction therapist. After receiving a diagnosis and a treatment proposal, the client begins the 4-week treatment program. The schedule for each weekday is a fixed one consisting of a morning meeting, lecture, group therapy, peer group therapy, and story group in which each client tells her or his story of substance abuse. The addiction therapists also individually counsel the clients. In the evenings, time is reserved for the clients to attend AA and NA meetings. These are held inside the clinic, where AA groups organise meetings daily, as well as outside the clinic in other locales. Evenings are closed with a farewell ritual, where the departing clients are wished sober days, or with an evening circle where each client has an opportunity to talk about their day, etc.

**Data and Methods**

Two types of data were collected for the study. First, videotaped materials of various situations were collected for the analysis of situated interactions, and secondly, ethnographic field notes were taken for the exploration of participants' interpretations of situations and of the treatment process in its entirety. The videotaped materials cover four types of situations: 1) group therapy (19 sessions of two therapy groups taped during a two week period), 2) peer-group therapy (18 sessions of two therapy groups during taped during a two week period), 3) individual counselling (16 sessions by three therapists), and 4) multiprofessional team meetings, in which the progress and the treatment motivation of individual patients are discussed (7 sessions). Each group therapy session was about 45 minutes long; individual counselling and multiprofessional team meetings were of varying duration. Most of the recordings were done during a two-week period in 1997, while some individual counselling sessions were recorded afterwards. The tapes include about 40 hours of live interaction. They were all transcribed according to the conventions of CA (see Atkinson & Heritage 1984) and were collected with the permission of all the participants.

The primary goals of the ethnographic research were: to provide descriptions of recurring types of situations in the treatment program, to elaborate the relationships between the different situations to offer an overall view of the treatment process, and finally to elaborate the treatment process from the points of view of both the treatment professionals and the clients. Besides ethnographic observation, some written materials, such as psychological test forms used by the clinic, official treatment plans, lecture notes, etc., were included in the materials. The bulk of the ethnographic fieldwork was carried over the course of three months in 1997. The typewritten field notes from this period comprise about 300 double-spaced pages. A combination of discursive ethnography and conversation analysis (CA) was used in analysing the materials (cf. Miller 1998). The ethnographic investigation was envisaged as providing an overall view of the treatment process as well as giving contextual information for more detailed analysis of situated interaction.

## Clients' Undesirable Actions and Speech as Seen by Professionals and How it is Dealt with in Face-to-Face Interaction

In this ethnographic part of the chapter, it is our aim first to show what aspects of the clients' actions and speech the professionals see as problematic. This is evidenced in the ways the professionals discuss clients and the feedback they believe clients could benefit from. Secondly, we show how undesirable actions on the part of clients are dealt with in practice in face-to-face interaction between professionals and the clients.

Evaluating how clients are progressing in their treatment is a very important part of work carried out by professionals. Without monitoring how a client is coming along, treatment professionals are unable to interfere when problems occur. Moreover, the evaluation of the clients' progress is a way to construct and maintain a normative idea of an ideal patient who conforms to the professionals' view of addiction and the means and goals of recovery. In this fashion, confrontational communicative work does not just deal with problems and difficult clients, but also builds a normative framework that every client can use as a measure to evaluate their own progress. When the professionals make the breaking of norms visible by interfering in what the client has said or done, clients may be required to reflect upon their behaviour and estimate whether it conforms to the ideal made visible. In looking at these encounters, we have used data gathered mainly through field observation and in part also on notes made of video-recordings from the same setting. Comparing the latter material with the video-recordings themselves gives different pictures of the face-to-face-interaction between the participants and offers us a view of the differences between ethnographic and conversation analytic findings and to the ways these approaches construct their realities.

## Clients Who Are Not Getting Along Well

The two daily staff meetings and the meetings of the multiprofessional team several times a week constitute the main context in which the progress of the client is most often discussed among the professionals. In the morning and afternoon reports, the counsellors, therapists and other staff members inform each other about the proceedings of the day or the previous night. On these occasions, problems with certain clients may be discussed. Each client's situation is discussed by the team with the aim of helping the client's therapist find ways of intervening when a client is not progressing as desired.

In characterising a client who is progressing as desired, the members of the staff use the expression *to get along well*. Three main aspects of a client's behaviour discussed by staff as signs of **not** getting along well - and breaking the norm of an ideal patient - are as follows: The client 1) seems reluctant to adopt the identity of an alcoholic or a drug addict; or 2) does not show enough motivation towards the treatment program and its goals; or 3) seems reluctant to make a commitment to AA or NA.

## Adopting the Identity of an Addict

The written institutional charter of the clinic state as the first goal of the treatment, "to help the chemically dependent patient to recognise his/her illness and its consequences" (Anonymous source, n.d.). It is noteworthy that the members of the staff consciously and systematically call the clients *patients* which points to the idea of substance abuse as an illness and aims at making the clients acknowledge their illness. When the staff members discuss problems involving clients' self-identification as addicts, the concept of denial is often brought up. In the following example from a morning report, the counsellor and the therapists negotiate which client they should choose to be house-senior. This role, filled each week by a client, is a kind of mediator between staff and clients.

*(MT1-5 = Male therapists, FT = Female therapist, C = Counsellor, all clients' names, professions, etc. have been changed.)*

*MT5 tells the others about the house meeting held yesterday. Liisa, Sirpa and Make were nominated as the potential new house-senior. MT4: "Not Sirpa, that won't do." MT5: "Liisa could probably do the job." C: "She would be capable but I wouldn't choose her after her story yesterday, she was really good at avoiding the real issue." MT5: "Who the house-senior is will then of course affect the atmosphere in the house." C: "Well yes!" (...) FT: "In my opinion Liisa is in complete denial, and then she could just spend her energy being the house-senior and the denial would stay." MT5: "But that would give her some responsibility to bear." FT: "I don't think that carrying responsibility is her problem, she can do that." The conversation moves on to the house chauffeurs. MT5 says that Liisa should not be chosen because then she would just concentrate too much in the tasks of being the house-senior" (Field Notes, page 62).*

Here a client called Liisa is characterised as being in complete denial. The female therapist tells a new staff member (MT5) that Liisa's denial should be prioritised in her treatment. However, in dealing with most clients, underrating problems is the issue more often than complete denial. The majority of the clients seem, at least in public, to adopt the professionals' view of themselves as chemically dependent. In these cases, the problems perceived in the client's self-identification as an addict are subtler than those in the previous example. Clients who have acknowledged that they have a chemical addiction can still be seen by the professionals as minimising their problems, i.e., reluctant to acknowledge thoroughly the depth of the problem in such terms as quantity or frequency of substance use as well as the scope of its negative consequences. In the following example, a therapist tells other professionals in the multi-professional team meeting about a client who minimises his problem:

*(MT2 = Male therapist)*

*MT2: "I'm actually worried about this one. When I asked him today what are the things that make him an alcoholic, he listed all sorts of things but not the suicide attempts, nor that his wife has left him. I mean that the guy should see this issue more clearly. Last week he came to tell me that he can only attend AA every third week because of his work shifts, so he had already decided how things are going to go" (FN, page 129).*

In the therapist's view, the client does not realise the seriousness of his problem. The client does not connect his drinking problem to his suicide attempts or his wife's dissatisfaction. However, minimisation is rarely seen as a conscious effort by the client to disguise the truth or as unwillingness to deal with the problem. Professionals understand minimisation and denial as unconscious acts that the clients cannot help, but with which they need help to deal with effectively.

Finally, the special meaning of alcoholism in AA manifests itself in the nature of the identity the clients are supposed to adopt. In AA ideology, alcoholism is an illness from which one can recover only through abstinence achieved with the help of working through the AA program. Therefore, a client who either hints at the possibility of becoming a moderate drinker or does not perceive alcoholism as an illness, from the professionals' point of view, has not fully adopted the identity of an alcoholic or a drug addict.

### Motivation Towards the Treatment Program as a Sign of Motivation towards Recovery

The second goal of the four-week treatment program reads as follows: "To help the patient to accept that he/she needs help and to teach him/her to live with the illness in a constructive way" (AA, n.d.). When a client shows sincere motivation toward the treatment program, the client admits the need for help, whereas signs of bad motivation can mean that the client does not accept help. Some clients even resort to drinking or using drugs during the treatment. In these cases, the treatment is immediately terminated and the client is expelled without any further guidance. Also other minor ways of breaking the rules are taken seriously by the professionals and they can lead either to a warning or the termination of the treatment.

Well over half the clients are sent to the treatment by their employers. Some clients are sent by social workers concerned about the children of these clients. In fact, only few clients have come to the clinic of their own initiative. Consequently, not a few mandatory clients show low motivation. The professionals are aware of this situation and sometimes they share with the other members of the staff their observations about clients who are participating only to keep a job or children.

Omissions such as coming a few minutes late to a group therapy session, not returning one's diary on time to the therapist or neglecting one's homework are often treated as signs of insufficient motivation. In these cases, however, the lack of motivation in the professionals' view might not spring from lack of motivation towards the treatment itself but from inability to understand that "precision in little things" is important if one wants to recover. Furthermore, such precision maintains order in the clinic. In the following example a counsellor and two therapists discuss potential problems with clients who have been neglecting some parts of the program:

*(MT1-5 = Male therapists, FT = Female therapist, C = Counsellor, all clients' names, professions, etc. have been changed)*

*FT: "Any observations on Jaana?" C: "She seems to be getting along all right." FT: "She didn't come to the meeting yesterday, nor to the house meeting..." C: "Well, she's a really young girl." FT: "Despite that, the timetables should be followed, and people were also late to the housemeeting." MT2: "We have to pay attention to order, the patients have to realise that if they only think of themselves it makes it hard for others to get their work done. I've had a hard time with Anni with these things, she's been through two treatments here before and perhaps two would have been enough if no compromises had been made when it came to order. These are important issues" (FN, page 85).*

Finally, clients' reserved behaviour can be seen as a sign of low motivation. A client who does not reveal her thoughts and emotions, e.g., in the group therapy sessions, can be seen as concealing something.

## Accepting AA or NA as the Means of Recovery

The third and fourth goals of the Minnesota model treatment are: "To help the patient to recognise what he/she has to change in his/her life," and "To help the chemically dependent patient to change this understanding into action" (Anonymous source, n.d.). In practice, these goals mean that the professionals do their best to get the clients integrated into AA or NA. While clients are required to attend AA or NA meetings eight times during the treatment period, one treatment goal is that they will accept AA or NA as their means of recovery also in the future. Sometimes when a client expresses a single or repetitious criticism of AA or NA, it causes worry among staff that the client is not planning to recover in these mutual-help groups. In the following example, a female therapist characterises her client's difficulties with AA:

*(FT = Female therapist)*

*FT: "...she has motivation and willingness but, for example, when somebody had been swearing in the AA group yesterday, she only listened to the swearing... and it will probably be difficult for her to integrate in to AA treatment, there's so much resistance" (VN=Video Notes, Multiprofessional team 4).*

On the other hand, openly expressed criticism of AA or NA can be seen and appreciated as honesty, especially when the client intends to attend AA or NA after the treatment despite his/her critical attitude. Sometimes, without any criticism of AA or NA, a client tells his/her therapist that he/she will not likely attend AA in the future, for instance, because of difficult work-shifts or out of a conviction that AA is not necessary for staying abstinent. In the next example, the multiprofessional team discusses a client who has shown motivation during her treatment to stop drinking but reluctance towards recovery in AA:

*(FT = Female therapist)*

*The nurse is reading the doctor's statement: "... The patient was here in '85... she didn't go for any aftercare after her previous treatment and the reasons for this have to be found out. This time, effort should be made to get her to make a commitment to aftercare." FT: "She's been sober since '85, it's been a good period. She connects her relapse to her husband who was looking at another woman on a holiday trip... Again her plan is to stay sober on her own. She's unable to accept help..." (...) Psychologist: "... She's trying to cure alcoholism by being good and working hard, that's like starting to chop wood with a toothbrush" (VN, Multiprofessional team 3).*

When the doctor refers to aftercare in his statement, what he actually means is attending AA.

## What Should Be Done with Clients Who Are Not Getting Along Well?

Now we will briefly look at how the professionals discuss what actions to take with clients who in their opinion are not getting along well. This takes place most often in the multiprofessional team meetings where the progress of each client is discussed in turn. The team members give suggestions to the client's therapist about feedback from which the client might benefit. The suggested feedback is usually directed either at the client's emotional life (e.g., how the client could learn to cope with feelings of anger) or at the client's other problems with progressing in the treatment. The most commonly suggested advice is to give the client some homework, that is, tasks to do in her/his free time during the treatment. For example, the psychologist suggests to the therapist that a client who is seen as being critical of AA should write down the experiences or emotions he/she has identified with in AA meetings. When a client is seen as engaging in denial or minimisation, it may be proposed that the doctor should talk to the client about the medical facts (e.g., damaged liver), or that the client's employer should be invited to a network meeting where the client's addiction-related problems at work could be discussed. At the end of the day, the client's therapist must then choose which course of action is taken.

## Confronting Clients in Face-to-Face Interaction

So far we have looked at what kinds of issues are brought up when the professionals discuss problems related to the clients' progress and the feedback that might help clients to see their situation more in line with views of the professionals. Let us now look at what happens in face-to-face interaction when the professionals respond to the clients' undesirable aspirations or attitudes. First we will look at confrontation through some ethnographic characterisations of the situations, and subsequently, in the following section, conversation analysis will be employed to get a closer look at the interactional organisation of confrontations.

Confrontation takes place regularly if the professionals feel that a client is minimising the addiction or has a negative attitude towards recovering in AA or NA. In the following example, the therapist confronts a client who has presented his aftercare plan in the group (a task every client has to do during the last week of the treatment). In his plan Osmo was vague about attending AA in the future and another client, Erkki, said that maybe Osmo would manage on his own (without AA) since he claimed to have drunk only during holidays. Following the other clients' comments to Osmo, the therapist confronts the client about being a holiday drinker:

*(MT1 = Male therapist, all clients' names and professions, etc. have been changed)*

*MT1: "Osmo, who told you to come here to this treatment?" Osmo: "My employer." MT1: "The employer. Erkki made some good observations but there was still something a little bit... Employers don't tell people who only drink during their holidays to go to treatment." Osmo: "... there's never been anything at work, it was just that after the holiday I didn't..." MT1: "Yes, you didn't remember to go to work." The therapist walks to Osmo's figure on the wall and says: "1996 you were sent to treatment twice" (VN, Group therapy session 12).*

It is rather obvious that Osmo had been minimising his problems with alcohol by calling himself a holiday drinker. When clients minimise their addiction, the therapist often interferes by bringing in contradictory evidence. Therapists regularly identify some ways of talking as expressions of minimisation. At least two therapists require that the clients use their real names in the group sessions since using nicknames would in their view weaken one's effort to recover. Furthermore, slang expressions for things such as alcoholism or suicide are not to be used for similar reasons: namely, that slang words make the issues less serious. Finally, some therapists treat the use of passive forms of verbs to refer to oneself as a form of minimising. In the following example, a client is telling the group about the negative consequences of his drinking. This is a task every client is required to do in the group. The therapist interferes in the client's use of the passive form of a verb.

*(MT2 = Male therapist, all clients' names, professions, etc. have been changed)*

*Pasi explains that when he was a student, the drinking didn't really matter, "it was easy to be away from lectures and end up going with friends and..." The therapist interrupts: "Yes, who ended up going?" Pasi laughs: "Well Pasi did and Pasi was drinking." The therapist also joins in the laughter. MT2: "But those friends aren't here now, just you." Pasi: "Yes but many of them would have a reason to be here." MT2 says a couple of times: "Yes, but it's only you who ended up here"(FN, page 105).*

Criticism of individual AA meetings is another topic that arises regularly as the topic of confrontation. The therapists usually comment on this criticism, e.g., by saying that there are very different kind of groups and maybe the one criticised was not the right group for the client in question. Alternatively, the therapist may try to direct the conversation from clients' criticism of, e.g., smoking or swearing in an AA group, towards the putative substance of the meeting, that is, towards what was said there and how the participants had managed to stay sober.

Another thematic context where confrontations arise in connection to AA (or NA) is situations where clients express unwillingness to attend AA or NA in the future, or to contact the assigned support person from AA or NA. On these occasions, the therapist usually interferes by stressing the importance of having a support person and the difficulty (or impossibility) of recovering without the help of AA or NA. In the following example drawn from ethnographic notes about one group therapy session, the therapist talks to a client who has just presented her aftercare plan in which her job and hobbies play a central role. The therapist's criticism is directed at the absence of AA in the plan:

*(MT1 = Male therapist, all clients' names and professions, etc. have been changed)*

*MT1: "What's good about this is that it has been done and that it's honest. But what has gone missing is that it's an afterCARE plan. If*

alcoholics would recover just through hard work you'd all be sober."
Sanna: "I can't write that I'll start going to AA since I don't know if I
will." MT1: "Yes, the honesty is good... What about an agreement that
you'll phone your support person and decide on the first visit to AA before
you get the medical certificate? Shall we make this kind of an agreement?"
(...) Sanna: "Well, I supppose I must in order to get that medical
certificate." MT2: "You don't have to but it's for your own sake" (VN,
Group therapy session 10).*

In the above example the confrontation seems to be direct and face
threatening to the client: the therapist's disagreement is expressed openly
and straightforwardly, and the client is not left with much chance to
disagree with the therapist's suggestion. This is, however, the point at
which the ethnographic and the CA approaches constitute their realities in
somewhat contradictory ways. When the above-cited note was compared
with the video recording of the instance and a conversational analytical
reading of it, it was revealed that the notes - due to their unavoidably
summary character - leave out some important aspects of the interaction.
These aspects, such as laughter, pauses and even some sentences that were
missing from the notes, are the devices the participants use to make the
confrontations less direct and more face-saving. The analysis of the
ethnographic material (notes written on the basis of the field observation
and on the video recordings) has so far offered us an understanding of how
the professionals understand what aspects of the clients' behaviour require
intervention, and also of the thematic contexts where the therapists confront
their clients. However, in order to understand in more detail *how* the
confrontations are carried out on the micro-level of conversation, it is
necessary to turn from the ethnographic notes to the video recordings and a
conversation analytical analysis of these.

**Confrontations as Interactional Products**

Thus far we have seen that both clients and professionals in this 12-step
treatment program treat some types of actions and aspirations as
undesirable. In this section, through CA, we will offer a detailed
examination of treatment interaction *per se*. We will deal with one instance
in which a therapist confronts a patient who expresses ambivalence towards
the goal of the treatment. So far in the text the clients have been referred to
as clients. In this section which is based on CA, the word patient will be
employed since this is the word used by the participants themselves - both

therapists and clients. Even though we present here only a single case, the aim is to point out generic strategic moments of the therapeutic interaction in which, at least in principle, the participants could choose between alternative courses of action.

Our analysis demonstrates that participants' choices are limited by their participation in social interaction that poses seen-but-unnoticed interactional constraints on the parties. That is, actions by the participants such as confrontations are conditional to the primary task of maintenance and management of intersubjective sociability. Therefore, we must note that responses to clients who act against their best interests are ought not be seen as autonomous, independent actions but rather as occasioned outcomes in, and through, interaction between parties in the treatment clinic.

Here, we will analyse an instance of a group therapy session in which the therapist treats the client's turn as troublesome and in so doing initiates a confrontation. The data segment in its entirety can be found in Appendix 2. If the reader wishes to scrutinise the data independently, the segment should be read now before our analysis of it. We will first briefly summarise the episode in question, and then focus on its strategic moments.

In lines 1-2, S (the female patient) introduces a story-able item, her dream about the impossible choice between mathematics and humanities in the matriculation exam. In lines 8-9, an abstract of the story foreshadows its moral point, the teller's ambivalence and struggle with AA. The story about the dream is subsequently told (lines 11-28). In lines 30-31, S draws a conclusion about her dream. At this point (32), the therapist nods, thereby displaying his active recipiency, but does not (yet) take the turn. Following the non-response to her story, as marked by her "well that's all then" (33), S relates a positive experience. The pauses at lines 35 and 37 demonstrate that S would be willing to give the floor to another speaker. In line 38, S reinitiates some trouble talk about her present day concerns. Not until a lengthy pause (49, 51) does the therapist initiate his response (in line 54). S receives the therapist's response with a minimal acknowledgement. In lines 76-77, the therapist concludes his response with some laughter in his voice. The humour hinted at in the therapist's voice invites S to produce some delayed and constrained laughter mixed with coughing (81). In line 83, R (co-patient) poses a question to S about the end of the story. An extended repair-sequence follows in which the referent of the question is clarified: i.e., whether it concerns the dream, or the matriculation exam during her school years, 85-100. After S's answer, "both" (101) and J (co-patient) burst into laughter (104). Then J draws his conclusion about the point of the story, "drink and attend AA" (110). In lines 111 and 113, the therapist presents his evaluation of the outcome of the conversation. From lines 114 to 121, talk starts to fade away. Finally, the therapist alters his conclusion, underlining the positive side of the story. In lines 128-129, the therapist turns towards another patient and initiates a new cycle.

The data segment chosen includes what we may call a complete therapeutic cycle in group therapy. First, a patient makes her contribution (here tells a story about a dream). Second, the patient's contribution gets a response from the therapist (notably, an institutional order prevails in which all the parties are oriented to the therapist giving the first response). After the therapist's response co-patients then take their turns participating in the evaluation of the patient's contribution. Finally, the therapist closes the sequence and initiates a new one. As a whole, this segment provides us access to the microcosmos of therapeutic reality coconstructed by all the constituents in this process. For instance, through the therapist's response to the patient, we can recognise the specific type of therapy that is being practised. The therapist does not aim at interpreting the dream or explicating the patient's hidden psychodynamic tensions, but focuses on the patients' current situation and future-oriented solutions. In this way, the parties' talk both constitutes the situation and provides analytic resources for the researcher to identify the type of ongoing action.

Next we will focus on three strategic aspects of the therapeutic cycle involving S, the therapists and other members of the therapy group. These are: 1) the sequential placement of the therapist's response, 2) the relevance of the co-patients' presence for the participation framework of group therapy and the role of the co-patients' contributions, and 3) the consensus-orientation of the closings. These strategic aspects are interrelated and through their analysis we can understand some central aspects of the group therapy process central to 12-step treatments. Finally, with the help of our enhanced understanding of this process we can also get a view of the range of possibilities for confronting patients who are acting against their best interests.

**The Sequential Placement of the Therapist's Response**

Although the content of the therapist's response to the patient is unquestionably to our interest, we will start our analysis with the location of the response. In this fashion, we can illuminate the interactional dynamics of confrontations in these group contexts. When we return to our segment of data, we can observe a clear pattern in the design of the therapist's response, in that it is considerably delayed. The therapist does not initiate his response after the first projectable completion of the patient's turn, but allows several transition relevance places pass, that is, the therapist comes in only after several possible places in which the floor would be open for a speaker transition.

In line 31, S (the patient) has drawn her story to a conclusion that would allow recipients to come in and show their evaluation and appreciation of the story. Instead, a pause of a second is opened during which the therapist nods, thereby displaying his recognition of the completion point, but in so doing allows the opportunity to respond to pass. In her next turn, S recognises this lack of uptake with her sequential marker "well that's all then" (33), and goes on to introduce a new talk-able item: her good mood on the previous day. In this way, the therapist's minimal response (nodding) worked here as a continuer so that it allocated the turn back to the patient S. The therapist's withholding from taking a verbal turn, which was also acknowledged by S via her sequential marker, invited S to continue her turn further. Subsequently, the therapist still delays his response, and pauses in lines 35, 37, 49 and 51 emerge after potential completion points at which S would have allowed recipients to take the turn. At least the later part of S's turn (from line 32 on) is enabled by the therapist and co-patients through their refraining from turn taking at potential transition places. We may now state our first finding: the delay in the therapist's response has some strategic importance here; it is a therapeutic resource to make the patient to talk more.

In addition, a recipient's decline to make a response may be understood as providing the speaker with a base to anticipate a disagreement or disaffiliation. Agreements and affiliations are nonmarked responses that normally follow immediately and straightforwardly (Pomerantz 1975, 1984). Therefore, the emergence of a pause before a response gives the speaker a basis to anticipate an upcoming disagreement or disaffiliation (Davidson 1984, 1990; Schegloff 1988). In our data segment, too, the delay was followed by disaffiliation. When the therapist finally comes in (line 54), he states that the patient is an adult and should be able to make up her mind, thereby undermining the patient's suggestion of ambivalence and struggle. As for its semantic content, the therapist's response was clearly a strong confrontation: it offered a view directly opposing that which the patient herself has of her situation. However, in terms of its interactional delivery, the confrontation was mitigated through its non-preferred format, through its production only after a considerable delay. Through this mitigation of disagreement, the therapist maintains an orientation to social solidarity. Had the therapist presented the disagreement straightforwardly and without any delay, this might have precipitated an argument and chosen an argumentative genre in which no orientation to social solidarity would be able to prevail (cf. Goodwin 1990; Berg & Mäntynen 1992). In all, we have found an interactional basis for the mitigation of confrontations. Namely, a straightforward confrontation would not only be heard as an argumentative exchange but as a refusal to maintain solidarity, that is, as an overtly aggressive and hostile move. Clearly, therapists have some good interactional reasons to avoid overt, unmitigated confrontations even if patients act against their best interests. Besides avoiding an open conflict, the therapist's delayed response allows the emergence of a reflexive space for the patient. Namely, after the therapist declines to take a turn, the patient is implicated to talk more. As the patient anticipates forthcoming disaffiliation, she may try to reformulate her narrative so that it reflects the way she imagines the therapist would like her to see things. In this way, the delaying of a response is an indoctrinating technique. Note, however, that the therapist's power to indoctrinate is limited. It is optional and depends on the patient's willingness to be indoctrinated. In our example, the therapist's success is strictly restricted. Here, the patient does not go on to reflect on her earlier talk but chooses instead to initiate new subjects to talk about. In some sense, however, the patient seems to have recognised the therapist's aim. In line 50, the patient says "well," and shrugs her shoulders providing a signal that she has completed her turn but, perhaps, also an expression of dissatisfaction with her own contribution, as if she feels that something else, or more, was still expected of her.

## Participation Framework and the Role of the Co-patients

Co-patients are especially significant in group therapy at least in two respects. First, of course, the co-patients may produce verbal contributions enhancing therapeutic processes. Second, in a less obvious way the presence of co-patients plays a role in the organisation of the participation: the participants are oriented to multi-party interaction rather than two-party exchanges. In confrontations, co-patients may play the role of mitigators. When we look at the therapist's confrontation with the patient in our data segment (lines 54-77), we can see here how co-patients play mitigating roles. In this respect, the laughter in the therapist's voice in lines 68 and 76-77 as he closes his confrontation is of special interest.

Overall, patient S receives the therapist's confrontation with a very limited amount of response. Only in line 57 does S produce a minimal acknowledgement, "mm.", accompanied with a nod after the therapist initiates his confrontation. Subsequently, S refrains from producing any verbal responses and she sits still and stays passive in a frozen-like posture (58-77). This kind of passive reception of counselling talk has been called passive resistance (Heritage & Sefi 1992; Silverman 1997, 134-153). Additionally, we may consider the patient's declining to display an acknowledgement as an indicator of trouble and a lack of alignment between parties. S has only acknowledged the preliminary component of the therapist's confrontation "now then you're an adult... you've got to make up your mind..." (54-55). The therapist's confrontational and ironic advice "go back drinking" (58-9) is met with silence (60), and the therapist's next suggestion "do not go to AA" (61) does not receive any immediate uptake (62-63).

In a group situation, passive resistance opens a specific interactional challenge: namely, that if silence develops, to whom does the turn then belong? Here the therapist himself orients to the interactional problem, and after his second suggestion does not receive a response immediately, he utters "yes" [joo] with a heavy inbreath (64). This kind of "joo" is normally used to register the recipient's response (Sorjonen 1997, 297-309), here it simply registers the lack of uptake. Again this "joo" could allow a speaker transition, but neither the patient nor the co-patients come in (65-67). In this context, when a patient is met with a confrontation and subsequently declines from verbal interaction, silence among co-patients works as a supportive gesture as it allocates the turn back to the therapist and makes its revision relevant. When both the patient and the co-patients refuse to acknowledge the therapist's proposal, the therapist is put in the position of working his way out of an interactional cul-de-sac. At this point, some laughter emerges in the therapist's voice in line 68 as he says something softly. The utterance itself is barely audible, but it sounds as if he is taking back his words "I don't now", i.e., he is implying that he has not been serious. However, the patients still withhold from taking a turn (69-75), after which the therapist produces his future-oriented proposal "do it the other way round, do not please the teacher" with some laughter in his voice. Again some delay emerges before S comes in with a constrained laughter token (81). Through her joining in the laughter, although only after some delay (78-80) and in a constrained form, the patient finally has produced some minimal acknowledgement and the interactional dead-end has been surpassed. In this instance, the therapist used laughter to make his confrontation softer but only after the patients forced him to do so. In this way, the patients can form a team that balances the power relationships in group therapy (cf. Kangasharju 1996, 1998).

After the therapist softened his confrontation with laughter, and S acknowledged this confrontation with some constrained laughter, the co-patient R asks about the end of S's story. In this context, the co-patient's question offers an exit from an uneasy moment as he topicalises a new talkable. In conversations about troubles, a recipient of a troubles-talk may topicalise an ancillary matter to provide a gateway to a safer topic (Jefferson 1984). This appears to be the case here, too. Namely, an extended repair sequence follows (84-100) concerning the referent of R's question, which shows that the topicalised issue was not immediately present in S's mind. In this fashion, R's question about the end of the story shifted the interaction to a new direction, thereby outlining a route away from the troublesome moment that arose in the confrontation. Finally, when S answers R's question (101), another co-patient, J, bursts into loud laughter, subsequently, giving his interpretation of the point of the story: "this is the STORY: DRINK AND ATTEND AA" (107, 110). The co-patients' intervention into S's story has made public a transgressive moral, which is exactly the opposite of the 12-step treatment ideology. To conclude, in environments of non-affiliation, patients may form teams to give moral support to each other. This may lead to an outcome in responding to interventions made by a therapist that is antithetical to the therapist's intention.

**Orientation to a Consensus in the Closings**

Closings of interactions have strategic relevance in that they stand for the outcome of interaction (Arminen 1998, 141-178). That is, closings are a place in which parties can display their understanding of what has been accomplished in the activity. In our data segment, the therapist works to repair the unfortunate outcome of the confrontation. As one of the co-patients, J, states the transgressive moral of the story "drink and attend AA" (110), the therapist comes in immediately with a last item overlap at line 111. Through taking a turn at the earliest possible place, i.e., briefly overlapping with J's turn just before its first possible completion point, the therapist curtails J's and others' chances to continue the moral transgression. Instead, the therapist starts to produce his conclusion: "yeah now this went a bit badly, this was bad". In this way, the therapist draws a negative conclusion about the episode's value. However, the therapist does not let this negative statement pass as his final say. After some delays, the therapist comes in to alter the evaluation of S's experience, and in one sense, of the whole interactional episode (122-126).

In his final conclusion (122-126), the therapist changes his focus and moves to the meta-level above the actual concerns of the participants. In his conclusion, the therapist no longer addresses the potentially problematic and distressing fact that S is unable to decide whether to accept AA (the ultimate goal of the treatment). Instead, he stresses the benefits of S's ability to reflect upon these things. The therapist states that it is not only good for S that she is able to reflect but it also helps others. This meta-level provides an opportunity for the therapist to draw an auspicious conclusion about matters that otherwise might seem worrying. Finally, this trouble-free conclusion occasions a suitable environment to terminate the episode and to initiate a new activity. After the conclusion, the therapist turns towards another patient and poses a question, which initiates a new therapeutic cycle in the group (128-129).

The orientation towards consensus not only prevails at the very end of the therapeutic cycle but also at the closings of its subsequences. When the therapist's confrontation was met with the passive resistance of the patients, he lightened his confrontation with laughter. In a similar way, the co-patients' intervention in S's story ended with J's laughter, which also invited the therapist to laugh (the therapist's turn at lines 111 and 113 was uttered with laughter in his voice). In all, this orientation to the maintenance of social solidarity provides a working consensus for the group therapy process, which may also forestall sharp conflicts having the potential for dividing the group or turning patients against the therapist. All the same, the orientation towards consensus may again set some limits on a therapist in confronting the patients.

## Interaction Order and Confrontations

We have seen that both the initiations and the closings of confrontations are constrained by the participants' orientation to the maintenance of conversational interaction. Professionals have to avoid excessively straightforward initiations of confrontation that might be interpreted as overtly hostile and aggressive moves, endangering the co-operative nature of the occasion. In closings, the therapist faces the necessity of providing formulations that guarantee sufficient alignment between parties so that the therapy process can go on. In addition, the group situation makes possible the formation of teams among participants, which further motivates the therapist not to induce such dynamics. As a whole, through CA we have traced the intersubjective basis of therapy, which is often taken for granted and whose implications for the therapy process have therefore been neglected.

Our analysis has shown that the dilemma of two cultures is embedded in the matrix of social interaction. Interactional constraints limit the options available for a professional in confronting a patient. The professional has to produce an interactionally adequate response to the patient's seemingly counterproductive aspirations. Our excerpt gave some examples of the alternatives open to a therapist dealing with such a dilemma. Through a delayed response, a therapist - as we have shown here - may be able to carve out a space in which a patient is induced to reflect on her/his stance. Further emphasis should be put on the study of the options available to the therapist to work inside the patient's therapeutic space, that is, on those occasions when the patient is reallocated the turn and thus implicated to continue and to reformulate the ongoing turn. The therapist's indirect ways of influencing the patient's own reflection would also merit further consideration. As a whole, the study of interactional accomplishment of confrontations has stressed the therapeutic techniques to produce mitigated and indirect confrontations. This suggests that perhaps the greatest chances and challenges for the development of the therapeutic talk may lay in the indirect ways of influencing on patients' self-reflections.

**Discussion**

Confrontational communicative work is central to the therapeutic work in 12-step treatment institutions. The centrality of confrontation can also be seen from the stories therapists tell one other about what they have said to clients who have expressed undesirable attitudes, etc. These narratives not only inform others about problematic clients but also about the therapists' moments of success. In these narratives, therapists are often described as having reacted to a client's expressions of undesirable attitudes in spontaneous and contradictory ways so that the client has realised how wrong she/he has been thinking and acting. Such stories reveal the therapists' ideal of what confrontation in face-to-face interaction should be like. This is illustrated in the following excerpt from our data.

*(MtX=Male therapist X, all clients names, professions, etc. have been changed)*

*MtX: "Tauno told his story yesterday and it was pretty mild, so the group gave him the feedback that you seem to be a moderate drinker. I said that if we would put all the bottles Tauno has emptied on the floor, a sensitive guy might well faint. I would faint myself, Tauno said" (FN, page 12).*

In their stories, therapists relate how they use confrontation as a tool to deal with pivotal adversaries of the recovery process. These adversaries, they often label under the category of denial. The patient's refusal to admit problems, minimisation of problems, lack of motivation and weak or unrealistic aftercare plans are seen as aspects of denial. Through confrontations, the therapists aim at breaking the patient's denial and facilitating an identity shift that would enable the beginning of recovery. Thus confrontation does not stand for the therapists only as a sign of trouble or as an index of a difficult patient, but is also a generic tool for doing therapy. The therapists' stories about confrontations are also success stories. In these narratives, the therapists present themselves as skilful, even heroic characters who are capable of working with clients and successful in their attempts to change the clients' ways of seeing themselves.

*(MtX=Male therapist X)*

*MtX tells about having had a word with a dentist who had just gone through the evaluation period and who was seemingly anxious. MtX imitates the patient with a snuffle: "Sure I cope with this, I am really determined, it's just that all these things have happened to me lately." (The snuffling ends, MtX starts to talk with his own voice.) "I said to him: 'Listen to me, a year ago I had here a guy who was a Finnish champion in his sports, but even he wasn't determined enough'. She just stared at me" (MtX lets his eyes pop out) (FN, pages 26 - 27).*

These stories are revealing in terms of the therapists' self-understanding of their work and communication situations. Further, these stories are undoubtedly a valuable resource for the therapists in helping them to maintain positive self-images through which they can cope with their stressful work. However, the picture of their work becomes much more complicated as soon as we witness actual confrontations as captured on videotapes. In real-life interactions, therapists do not straightforwardly impose their own views on patients or argue with the patients, nor do the patients display sudden, clear changes in their beliefs due to the therapist's confrontation. Although we have analysed only one actual confrontation in this chapter, other available materials suggest that confrontations are highly delicate and sensitive activities that the professionals are inclined to pursue with a great care and circumspection (Arminen & Halonen forthcoming; Halonen forthcoming).

Actual confrontations are not simply one-way processes that are unilaterally directed by the professional. Instead confrontations as they occur in face-to-face processes of interaction are collaborative constructions in which both (or all) parties orient to one another to maintain inter-subjective understanding of the ongoing activity and to preserve the faces of parties to sustain the collaborative nature of event (cf. Peyrot 1987; Peräkylä 1995, 103-143; Silverman 1997, 63-88). Because of this, their outcomes are not simply public displays of distinct change in client identities but rather are acknowledgements of the existence of more than a single view of the issue debated. In contrast to the therapists' self-understanding in the above-cited narratives, confrontation is not just a technique for conquering the dilemma of two cultures. Our findings indicate that confrontations themselves involve elements maintaining the existence of two cultures as well as elements combating this existence (see Miller & Rollnick 1991).

To sum up our main findings, through ethnography we have documented that professionals see confrontation as a central tool in addiction therapy. This, of course, is what the 12-step therapy literature also maintains. Confrontation is a device through which the professional can make visible a client's deviations from the ideal patient's role and comportment. In this way, confrontation is used as a method to make publicly available an understanding of how the patient ideally should behave and see things. However, whether clients actually identify themselves with this ideal is another story, of which we have gained some glimpses through analysis of treatment interaction.

Our investigation of a segment of actual treatment interaction shows that confrontation is an activity, in which engaged parties display overt caution toward one another. The delicacy of the interactional orchestration of a confrontation manifests itself in several stages and aspects of these activities. The initiation of confrontation is systematically delayed so that the professional then initiating the activity avoids giving an impression of overt aggression. In group therapy contexts in particular, the therapist must avoid actions that might induce the patients to team up against the therapist. Finally, in closings, the parties orient to consensus in order to create a suitable environment to terminate the activity and to introduce a new one.

In this fashion, the interaction order entails a conservative tendency that constrains the parties' possibilities to engage in radical actions that might disrupt the intersubjective understanding of the situation as well as social solidarity serving as a constitutive basis for social actions. For these reasons, we suggest that in developing confrontational practices, further emphasis should be put on the various ways of engaging in mitigated and indirect confrontation.

Our study has shown that the existence of the dilemma of two cultures is a social fact that the therapists must take into account while designing their confrontational interventions. Therefore, the paradox of treatment outcome studies showing that different types of therapies produce almost the same results appears to have a processual basis. Our data indicate that confrontational encounters are double-edged swords that may enforce the desired outcome but may also make available a goal for resistance, and thus lead to an outcome that is antithetical to what was intended. In this way, we may have found the most primitive cell of Foucaultian micropower permeating all societies and operating always as a two-way process.

Finally, we may return to the methodological questions concerning the use of both ethnography and CA. The strength of ethnography lies in its capability to cover a global sense of action and address parties' understandings of these actions. Ethnography has allowed us to comprehend the professional's understanding of the role of confrontation in addiction therapy and given us a view of the different situations where confrontation is used. However, the ethnographic method is limited when it comes to analysis of the details of the participants' interaction and thus to understanding the construction of situated meanings. Therefore, CA, which relies on recorded materials and their detailed transcriptions and focuses on systematically analysing the taken-for-granted details of the orchestration of interactional events, can complement and deepen ethnographic findings. On the other hand, because of its focus on conversational details, CA is much less efficient than ethnography in getting a hold of the broader context of the interaction, and consequently CA studies can benefit from ethnographical findings. Meanings of interactional patterns and the maintenance of institutional contexts can be better understood when ethnographic and CA methods are combined, and the reflexive relationship between the interactional patterns and their context of use is taken into account. Such patterns are affected by and gain their meaning through their tie to the context in question, and the context is maintained with the help of the interactional practices.

# Acknowledgements

We wish to thank Mia Halonen for the insights she provided us as well as permission to use materials from her study of therapeutic sessions.

## Appendix 1: Transcription Symbols

The speakers' names, and possibly some other details, have been changed in order to secure the anonymity of the persons involved. Due to space restrictions only the translation of the original materials will be presented here (for the original materials, please, contact Ilkka Arminen [e-mail: ilkka.arminen@stakes.fi).Transcription symbols and conventions of conversation analysis are used throughout the extracts (see Atkinson & Heritage 1984).

| | |
|---|---|
| [ ] | simultaneous speech and voices, its start and end |
| = | immediately continous talk, no interval |
| (0.6) | pause and its length in seconds |
| (.) | micropause, shorter than 0.2 seconds |
| .h | in-breath |
| hh | out-breath |
| __ | emphasis |
| : | stretch |
| YES | loud |
| . | falling intonation |
| , | continuing intonation |
| ? | rising inflection, not necessarily a question |
| ?, | weak rise in intonation |
| 8 | marked rise in pitch |
| 9 | marked fall in pitch |
| - | dash at the end of the unfinished word marks a cut off |
| > < | pronounced faster than the surrounding speech |
| < > | pronounced slower than the surrounding speech |
| $ $ | laughter in the voice |
| @ @ | animated voice |
| E E | diminishing voice |
| # # | shivering voice |
| rrrr | bell |
| tttt | applause |
| hah | laughter |
| (( )) | researcher's comment |
| -> | target line; crucial instance for the analyzed speech |

## Appendix 2: Uni "Dream"

[PR11; 13] (S=female patient, TM=male therapist, Mf=female co-patient, R=male co-patient, J=2.male co-patient, M=unidentified male voice, N=unidentified female voice)

```
1    S: then the night between (.) saturday and sunday
2    I had?, (.) such a dream I >I don't know have you read<
3    my #EdiaryE#.
4    (0.8)
5    S: just th[at, ]
6    TM:     [8mm,]
7    (0.5)
8    S: which I feel describes well my struggle with the
9    AA (EthatE).
10   (1.8)
11   S: erm #we:ll#, (2.0) I was like POW. .h (.) in the school
12   again and (.) the matriculation exam was [coming closer and,
13   ?: [heh heh
14   S?: .nff
15   (0.8)
16   S: I myself wa- humanities and mathematics were as alternatives
17   and uh I myself wanted to take mathematics
18   and the teacher was like tellin' me that you have to take
19   humanities. (1.0) .hh and well then she was like that I don't
20   do well in the 8mathematics and?, (0.8) .MT then I just
21   thought that I don't have time to read humaties and .nf th-
22   I realized likewise that really I don't know much or anythin'
23   in 8mathematics but still I want to take the
24   >8mathematics< and, .hh (0.5) e- I just got such a feeling
25   that the teachers?, (1.7) wanted that the avarage of the school
26   shouldn't 8fall, (1.1) but I thought that what the heck
27   (0.3) if I failed that at least I'd got chance to try
28   just the way I #wanted#.
29   (1.2)
30   S: Bwell:Bmh (1.0) I felt that it was terribly clearly a description of e:rm
31   (0.3) my:, (0.3) feelings toward AA,
32   (1.0)
33   S: well that's all the(n) the yesterday was really (.) peaceful
34   (0.3) a good mood #I liked to take a walk out#.
35   (1.0)
36   S: (well) (0.8) it was so #wonderful weather#.
37   (1.1)
38   S: today then the 8lecture was disstressing I noticed that,
39   (0.7)
40   ?: .nff
41   (0.7)
42   S: >as the one< from the treatment association, (.) return to
43   work place (.) or (the) lecture erm, (0.6) sure I noticed that
44   it distresses me that
45   (1.5)
46   S: Its a disstressing thought to go back to the work place uh I got (1.8)
47   got a bit kind of bad feelin' that I was wondering how things y-know
48   are there.
49   (3.3)
```

50   S?: well
51   (1.8)
52   TM: mm8m.
53   (1.8)
54   TM: .thh well n̲o̲w then you're an 8a̲dult .mhhh so n̲o̲w y-know
55   you've to make up your mind don't you.
56   (0.3)
57   S: mm.=
58   TM: =wouldn't that be good. (.) How about that I order you
59   to go back drinkin'.
60   (3.5)
61   TM: and then I forbid you to go to EAAE.
62   ?: .nff
63   (.)
64   TM: B.yes:B. ((pronounced with a heavy inbreath))
65   (3.5)
66   Mf: ÖHHy ((coughing))
67   (0.8)
68   TM?: B($I'm not now(h)$)B.
69   (1.0)
70   ?: EkryhymE.
71   (.)
72   ?: .nff
73   (0.4)
74   ?: .mt
75   (0.3)
76   TM: you do?, (.) now the other way round then you tried to $please
77   the teacher@ and,
78   (0.5)
79   ?: .nff
80   (0.3)
81   ?: krhym
82   (0.8)
83   R: so how did it 8go then.
84   (1.2)
85   R: in the matriculation in its time.=
86   S: =e- well it wasn't settled.
87   (.)
88   R?: BI seeB.
89   (0.4)
90   TM?: did you get-?
91   (1.0)
92   TM: well then which one did you take.
93   (0.3)
94   S: .h #ee- e-# no it, it didn't become clear in the dream it
95   remained (.) [open.
96   J?: [yea- (.) but in a 8re̲al world [which one did
97   TM: [yes but
98   then (>as<)]s-? #uh#=8<m̲a̲t>riculation was so

99    J: you take]
100   TM: ho[w was it?
101   S: [both
102   (.)
103   M: [(I see.)
104   J?: [hah hah HAH [HAH HAH HAH
105   M: [(---)
106   M: (oh yeah -[--)
107   J: [this is? (.) this is
108   N: [(-[--)
109   109   M:          [(---)
110   J: the STORY (.) 8DRI:NK AND ATTEND A[A.
111   TM: [$yeah now this went [a bit]
112   ?: [.nff]
113   badly$ this was bad,
114   (0.8)
115   ?: .nff
116   (0.3)
117   TM: yeah,
118   (1.2)
119   J?: kröh[öm.
120   TM: [(--)
121   (1.0)
122   TM: yes. (.) yeah surely they: #m u:h# now you're nicely
123   (1.0) nicely well erm well, (.) honestly goin' through
124   erm, (2.0) sure many find that helpful many do this
125   thing more (quiet and), (.) secretly but Its 8quite
126   alright that (.) #you tell about it#.
127   (2.0)
128   TM: .hh yeah .h 8what was there so good, (0.3) in the group as
129   you said that >it was nice<.

## Bibliography

Anderson, Daniel J. (1981) The Psychopathology of Denial. *Professional Education* (9) Minnesota: Hazelden, Center City.

Anonymous source. Not dated. Unpublished material from the clinic under study.

Arminen, Ilkka (1998) *Therapeutic Interaction. A Study of Mutual Help in the Meetings of Alcoholics Anonymous.* Helsinki: Finnish Foundation for Alcohol Studies.

Arminen, Ilkka and Halonen, Mia (1999) Talk at Work in the Addiction Treatment. In Rhodes, T. (ed) *Qualitative Methods for Drug research* London: Sage.

Atkinson, J.M. and Heritage, J. (1984) (eds.) *Structures of Social Action.* Cambridge: Cambridge University Press.

Berg, Maarit and Mäntynen, Anne (1992) *Väittelyn rakentumisesta. Erään arkikeskustelun analyysi.* [On the Organization of Argumentation. An Analysis of an Everyday Conversation.] Unpublished Masters thesis. Helsinki: Department of Finnish language.

Davidson, Judy (1984) Subsequent Versions of Invitations, Offers, Requests, and Proposals Dealing with Potential or Actual Rejection. In J.M. Atkinson and J. Heritage (eds.) *Structures of Social Action*. Cambridge: Cambridge University Press.

Drew, Paul and Heritage, John (eds) (1992a) *Talk at Work - Interaction in Institutional Settings*. Cambridge: Cambridge University Press.

Ford, Cecilia and Thompson, Sandra (1996) Interactional Units in Conversation: Syntactic, Intonational, and Pragmatic Resources for the Management of Turns. In Ochs, E. (ed) *Interaction and Grammar,* Cambridge: Cambridge University Press.

Goodwin, Marjorie (1990) *He-Said-She-Said. Talk as Social Organization among Black Children*. Bloomington: Indiana University Press.

Halonen, Mia (Forthcoming) *12-askeleen ryhmäterapia*. [12-step group therapy]. PhD dissertation in progress. Helsinki: Department of Finnish language.

Heritage, John (1984) *Garfinkel and Ethnomethodology*. Oxford: Polity Press.

Heritage, John and Sefi, Sue (1992) Dilemmas of Advice: Aspects of the Delivery and Reception of Advice in Interactions between Health Visitors and First-time Mothers, In Drew, P. and Heritage, J. (eds.) *Talk at work - Interaction in Institutional Settings.* Cambridge: Cambridge University Press.

Hutchby, Ian and Wooffitt, Robin (1998) *Conversation Analysis. Principles, Practices & Applications*. Cambridge: Polity Press.

Institute of Medicine (1992) Prevention and Treatment of Alcohol-Related Problems: Research Opportunities. *Journal of Studies on Alcohol* (53)1, 5-16.

Jefferson, Gail (1984) On Stepwise Transition from Talk about a Trouble to Inappropriately Next-positioned Matters. In Atkinson, J.M. and Heritage, J. (eds.) *Structures of Social Action*. Cambridge: Cambridge University Press.

Kangasharju, Helena (1996) Aligning as a Team in Multiparty Conversation. *Journal of Pragmatics* (26).

Kangasharju, Helena (1998) *Agreement in Disagreement. Conflicts in Multiparty Talk*. Ph.D. Monograph. Helsinki: Department of Finnish language.

Keso, Lauri (1988) *Inpatient Treatment of Employed Alcoholics: A Randomized Clinical Trial on Hazelden and Traditional Treatment*. Tampere: Tamprint.

Koski-Jännes, Anja (1992) *Alcohol Addiction and Self-regulation. A Controlled Trial of a Relapse Prevention Program for Finnish Inpatient Aalcoholics*. Helsinki: The Finnish Foundation for Alcohol Studies.

Lausvaara, Jari (1990) *Hoidon käsite Minnesota-mallissa*. [The Concept of Treatment in the Minnesota Model] Unpublished Master's Thesis. Helsinki: Department of Theology.

Levinson, Stephen C. (1983) *Pragmatics*. Cambridge: Cambridge University Press.

Longabaugh, E. (1998) Network Support for Drinking, Alcoholics Anonymous and Long-term Matching Effects. *Addiction* (93) 9, 1313-1334.

Miller, Gale (1997) Toward Ethnographies of Institutional Discourse: Proposal and Suggestions. In Miller, G. and Dingwall, R. (eds.) *Context & Method in Qualitative Research*. London: Sage.

Peräkylä, Anssi (1995) *AIDS Counselling - Institutional Interaction and Clinical Practice*. Cambridge: Cambridge University Press.

Peyrot, Mark (1987) Circumspection in Psychotherapy: Structures and Strategies of Counselor-Client Interaction. *Semiotica* (65) 3/4, 249-268.

Pomerantz, Anita (1975) *Second Assessments: A Study of Some Features of Agreements/disagreements*. Unpublished PhD dissertation. Irvine: University of California.

Pomerantz, Anita (1984) Agreeing and Disagreeing with Assessments: Some Features of Preferred/dispreferred Turn Shapes. In Atkinson, J. and Heritage, J. (eds.) *Structures of Social Action.* Cambridge: Cambridge University Press.

Pomerantz, Anita and Fehr, B.J. (1997) Conversation Analysis: An Approach to the Study of Social Action as Sense Making Practices. In van Dijk, T. (ed) *Discourse Studies: A Multidisciplinary Introduction, Vol. 2.* London: Sage.

Project Match (1997) Matching Alcoholism Treatments to Client Heterogeneity: Project MATCH Posttreatment drinking Outcomes. *Journal of Studies on Alcohol* (58)1, 7-29.

Schegloff, Emanuel (1988) On an Actual Virtual Servo-mechanism for Guessing Bad News: A Single Case Conjecture. *Social Problems* (35) 4, 442-457.

Schegloff, Emanuel (1996) Turn Organization: One Intersection of Grammar and Interaction. Ochs, E. (ed) *Interaction and Grammar.* Cambridge: Cambridge University Press.

Silverman, David (1997) *Discourses of Counselling. HIV Counselling as Social Interaction.* London: Sage.

Stenius, Kerstin (1991) The Most Succesful Treatment Model in the World: Introduction of the Minnesota Model in the Nordic Countries. *Contemporary Drug Problems* (Spring) 151-179.

Stenius, Kerstin (1999) *Privat och offentlig i svensk alkoholistvård. Arbetsfördelning, samverkan och styrning under 1900-talet.* Lund: Arkiv förlag.

Toiviainen, Seppo (1997) *Kantapöydän imu. Juoppokulttuuri valintana ja pakkona* [The Draw of the Regular Table. Culture of the Drunkard as a Choice and Constraint]. Hämeenlinna: Hanki ja jää.

Wieder, Lawrence D. (1974) *Language and Social Reality. The Case of Telling the Convict Code.* The Hague: Mouton.

# 8 Who!? Identity in Institutional Contexts

LARS-CHRISTER HYDÉN

## Introduction

In modern society individuals are constantly confronted with identity problems and dilemmas in the sense that they have to state who they and others are in ever changing and new social contexts and situations. One reason for this is that, in modern society, individuals are part of a more or less infinite number of social contexts. These range from private and informal ones to formal and institutional. All these contexts require, demand and introduce various relevant identities to persons as private persons (father, parent, neighbour, etc.), as professionals (researcher, doctor, social worker) or as subjects in institutional contexts (patients, clients, pupils). It has even been argued that an essential trait of what is called the postmodern world is the fact that individuals constantly move between many social contexts, multiple and shifting identities. This implies - argue Giddens (1991) and Gergen (1991) - that identity becomes tied to self-reflexivity. That is, individuals have to actively state and display their identity in various social contexts by using and making aspects of their personal life and circumstances relevant.

A further important problem in modern society is how identity is established in institutional contexts - due to the central role of institutions in the lives of citizens. Most Western democratic countries subscribe to various ideals and norms about the relationship between citizens and the state. For instance, it is generally held that the relationship between citizen and state ought to be modelled in a way guaranteeing the integrity and equal treatment of citizens. Being treated equally and uniformly by various social institutions means that decisions, assessments or investigations involving citizens have to be made in rational and formal ways. These in turn are then subjected to critical examination and discussion. In modern society, professionals being paid for their work accomplish most of these administrative tasks. That means that they are seen as representatives of the institution and have to set professional standards for their work, such as being effective, just, impartial, etc. The various norms and standards guiding the work of social institutions have been part of the modern society's conception of it self since the late 19th century (cf. Sarangi & Slembrouck 1996).

As a consequence of these norms, representatives of institutions of the modern state have to disregard aspects of citizens that could be understood as personal. These, for example, may concern citizens' connections to specific social or ethnic communities or contexts, gender, colour, language, religious conviction, individual idiosyncrasies, etc. It is only those more or less abstract qualities and aspects of persons marking them as citizens that are supposed to be relevant, such as, being competent, of legal age, being a citizen of the country, etc. Further, representatives of social institutions have to disregard aspects of themselves that identify them as specific individuals. They are obligated to define themselves solely as part of the institutional context. Professionals have to disregard their own norms, preferences, values, views and impressions and represent only the standards and norms of the institutions. Their actions have to be subordinated to administrative and organisational procedures. As a consequence of this, individuals meeting in any institutional context have to make a clear separation between aspects and identities defining them as individuals and private persons and those designating them as institutionally defined persons.

Social institutions generally have certain more or less well defined functions and tasks, such as providing economic and social support to persons in need, educating young citizens, etc. These tasks are often accomplished in more or less routine ways. Furthermore, these work and administrative processes are often controlled and regulated by formal and informal rules, norms, traditions and procedures. These apply to every actual encounter between a citizen and institutional representative leading to constraints on their relationships and possible identities the participants may assume (cf. Drew & Heritage 1992). [1]

In the following chapter, it will be argued that the procedures of establishing, displaying, and communicating identities in institutional contexts involve certain pervasive problems connected to specific traits of the institutional context. This discussion will focus on interaction and conversations between social workers and clients at social welfare agencies in Sweden. In the late 1980s, a data corpus consisting of 20 encounters between social workers and clients was collected. All of the encounters took place at social welfare agencies in Stockholm. The conversational interaction between clients and social workers was recorded on tape and later transcribed. Fifteen of these 20 encounters concerned applications for cash public allowances and constitute the material in the present analysis.

The general structure of the 15 encounters has been analysed and discussed in earlier works (Hydén 1996; also cf. Linell & Fredin 1995). To become a social welfare client in Sweden means going through a selection process, generally starting at the switchboard of the social welfare bureau. The telephone operator here makes an initial screening of all incoming calls redirecting citizens who have called the wrong agency or are obviously not eligible for social welfare. Those overcoming this first obstacle are then directed to a social worker who is on call. This worker makes a preliminary investigation over the phone and the individuals found eligible at this stage then are given an appointment to meet a social worker. Before this meeting, the client is sent an application form in the mail. The form consists of questions concerning the applicant's date of birth, address, civil status, income, rent, and other basic social and financial information considered relevant for the assessment of eligibility for social welfare benefits.


## Identity

The identity concept is multifaceted and has been used to denote a number of different phenomena by various authors during the last three or four decades. Today identity is often substituted for the conception of self. Psychologists and social psychologists view identity either as something given or as something inherently problematic. For some identity is more or less a self-evident and given entity and these writers see no problems existing in displaying identity. For some of these writers, identity is viewed as something externally given by the social or institutional "structure". For other, however, identity is problematic because of either being tied to personal crises or trauma, or by reflecting problematic social organisation and/or social structure.

In either case, one problem is that identity not only has to be displayed, but also communicated. Participants have to share the same view of their identities at a particular moment, which means that identity have to be interpersonally established. Further, in professional as well as informal contexts, participants may shift between several different identities, from the past as well as the present, which have to be signalled and established. Finally, identity is simply not a thing, an entity or something neatly delimited, but a way of establishing continuity and responsibility for actions (especially utterances) in a temporal and spatial context.

Identity is not simply an <u>analytical</u> concept that can be used, for example, by researchers and psychologists analysing data or an individual's problems. Identity is also a concept that can be actively used by participants (both speaker and addressee) as an *interactive resource*. In interaction, persons may actively talk about their identity in terms of their professional, personal, political or ideological identity as well in terms of experience. Identity talk has also become a widely spread and used resource in political and ideological contexts. This is clearly seen in the movement towards "identity politics" (cf. Anspach 1979). In this sense, the concept of identity can also be politically charged, such as being recognised as a certain type of person or being member of a certain ethnic group (cf. Taylor 1991).

Identity is not a name for a more or less homogeneous entity existing in the mind of the speaker. Rather, it is a class of *self-representations* that participants can use for various purposes (Schafer 1976). As such, identity exists in the vocabulary of participants in the form of words, expressions, ways of speaking, etc. Further, identity is part of activities when participants represent themselves in communication, either directly or indirectly. In other words, identities do not exist independent of communicative contexts.

Both as an analytical tool and interactive resource, identity is multifaceted and covers several different types of phenomenon. The multiple meanings of the identity concept point to some basic aspects of communicative activity. First, identity indexes and points to one specific person among several persons in for example a family or a group. This could be called identity's *spatial* aspect. Of central concern here is the indexing and identifying of the present speaker or addressee together with the anchoring of the ongoing interaction in the context. This is done, for instance by using name, pronoun and such categorisations as kinship, professional, social or the like (Hanks 1990, 154). Social identification typically can be seen as the identification of a person with the help of social categories (cf. Antaki 1997; Antaki & Widdicombe 1998). Second, by identifying someone, this establishes a continuity of this person over time. This is exemplified by figures in a life story or narrative actually referring to the same person, albeit in the form of baby, child, youth, adult, etc. This could be called the *temporal* aspect of identification and identity (cf. Tugendhat 1992). These aspects of identity have been discussed by Erikson among others in his theory of the individual's epigenetic development (1950) and by many life historians (Josselson 1996). The common denominator for both spatial and temporal identification is the fact that both types *individuate* - i .e. indicate one person among several. In individuating a person by identifying him or her, it also become possible to assign a relation between the depicted agent and an action, whether this is physical, gestural or verbal. Central to the relation between agent and action is the *responsibility* for the action. By assuming or ascribing various identities to persons, it is possible to negotiate responsibility for action. For instance, a person identified as a small child or baby is generally not held as responsible for his or her verbal actions, as is an adult.

In modern society, a new type of identity has emerged, namely the bureaucratic or *administrative identity*. Historically, as a result of the need to organise and surveil the growing population, various forms of archives cataloguing information about individuals were established, passports and identity cards issued, etc. Consequently, various proceedings to establish and keep track of individuals' identities were developed. Those procedures and criteria for identities that developed as a result of these changes seldom had any immediate relation to an individual's experience of identity or possibilities of correcting an identity. The truth of administrative identity came in this way to be found in archives and case summaries all having lives of their own (Harré 1983; Hydén 1997) and being closely connected to institutional contexts.

**Interaction and Identity**

Identities are displayed, negotiated and established in activities, where people do things together, i.e., in joint activities in face-to-face interaction. Activities of this sort, for instance, applying for and investigating entitlements to social welfare benefits are accomplished through interaction between two or more participants. By organising and structuring sequential interaction participants create and interpret meaning by identifying themselves and the other while enacting their relationships.

In most joint activities, interaction between participants consists of talk. That is, it is by using language that participants act and accomplish their activities. In joint activities like conversations, identities are established as a way of connecting the ongoing verbal interaction with the participants in the speech situation. This makes specific features and aspects of the participants relevant for the activities.

As already indicated above this can be done by using several culturally relevant procedures. Three types of procedures seem especially important for identifying. One of the most common ways is by <u>indexing</u> participants in using pronouns: "I" for speaker, "you" for addressee, and "he" or "she" for third parties, like audiences, overhearers or non-present persons. A pronoun may index the physical aspects of the speaker or the addressee but most often index what Goffman calls the *principal* (1974, 518-519), that is, the person in the sense of either being responsible for the utterance or the person viewed a responsible addressee. A second possibility to identify someone is by *reflexive* use of categorisations such as "social worker", "skinhead", "drug addict" by using what Sacks called "membership categorisation" (Sacks 1992). Identity in this sense may be established by *describing* persons or oneself as being of a certain type. This may be done either explicitly by invoking a social category or implicitly by establishing a social identity *in action*. The latter may be accomplished by doing something that identifies the actor or other participants or persons as being of certain type. By asking a person for a menu in a restaurant, the addressee is identified as a waitress or waiter and the speaker as patron - although the categorisation is implicit. A third possibility is to refer to and use *iconic* aspects of identity. That is, a person may look the same or like a younger version. Or she/he may look like someone else or like a person of a certain type. Here, various iconic, pictorial or physiognomic aspects - "looking like" - are utilised in establishing identity. These types of procedures are often used in looking at photographs in family albums, recognising persons not encountered in many years and showing a passport or identity card.

Establishing identity is something that both contributes to and anchors the participants and their actions in the social organisation of the speech event. In this way the speech situation is widened to include not only the physical present participants as animators or "actual sounding boxes" (Goffman 1974, 517), but also the various positions, roles and relationships that participants may take up in relation to each other. In doing this, a *participant framework* is established (Goffman 1981). That is, the organisation of shifting and temporary relationships between the participants and between the participants and the ongoing actions. The uses of for instance the pronoun "you"[2] casts a participant as an addressee; the use of social categories or kinship categories casts other participants in the social roles of client or father. In this sense, the use of pronouns or social categories is not only or even primarily a reflection of a social structure, but rather the creative introduction of social relationships and social structure (cf. Silverstein 1976).

By organising and structuring interaction in more or less systematic ways, it is possible to enact certain more or less constrained relations between participants, possible participant identities, and their understanding of the situation. This is what happens in conversational interaction in what is called *institutional contexts*. If, for instance, one person systematically ask questions and the other answers these, a relationship is created that constrains the possible participant identities and interpretations of the situation.

Viewed form this perspective, it can be argued that establishing and interpreting identities in institutional contexts is done in a way that differs somewhat from what occurs in informal contexts. The first of these ways involves active categorisation and re-categorizion of clients. The second involves the use of pronouns creating a type of preferred relationship between a client and a representative of the institution, which excludes other possible relations. The third involves the use of identity procedures that are specifically administrative.

**Categorisation**

One way to identify participants and establish identity is by categorising participants, either by self categorisation or categorisation by the other. As Sacks (1992) pointed out, social categories have several interesting properties. One of these is that we generally tend both to speak and to hear as if a connection between being a certain type of person and certain types of actions exists, and vice verse. This is what Sacks called "category-bound activities" (Sacks 1992). Participants can utilise this in categorising each other. Categorisation can be made directly and explicitly by invoking a social category, like "client" or "alcohol abuser". From this categorisation, certain types of behaviour are inferred, i.e., it is heard as if they are connected to a person of this sort. In the same way certain types of actions or behaviours can be made relevant in the interaction, indicating that the agent of these actions belongs to a certain social category. These actions and behaviours can be made relevant by describing them in a conversation or they can be acted out. In this way a participant may propose a certain social category as relevant by acting in a certain way or by describing certain types of actions. This would be an *implicit attribution* of a social category.

Institutions in general have a set of social categories that are relevant due to organisational and administrative routines (Prottas 1979; Lipsky 1980). Eligibilities are generally tied to these social categories. The social welfare agency is a typical example of this (cf. Hydén 1999). For the social worker it is important to be able to describe and categorise the client as deserving, as one actively looking for a job, not using alcohol or drugs, etc. In categorising the client, the social worker offers in this manner an identity that is grounded in the slots and categories of the institution. An example of a fairly unproblematic categorisation is shown in the following:

*Example 1*

Those present are a female social worker (S), a female client (K) and a female research assistant. It is the first time the client visits a social welfare agency. From the start of the conversation:

```
1   S:   å du kommer för å söka socialbidrag förstår jag
2   S:   so you've come in order to apply for financial benefits
3   K:   ja
4   C:   yes
5   S:   eftersom du kommer till mej
6   S:   while you came to see me
7   K:   ja
8   C:   yeah
```

Very early on in the encounter, the social worker self-reflectively suggests identities both for herself and the client. She does this by saying that this is inferable from what the client wants by knowing who the present speaker is, that is, a social worker (turn 3). By invoking her own institutional identity here it is possible for the social worker to position the addressee as a client. The client accepts the social worker's suggested inferences (turn 2 and 4) and by doing so accepts identification as a client. This indicates processes of suggesting and accepting identities are generally joint accomplishments. Also, this suggests identity in institutional settings is tied to available social categories.

Assuming an identity through an implicit social categorisation is the most common way to assume identities in the social worker material. Rarely does the social worker make an explicit self-categorisation, although it sometimes happens as in the following:

*Example 2*

Those present are a male client (K), male social worker (S) and a female research assistant.

1   S:   Jag heter alltså Carl mitt förnamn och efternamn Andersson / K: m /
1   S:   My name is Carl first name and last name Andersson /C: m/
2        socialsekreterare på den här grupp tre kallas den vi är ansvariga för dom som är
2        social worker in what's called here group three we are responsible for those
4        till för dom som bor i detta område. Det är därför du har hamnat här       ,
4        living in this area. That's reason you ended up here

In this example, the social worker refers to himself as a social worker by using an explicit social category: "social worker in what's called here group three" (sw: "socialsekreterare på den här grupp tre"). Further, he implicitly categorises the addressee as client by including him among persons living in a certain geographical area.

When social workers categorises clients this is something they generally are entitled to do. Further, such categorisation has consequences in terms of clients' eligibility for social welfare. Clients are generally eager to present themselves as being persons of a certain category. That is, both the client and the social worker in an encounter can be expected to have categorisations that which they prefer. When one participant categorises another, a central problem is whether the categorised participant accepts this categorisation or not. The proposed categorisation may in some way affect the standing of the participant, for instance, by suggesting that he or she is not eligible for certain rights.

*Example 3*

Those present are a female social worker (S), male client (K) and female research assistant. The social worker and client have met on several earlier occasions.

1   S:   Vet du va ja tänkte på när du kom in här i rummet /K: m/ vi har träffats en gång förut i januari /K: ja/ å då tyckte ja att du såg drogad ut å då frågade ja dej /K:jae/ å då prata du om att du fick att du åt tabletter va att du va +sjukskriven
1   S:   Do you know what I thought when you entered the room /C: m/ we met once before in january /C: yes/ and then I thought you looked high and I asked you /C: yeah/ and then you talked about

|  |  | having that you were taking pills and that your were +on sick leave |
|---|---|---|
| 2 | K: | +jaa att jag hade tage nervlugnande ja också |
| 2 | C: | +yeah that I was taking sedatives an' also |
| 3 | S: | +och nu tänkte ja |
| 3 | S: | +and now I was thinking |
| 4 | K: | +sömnmedicin |
| 4 | C: | sleeping pills |
| 5 | S: | precis å nu tänkte ja tänkte samma som nu då du kom in i rummet /K: nä/ tänkte ja också på mej gör du intryck av å vara drogad |
| 5 | S: | exactly and I was thinking the same thing now when you entered the room /C: no/ I thought you impressed me also now as being high |
| 6 | K: | näe [skrattar] ja ä inte de |
| 6 | C: | no [laughs] I'm not |
| 7 | S: | ä ä det ovanligt ä ha den enda som säjer de här till dej ä de nån annan= |
| 7 | S: | is it uncommon is I'm the only one that tells you this is there someone else= |
| 8 | K: | =på sista tiden ä de bara du som har sagt men nu nu nu ä ja inte riktigt frisk va de var likadant i går när jag sökte jobb så där kände mej skitkonstig så där skakade å vart dålig i magen å de å förra veckan hade ja feber å de |
| 8 | C: | =lately it's only you that's said but for the moment I'm not totaly healthy hm it was the same yesterday when I was looking for a job I felt strange shaking and had an upset stomach and so on and last week I had fever |
| 9 | S: | m men du säger på sista tiden ä de ingen annan som har sagt de till dej |
| 9 | S: | yeah but you say that lately no one else has told you |
| 10 | K: | näe de ä de int |
| 10 | C: | no no one has |
| 11 | S: | För va ja tänker de ä att de= |
| 11 | S: | 'cause I'm thinking that it is= |
| 12 | K: | =däremot så ä ja lite nervös å så nu visst fan ä ja väl de /S: m/ va ja fick lite tabletter sen å dom ä ju slut |
| 12 | C: | =but I'm a bit nervous right now that's for sure /S: m/ I got some pills earlier and they are gone |

In the preceding example the social worker suggests a social categorisation the client resists. The social worker opens the meeting by suggesting that she suspects that the client is under the influence of drugs (turn 1 and 5). She does this by describing her own experience of seeing the client enter the room. In turns 2, 4, 8 and 12, the client tries to reframe his use of drugs, from being abusive, to being connected to being ill (turn 8) or "nervous" (turn 12).

When the social worker says she suspects that the client is on drugs, she accomplishes at least two things in the interaction. First, by starting aggressively and describing and questioning the client, she implicitly defines herself as social worker; she is in a position entitling her to do what she does and the client is the one who has to answer her accusations. In a similar manner, by accepting his position as the one having to answer questions and accusations (turns 2, 4, and 8), the addressee assumes the identity of being a client. Second, in describing her experiences the social worker indicates a social categorisation of the client as a person who uses drugs. She does this by pointing to behaviours connected to drug abuse. The client reacts negatively to this (turns 6, 8, 12) by denying and reframing his use of drugs. Being categorised as a drug addict would most certainly have negative consequences for him since it would affect his possibilities for receiving social welfare benefits. It is a process that in many ways resembles what Garfinkel called a degradation ceremony (1956).

The explicit and implicit use of social categories is a way of pointing out various conventionalised and institutionalised social roles participants may assume in the interaction. This categorisation draws on the participants' common cultural knowledge about how actions may be heard as belonging to certain social categories. Further as well as expressing relationships between belonging to a social category and the entitlement of certain rights or social positions. This kind of categorisation is sometimes too coarse and needs to be finely tuned to serve interactional needs. One way of achieving this is by using pronouns and invoking various participant frameworks.

## Pronouns and Identities

In institutional contexts, professionals make a systematic distinction between themselves as private persons and as professionals in an administrative organisation. As private persons, they may hold personal opinions, norms, and moral standards and have feelings and experiences that as a rule are not to be allowed to interfere with their professional work. As professionals they have to represent professional standards, organisational norms, provide equal treatment to all, follow administrative routines, etc. - irrespective of their own views, feelings or ideas about the persons they work with. This is the classical bureaucratic ideal that has governed work in public institutions for at least a century in Europe and elsewhere.

The shift between various identities and positions is not specific for bureaucratic contexts. Individuals normally take on different identities in relation to various social contexts: at home, with friends, at work, with superiors, etc. What is specific to the institutional context is probably the fact that identities associated with private and informal spheres have to be suppressed in favour of institutional identities. Further, persons having contact with institutions are assigned identities in relation to the institution, for example clients and patients.

This means among other things that ordinary and frequently used pronouns like "I" and "we" have to be assigned specific meaning in institutional contexts, both for professionals and citizens. The distinction between the private and professional may assume central importance.

The use of pronouns presupposes a framework that makes clear what they indice. In institutional conversations a decentring of the actual speech situation to an institutional framework is made. This often is exemplified in institutional representatives' pervasive use of "we" in institutional contexts as ways of referring to themselves as speaker instead of "I".

*Example 4*

Those present are a male client (K), male social worker (S) and a female research assistant recording and observing. The client and social worker have not met before. In the early part of the conversation the social worker tries to survey how the client's contact was initiated.

1   S:   du har bott tidigare här i socialdistrikt 13 du vet inte hur på vilket sätt har du tagit kontakt med oss eller va de eller har vi tagit +kontakt me
1   S:   you lived earlier in social district 13 you don't know in what way have you contacted us or did or have we contacted +you
2   K:   +ja tog kontakt me er nu när jag fick de här jobbet va för ja måste ha mat måste ha råd me å käka å resor å

2    C:    +I took contact with you now when I got this job 'cause I need
            food I must have money for food and travels and

In this example a structuring of the relationship between client and social worker is accomplished by the use of various pronouns. In turn 1 the social worker addresses the client with the pronoun "thou" ("du" - second person [informal] pronoun - T-type) and refers to himself as "us" ("oss" - a reflexive first person plural pronoun) and "we" ("vi"- a first person plural pronoun). In turn 2 the client addresses himself as "I" and the social worker as "you" ("er" - second person plural pronoun). This example is taken from the early part of the conversation when the social worker begins his investigatory work (cf. Hydén 1996). Both social worker and client used this vocative form throughout this phase of the conversation. As a result, identities appear to be established both in terms of the *individual speakers* and their relationship to *social contexts* as well as the *relationship* between the speakers.

The social worker's use of "thou" identifies the addressee as the person sitting opposite the social worker and in that sense anchors the utterance in the spatial arrangement of the room where a research assistant is also present. The pronoun in this sense picks out one of three present persons as addressee. When the social worker in turn 1 addresses the client with "thou", he uses an informal address, "thou" instead of the more formal "you" ("Ni" - the so-called V-type) or some other type of direct address such as "mister" or an indirect circumlocution. The use of an informal pronoun was fairly common in everyday Swedish at the time of this encounter and is in that sense, unmarked, although it does project an egalitarian and non-hierarchical relationship (cf. Brown & Gilman 1960, 1972). The client initially identifies himself by the word "I" and makes use of no other pronoun in referring to himself throughout the entire conversation.

The social worker refers to himself by using "we". It must be noted that there are several types of "we". Both Bühler (1990) and Fillmore (1997) distinguish for instance between the excluding and including "we" depending on whether the addressee is included or not. This typology could be further differentiated in subgroups if we think that the speaker using "we" could refer to as well as include or exclude several other persons. This could be other participants in the interaction (either Addressee or other Participants) as well as persons not participating in the interaction (here called "Persons outside the speech situation").

**Table 1  Including and Excluding We-Forms**

The sign + indicate inclusion and - exclusion.

**(1)  Including "we"**
(a)   +Speaker, +Addressee
(b)   +Speaker, +Addressee, +Participants
(c)   +Speaker, +Addressee, +Participants, +Persons outside the situation

**(2)  Excluding "we"**
(a)   +Speaker, -Addressee, -Participants, -Persons outside the situation (the regal we)
(b)   +Speaker, +Participants, -Addressee, -Persons outside the situation
(c)   +Speaker, +Participants, +Persons outside the situation, -Addressee
(d)   +Speaker, +Persons outside the situation, -Addressee, -Participants

When reference is made to persons not present in the speech event - such as in 1c and 2c, d in Table 1 - a problem is, of course, whom these persons referred to may be. One way for a listener to solve the problem is to assume that it refers to persons belonging to some type of social group or collective as the speaker - that is, to persons who can be categorised in some way, like family members, Swedes, social workers, etc. In that way the pronoun "we" is used as a substitute for the name of this category (cf. Sacks 1992, 571 ff.). The relationship between the Speaker and the category is to be as understood as meaning the Speaker is a member of the category.

Using this typology, it becomes clear that the subtype of "we" that the social worker uses in example 4 is a "we" that includes the speaker, excludes the addressee and the third participant in the situation, the research assistant. Simultaneously, this "we" also includes persons outside the speech event ("have we contacted you"; sw. "har vi tagit kontakt me"). The social worker seems here to be referring to a collective which he is part of as a representative and which exists outside the current situation. In this case, he obviously is referring to the local social welfare agency that he works for, and even more specifically the group of social workers he belongs to - something that become clear later on. During the remainder of the conversation, this is the only type of "we" that the social worker uses. That is, he has a very strong preference for this type of pronoun use.

When using "us" and "we", the speaker by indexing refers to an institution of social welfare agencies and positions himself as a ventriloquist for this organisation. In that sense, he is not individuated as a specific person but is speaking as a collective. This is a case of *individuation by collectivising*. This form is probably prototypical for pronoun use by institutional representatives in institutional contexts, where the pronoun "we" become a substitute for the category of persons working for the agency.

Shortly after the above exchange the social worker starts to fill in a form and is apparently reminded that he has not presented himself to the client. In doing this, the social worker then shifts from "we" to "I".

*Example 5*

Same participants as in example 4 above.

| 1 | S: | [harklar sig] om jag börjar med dom här personalia [5 s] jo jag vill bara säga |
| 1 | S: | [clears his throat] if I start with these personal information [5s] I just like to say |
| 2 | | att du kanske inte hörde det i all hast du kan ta min [tar upp ett kort och räcker till klienten] |
| 2 | | that you perhaps didn't hear it you can take mine [takes up a card and gives to client] |
| 3 | S: | jag heter alltså Carl mitt förnamn och efternamn Andersson / K: m / |
| 3 | S: | my name is Carl first name and last name Andersson /C: m/ |
| 4 | | socialsekreterare på den här grupp tre kallas den vi är ansvariga för dom som är |
| 4 | | social worker in this it's called group three we are responsible for those |
| 5 | | till för dom som bor i detta område. Det är därför du har hamnat här. |
| 5 | | that live in this area. That's reason you ended up here |
| 6 | | De är alltså en ren slump att du hamnat hos mej |
| 6 | | You came to me by mere chance |

In this example, the social worker refers to himself by using the pronoun "I" when he starts to fill in the form placed before him on his desk (line 1). Up to this point in the conversation he has only used the first person singular pronoun once, when he asked the client "can I trust what you are saying?" (sw. "kan jag lita på det?"). In both instances the social worker individuates himself in relation to the institutional collective. He continues this individuation by presenting his name (line 3) and then places himself in the organisational structure of the social welfare bureau. In so doing, his individuality is framed not as the private person "Carl Andersson", but as a social worker belonging to a specific organisational unit ("group three"). This organisational unit is then described as having specific functions ("we are responsible for those that live in this area"; SW: "vi är ansvariga för dom som är till för dom som bor i detta område"). His "I" is the "I" of the individual *social worker* - not the private person.

In presenting himself in this way, the social worker also positions the client in a wider social and organisational context. The social worker tells the client that "his" organisational unit is for "those" (SW. "dom" - reflexive third person plural pronoun) living in a specific geographical area. When the social worker, in line 5 then addresses the client by using "thou" he individuates the client as a person being part of "those", i.e., the collective of inhabitants of a certain area. The social worker further stresses that the relationship between himself (SW. "mej") and the client ("thou") is accidental ("You came to me by mere chance"; sw. "de är alltså en ren slump att du hamnat hos mej", lines 5-6). In other words, their relationship is determined by certain organisational circumstances, not by any personal preferences or dispositions.

It is by primarily using the pronouns "I" and "we" that the social worker and the client establish who they are and their relationships. By placing the pronouns in various participant frameworks the speaker is able to actualise various aspects of his identity that he wants to make relevant in the interaction. Central to this effort is establishing and upholding the distinction between the social worker as a private person and the social worker as a representative of the institution. In the same manner, the distinction between the client as a private, biographical person and the client as an incumbent of a social position defined by the social welfare system is upheld. This is something that seems essential in the institutional context as a way of producing and upholding a bureaucratic relationship and processing of the client and his or her needs.

## Shifting Identity

If speakers establish identities by shifting use of pronouns in order to make various aspects relevant for the interaction, a central question is what these aspects are. In the conversation quoted above the social worker uses first persons singular or plural pronoun (I or we) on 71 occasions. Of these "we" is used on 43 occasions (61% of all occasions) and "I" on 28 occasions (39%). The social worker uses "we" nearly three times as often as "I". Example 6 shows some of the various ways pronouns are uses.

*Example 6*

a   S:   jag heter alltså Carl mitt förnamn och efternamn Andersson (201:3)

a   S:   my name is Carl first name and last name Andersson

b   S:   jag räknade ut (201:13)

b   S:   I worked it out

c   S:   kan jag lita på det? (201:2)

c   S:   can I trust what you are saying?

d   S:   annars får vi räkna er ihop och då måste vi ta reda på hennes ekonomi (201:13)

d   S:   otherwise we have to count you as a couple and then we have to find out about here financial situation

e   S:   vi kan skicka dej pengar vi måste först lägga upp en akt på dej (201:13)

e   S:   we can send you money we have to start by registering you

f   S:   men om man säger så här va att för 20 dagar är de här 1000 [kronor] va räknade jag här 510 [kronor] i uppehälle å så lägger vi till 800 kronor till din hyra (201:13)

f   S:   but if you put it this way for 20 days is these 1000 [Swedish crowns] I did count here 510 [Swedish crowns] for living expenses and then further 800 [Swedish crowns] for your rent

g   S:   jag måste fråga inspektören /K: m/ hur det är med det här (204:2)

g   S:   I have to ask my supervisor /C: m/ about this

As seen in (a) - (c) in example 6, the social worker tends to use the singular form "I" when he indexes himself as or his action as individuated. The "we" in (d) - (e) is used to index the social worker as acting as a representative for the social welfare bureau (although not necessarily his organisational unit). The last instance (f) uses a mix of both "I" and "we".

A closer look at the "I" in (a) - (c) shows three different types of individuation being accomplished, to create different relations between the social worker and the client. In (a), the "I" is used in a naming practice and indicates the social worker as the individual having the name "Carl Andersson". His "I" points to *the bearer* of the name.

In both (b) and (c) the "I" indicates the <u>agent</u> and in these cases, it indicates an individual agent in contrast to a possible collective agent. In both cases, the "I" indicates a relationship between the speaker and actions - the speaker is here "the principal" (Goffman 1974, 513). In using "I" in this way, a moral relationship is established between the agent and the action indicating the degree of responsibility of the speaker. In (b), the social worker points to himself as the person who actually did certain things ("I worked it out"; SW. jag räknade ut"). He is both the one who performed the action as well as who can be held as responsible for the doing. Here, there seems to be a shift in the relation to his actions and indirectly to the client. By individualising himself, the social worker establishes a direct relation between himself and his actions: he is personally responsible for what he is doing and will remain so until further notice.

In (c), the social worker establishes a relational and morally binding relation between himself and the client. The expression is elliptical in the sense that the promising subject - the client - is not mentioned. In view of the client's answer (not quoted here) and the local context, the sentence is heard as "Can I trust that you are speaking truthfully?" That is, by indirectly pointing to the client ("you") and himself ("I") the social worker is establishing a relation between himself and the client. This relation is based on the social worker and client as individuals and their relation as a moral one. The social worker obligates the client to speak only the truth.

In both (d) and (e), the social worker again indicates himself as agent, but now as a collective agent. His actions are not individual by choice, but are instead performed as part of administrative routines. They are based on the organisation's own standards and norms, not necessarily the social worker's own. In so doing, the social worker collectivises his actions. In this context, he also suggest a specific moral relationship between himself as speaker and agent and the actions he undertakes, namely a responsibility that is not personal but organisational. As a member or representative of the organisation he is responsible for the action - but only to a certain degree. The example in (g) indicates that the organisational responsibilities have certain limits, basically determined by to what degree the social worker can account for his or her actions. In this sense the collective agent has organisational limits outside of which his (or her) identity is taken over by someone else in the organisation.

Finally, in (f), the social worker indicates himself both as an individual and collective agent.

So by using the two pronouns "I" and "we", the social worker systematically can shift identity and relations to the client and his own utterances. These shifting alignments towards the addressee and the utterance are examples of what Goffman (1981) called *footing*. By shifting identity and relation the speaker makes various aspects of his or her potential identities relevant for the interaction. The social worker shifts footing in order to negotiate responsibility for his or her actions. This is done by invoking either a "we" form indicating the social worker acting as a stand in or representative for the social welfare agency; and "I" individualising the social worker as actor ("the principal") and stressing the interpersonal relation between him/her and the client.

## Confusion over Identity

The dependence of identity on the organisation of the participant frameworks is made very clear in cases where mistakes or confusion over identity are present.

*Example 7*

Those present are a female social worker (S), male client (K) and female research assistant. The social worker and client have met on several occasions before.

```
1   S:   om du söker om du söker bidrag till hyran de va de handlar om
1   S:   you're applying for help with your rent that's what it's about
2   K:   ja
2   C:   yeah
3   S:   så måste du ha ett godkänt andrahandskontrakt
3   S:   then you need a valid contract
4   K:   ja med de får ja ju
4   C:   yeah but I'll get one when
5   S:   också en sån här grundläggande sak
5   S:   that's like very fundamental
6   K:   de får ja ju inte här va
6   C:   I won't get one
7   S:   nä
7   S:   no
```

8   K:   som de vet ju inte va heter de vet ju inte hä dom vet inte ju inte
         om fastighetsägaren att ja hyr där förstår du
8   C:   they don't know what's it called they don't know the owner of the
         house don't know that I lives there you see
9   S:   ähm men än så längre som länge om du de handlar fortfarande om
         de bidragen gäller
9   S:   hmr but as long as if you it's still about the money
10  K:   mm till bostads
10  C:   for my rent
11  S:   ja just de
11  S:   that's correct
12  K:   ja ja vet
12  C:   I know
13  S:   eller att vi skall ta hänsyn till att du har nåra bostadskostnader
13  S:   or that we are going to include your rent
14  K:   men ja har ju
14  C:   but I have rent
15  S:   men ja [jag] låter så trött på rösten
15  S:   but I sound like I'm so tired
16  K:   vem
16  C:   who
17  S:   jag låter så trött på rösten
17  S:   I sound like I'm very tired
18  K:   varför då
18  C:   how come
19  S:   ja det är en intressant fråga
19  S:   yeah that's an interesting question
20  S:   ja tycker det här ä väligt grundläggande grejer å de tror ja att du
         gör också du ha
20  S:   I think this is very fundamental and I believe that you do the same
21  K:   ja jag vet
21  C:   yeah I know

The excerpt in example 7 is taken from the middle of a conversation between a social worker and client who have met several times before. The conversation takes place at a social welfare bureau in a large Swedish city. Both have been talking about for some time about various administrative points to be fulfilled in order for the client to be eligible for social welfare. In turns 1 to 14, they discuss whether the client has a lease for his apartment or not. The social worker positions the client as "thou" and herself as "we" (turn 13) and the client indicate himself by using "I". In turns 15 to 19, there is a sudden change in this interactional pattern. The social worker comments on herself that she sounds tired and the client apparently becomes confused about who is tired. After a further comments from the social worker, the interaction loops back to the previous discussion about contracts (turn 20, 21).

The relevant parts (turns 15 to 19) are marked in the conversation by a shift in voice from aggressive tones to softer and quieter ones by both social worker and client. This change also indicates a frame break, i.e., a new relationship between the participants (excluding the research assistant). This is a *reflexive frame break* in which the social worker makes a comment about the way that she sounds and about the quality of the interaction. In doing this, she decentres her previous speaker identity and relation to her utterances and to the participants. The addressee of utterance in turn 15 is unclear, in the sense that the words could be directed to her as well as to the other participants. This is what Goffman calls a response cry (Goffman 1981).

The "who?" of the client in turn 16 is apparently not related to the previous turn but is a further meta-communicative utterance asking for the principal of the previous turn: who is responsible for speaking these words. That is, there is no apparent confusion over the animator of the utterance but rather about what aspects of the animating person are relevant in order to understand the utterance.

In retrospect, it is through the use of pronouns in creative and differentiated ways that social workers as speakers establish and transform relations to clients and to utterances. As shown here, the relationship between the two persons in the speech situation is preferably cast as a relation between a "we-you", rather than a "I-thou" relation. Both the client and the social worker preferable stand out as representatives of collective social entities such as inhabitants of geographical areas or members of organisations. The social worker especially individuates actions in the institutional framework by shifting to "I".

## Administrative Identity: Criteria for Identity

A specific type identity that appears to be uniquely tied to institutional and administrative contexts is the *administrative* identity and the procedures for establishing this identity. In modern society, registers are kept and procedures used in order to identify persons as citizens (voting lists), patients (hospital records), clients (social welfare records), pupils (grades and gradecards/reportcards), etc. These registers give persons identities that are established, updated and maintained according to various administrative routines. Certain administrative identity tokens can be held by the individual, such as a passport or an identity card.

This type of identity differs from the interactional types of identities, earlier discussed. In suggesting or using an administrative identity it is not necessary that the person identified owns or experiences the identity. In this way, administrative identity is stripped from the person being identified. A person can be denied or attributed a certain identity without being able or having the power to correct the identity. Goffman's classic work on this process of identity stripping in institutional settings is found in his book *Asylums* (1961).

In everyday life, identities over time are generally sustained or argued, by interactionally invoking memories or by suggesting that a person look the same as he or she used to. That is, one important everyday procedure for establishing and sustaining identity is *iconic* similarity and recognisability. The person is who he or she is, she looks like the one he or she claims to be. This is probably a fairly recent way of both displaying, claiming and experiencing identity, most probably connected to the invention and use of photography (Benjamin 1969; cf. Davis 1983, for historical examples of contested identity). But these procedures do not necessarily have any impact on the administrative attribution and claiming of identity.

*Example 8*

A female social worker (S), an elderly male client (K) and a research assistant. The social worker and client have met several times earlier.

| | | |
|---|---|---|
| 1 | K: | du känner igen mej |
| 1 | C: | do you recognize me |
| 2 | S: | japp |
| 2 | S: | yeah |
| 3 | K: | utan skägg |
| 3 | C: | without the beard |
| 4 | S: | ja nä de gör ja ja mindes inte ens att du hade skägg |
| 4 | S: | well no I do I didn't even remember that you had a beard |
| 5 | K: | jag brukar ha helskägg för det mesta |
| 5 | C: | I usually have a beard |

6   S:   jaa
6   S:   yes
7   K:   men nu är de de att de blir så grått alldeles silver grått (...)
7   C:   but it's become grey totally silver grey (...)
8   K:   ja var upp till Lisett Bårker [name of social worker] tidigare
8   C:   I met Lisett Bårker [name of social worker] before

In example 8 the male client makes use of an everyday procedure for establishing his identity and to point out a change in his physical appearance. Very early in the conversation, the client asks the social worker "do you recognise me", putting forward the iconic aspects of his identity involving being recognised by looking the same as he did at their previous meetings. Here, the client suggests that he doesn't look the same because he has shaved off his beard. For the client, his beard was apparently an important mark of identity. As it turns out the social worker does not remember any beard (turn 4).

In saying that she doesn't remember any beard, she is in a way rejecting parts of the client's identity claim. It is as if how the client looks - that is his individual traits and marks such as the beard - do not have any relevance for the social worker. The client is not interesting as concrete individual in that sense to her. Somewhat later in the conversation, the beard and identity questions resurface.

*Example 9*

Continuation of example 8.

1   S:   har du ingen legitimation
1   S:   don't you have an identity card
2   K:   nej ja måste skaffa mej de
2   C:   no I've got to get one
3   S:   ja
3   S:   yes
4   K:   och ja måste fota mig för att ja har ju helskägg på dom fotona ja har
4   C:   and I have to take a new photo because I've got a beard on the ones I've got
5   S:   ja fast det ska ju inte vara någt hinder om du har skägg
5   S:   well it's no problem having a beard
6   K:   ja ja i Frankrike råka ja lite ille ut för tack vare att ja hade skägg

| 6 | C: | well when I was in France I had some problems due to having a beard |
|---|---|---|
| 7 | S: | m okej nu är de ju så eftersom ja känner igen dig så räcker det med det här då |
| 7 | S: | m okay well I recognize you so that will suffice for this time |
| 8 | K: | nu ska i gudarnas i ärlighetens namn sägas sägas att [continues] |
| 8 | C: | honestly speaking [continues] |

As it turns out, the client does not have an identity card. This is needed by the social worker in order to establish and verify the client's identity. In order for client to get an identity card, he needs a new photo of himself without beard. The social worker then says (turn 7) that he doesn't need to get an identity card since she recognises him and can vouch for his identity. This leaves the client with the puzzling question why did the social worker need his identity card in the first place.

## Identity Work and the Production of Bureaucracy

As we have seen, when a citizen and social worker meet in order to discuss, investigate and decide on a citizen's financial problem, they have a shared communicative problem. The ways ordinary used in establishing and displaying their identity in everyday situations doesn't work. The conditions for talk and interaction in institutional contexts differ from talk in informal contexts, in that special rules for talk but also for interpretation of the participants and their actions are at play. This conventions and rules have to do with the old and inbred conceptions in modern western societies of the relationship between citizens and representatives of the public sphere.

In modern bureaucracies, like the social welfare agency, it is important to establish and maintain a differentiation and boundary between both the citizen and institutional representatives as specific and concrete individuals and as citizens and representatives. For the institutional representative, this often involves a question of making a distinction between the private and professional person. For the citizen, it is a question about making a difference between the civic and private aspects of his or her person. Both parties therefor have to position themselves in the interaction in such a way that identities are used to uphold these distinctions. This makes it possible for the citizen to be received, treated and assessed in an impartial and objective way.

This identity problem is important for the participants to solve for at least two reasons. First, establishing and assuming identity is important in interpreting what is going on in the interaction and especially in the linguistic communication; that is, for inferring meaning (Gumperz 1982, 1992). Two aspects of the inference process are especially relevant. One is about the interpretation of the speech event, that is, the activity frame, and hence what type of activity the participants are engaged in. By assuming certain identities, such as professional identity, it is possible to infer something about the situation like what type of relationship is being projected. The other aspect concerns the interpretation of the linguistic means, that is, what is said. By knowing in what capacity someone says something, it becomes possible to delimit and interpret the meaning of an utterance. These two processes of interpretation have a reciprocal relation, each being necessary for the other.

Second, identity is used in order to establish, assess and negotiate responsibility for actions. This is especially important in bureaucracies where the institutional representative, like the social worker is not necessarily the author or the principal of what he or she does or says. As an animator of institutional norms and rules, the institutional representative on the one hand may preserve possibilities to sustain a private or informal identity of himself or herself as an individual. On the other hand by instituting a division between principal, author and animator, the representative can pose as a "mere" representative for a more or less abstract and impersonal administrative organisation. In the same way, only certain aspects of the client may become activated in relation to the administration thus giving little or no relevance to informal, private and life-world related identities.

It has been argued that participants may establish, display and communicate their identities in at last three different ways. First by using words to "point to" someone in the conversation, either the speaker or the listener. In this way words - especially pronouns - are used to <u>index</u> participants and relating them, not only to what is said, but also to the situation and to each other. A second possibility to identify someone is by the use of what is called *membership categorisations*. Identity is established by subsuming the other or oneself under a certain social category and hence being of a certain type. This is generally done by invoking a certain category or by description. It is a way of organising the participants by placing them in a *symbolic order*. A third possibility is to point to *iconic* similarities (or dissimilarities) between a participant and some image or picture of the person. This is a method that ties in to the administrative identity routines of modern society using identity cards as a way of presenting and displaying a certain identity.

The identity work of both the social worker and client is part of the larger production and reproduction of the social and symbolic order of the modern bureaucracy: it is part of *"doing bureaucracy"*. By making a distinction between various identities, it becomes possible to produce a sort of impersonal organisation not inhabited by and run by concrete living persons. Thus only certain administrative functions, like making decisions or calculating welfare benefits, are manifested in encounters, not the persons or their reasons for their actions. The actions are separated from the concrete persons, and turned into something existing independent of the concrete individuals performing them. In the same way, citizens, as clients or patients, do not appear in their capacities as persons in life-world context, but emerge instead only as bearers of certain social aspects that may entitle them to certain rights. Consequently, bureaucracy as an impersonal system is established and upheld as way of relating clients and institutional representatives to one another.

Finally, for social workers, these types of situations raise a challenge and a set of difficult problems. Who are they as actors in relation to clients, and what kind of relationships with clients is possible? This is a major and recurrent theme in the literature of social worker education as well as in books proposing "new methods in social work". Here it seems that two positions are suggested. The social worker may become a strict professional, identifying not so much with the bureaucracy, as with professional standards of the professional, she/he may become an impartial administrator. Or the social worker may try to surpass the limitations of these professional and administrative "roles" and develop a "genuine" relationship with the client; often identifying with clients and their situations.

Clients appear to have somewhat more awkward situation as compared to the social workers. Many lack routines and resources taught in professional education, for example in expressing and dealing with the various identities at their disposal in institutional contexts. As a consequence they may have more difficulties in using identity work as a *strategic resource* in their interaction with the social worker.

No final solution to these problems exists, but it is important with a continuing and ongoing critical debate about these issues. In that context, discourse oriented research about the encounters between social workers and clients may prove important in providing "problematisations" of the taken-for-granted everyday realities of the social welfare agencies. By showing how a social phenomenon like identity is not something natural or given, but is produced in and by the interaction between individuals in certain social contexts, where possibilities for critical reflection and discussion are created.

## Notes

1　Drew and Heritage (1992) suggest that it is possible to pinpoint three distinctive characteristics of institutional conversations. First, institutional conversations tend to have a goal and to be subordinated to that goal. In social welfare conversations, the goal may be to obtain the kind of information that the social worker needs to be able to arrive at a decision. Second, in institutional conversations, the turn-taking system - that is, the order in which the speakers are allowed to take turns - is either pre-determined or constrained. An important rule in social welfare conversations is that the social worker asks the questions and the client answers them - not the other way around. Third, special rules in institutional conversations are used to interpret certain phenomena in the conversation. In social welfare encounters, for example, silence on the part of the client may be interpreted by the social worker as a sign of doubt or resistance, and the client's "forgetting" of certain information may be perceived as an attempt to conceal facts that may affect decisions about financial benefits. Further discussions of these aspects of conversation between social worker and clients, are found in Hydén (1999).

2　In Swedish - like in many other European languages - a distinction is made between the address pronoun you ("du") in first person singular, the so called T-type of you, and you ("Ni") in second person plural, the so called V-type (cf. Brown & Gilman 1960, 1972).

## Bibliography

Anspach, R.R. (1979) From Stigma to Identity Politics: Political Activism among the Physically Disabled and Former Mental Patients. *Social Science and Medicine* (13A) 765-773.

Antaki, C., Condor, S. and Levine, M. (1996) Social Identities in Talk: Speaker's Own Orientations. *British Journal of Social Psychology* (35) 473-492.

Antaki, C. and Widdicombie, S. (eds) (1998) *Identities in Talk*. London: Sage.

Benjamin, W. (1969) *Illuminations*. New York: Schocken Books.

Brown, R. and Gilman, A. (1960/1972) The Pronouns of Power and Solidarity. In P. P. Giglioli (ed) *Language and Social Context. Selected Readings*. Harmondsworth: Penguin Books.

Bühler, K. (1934, 1990) *Theory of Language. The Representational Function of Language*. Amsterdam/Philadelphia: John Benjamins Publishing Company.

Davis, N. Z. (1983) *The Return of Martin Guerre*. Cambridge: Harvard University Press.

Drew, P. and Heritage, J. (1992) Analyzing Talk at Work: An Introduction. In Drew, P. and Heritage, J. (eds.) *Talk at Work. Interaction in Institutional Settings.* Cambridge: Cambridge University Press.

Erikson, E.H. (1950) *Childhood and Society.* New York: Norton.

Fillmore, C.J. (1997) *Lectures on Deixis.* Stanford: CSLI Publications.

Garfinkel, H. (1956) Conditions of Successful Degradation Ceremonies. *American Journal of Sociology* (61) 240-244.

Gergen, K.J. (1991) *The Saturated Self: Dilemmas of Identity in Contemporary Life.* New York: Basic Books.

Giddens, A. (1991) *Modernity and Self-identity: Self and Society in the Late Modern Age.* Cambridge: Polity Press.

Goffman, E. (1961) *Asylums.* New York: Doubleday-Anchor.

Goffman, E. (1974) *Frame Analysis. An Essay on the Organization of Experience.* Cambridge: Harvard University Press.

Goffman, E. (1981) *Forms of Talk.* Philadelphia: University of Pennsylvania.

Gumperz, J.J. (1982) *Discourse strategies.* New York: Cambridge University Press.

Gumperz, J.J. (1992) Interviewing in Intercultural Situations. In P. Drew and J. Heritage (eds.) *Talk at work. Interaction in institutional settings.* Cambridge: Cambridge University Press.

Hanks, W.F. (1990) *Referential Practice. Language and Lived Space among the Maya.* Chicago: The University of Chicago Press.

Harré, R. (1983) *Personal Being.* Oxford: Blackwell.

Hydén, L.C. (1996) Applying for Money. The Encounter Between Social Workers and Clients as a Question of Morality. *British Journal of Social Work* (26) 843-860.

Hydén, L.C. (1997) The Institutional Narrative as Drama. In B.-M. Gunnarsson, P. Linell and B. Nordberg (eds.) *The Construction of Professional Discourse.* London: Longman.

Hydén, L.C. (1999) Talk About Money. Studying the Interaction Between Social Worker and Client. *International Journal of Social Welfare.*

Josselson, R. (1996) *Revising Herself. The Story of Women's Identity from College to Midlife.* New York: Oxford University Press.

Linell, P. and Fredin, E. (1995) Negotiating Terms in Social Welfare Office Talk. In Firth, A. (ed) *The Discourse of Negotiation: Studies of Language in the Workplace.* Oxford: Pergamon.

Lipsky, M. (1980) *Street-Level Bureaucracy. Dilemma of the Individual in Public Services.* New York: Russel Sage Foundation.

Prottas, J. (1979) *People-Processing: The Street-Level Bureaucrat in Public Service Bureaucracies.* Lexington: Lexington Books.

Sacks, H. (1992) *Lectures on Conversation. Vol. 1 and 2.* Oxford: Blackwell.

Sarangi, S. and Slembrouck, S. (1996) *Language, Bureaucracy and Social Control.* London: Longman.

Schafer, R. (1976) *A New Language for Psychoanalysis.* New Haven: Yale University Press.

Silverstein, M. (1976) Shifters, Verbal Categories and Cultural Description. In K. Basso and H. Selby (eds.) *Meaning in Anthropology.* Alburquerque: School of American Research.

Taylor, C. (1991) *The Ethics of Authenticity.* Cambridge: Harvard University Press.

Tugendhat, E. (1992) *Self-Consciousness and Self-determination.* Cambridge: MIT Press.

# 9 Social Work or Bureaucracy?

ILMARI ROSTILA

## Introduction

This chapter describes how some social workers and clients talk with each other in social welfare offices in Finnish municipalities, and what can be said on the basis of this about the encounters between these professional helpers and those coming to them for help. The title "social work or bureaucracy?" reflects in a somewhat abstract way the possible forms these meetings may assume. This chapter draws from tape-recorded material analysed and discussed in earlier articles (Rostila 1995, 1997). In all these works, observations about the talk-in-interaction in social welfare-office are interpreted in the larger context of participants' activities and communicative work. Further, these findings are discussed from the point of view of implementing social welfare as a micropolicy of face-to-face-interaction.

There now exist a number of studies about talk-in-interaction in the encounters between social workers and clients in the social welfare offices in Nordic countries. The bulk of these are based on tape-recorded materials and deal primarily with clients applying for financial benefits (Cedersund 1992; Cedersund & Säljö 1994; Eräsaari 1995; Fredin 1993; Hydén 1991, 1994, 1996; Kullberg 1994; Sörensen 1995). The research has been most extensive in Sweden where encounters between social workers and clients have been interpreted very much in terms of institutional and sociocultural pre-existing models of talk. The theoretical frameworks used in these studies have tended to emphasise a dualism between the clients' life-world and the requirements of the system of the welfare state. The conversational pattern of the encounters is interpreted as a "speech genre" (Fredin 1993) resulting from the contradictions between these two domains of reality.

My research, on the other hand, is anchored to a tradition of conversation analysis developed in the works of British and Finnish researchers (e.g., Heritage & Drew 1992; Peräkylä 1995; Silverman 1997). This approach makes a claim of analysing institutional talk very strictly from the point of view of the participants' constructed meanings on turn-by-turn basis. Preserving a strong comparative perspective to so-called ordinary conversations, this approach is characterised by a extreme caution in issues involved with attributing any prescribed identities to participants, even though the event under examination happens to take place in some particular institutional setting (Schegloff 1991,1992).

## The Institutional Setting: Social Workers in Social Welfare Offices in Finland

All Finnish residents are entitled to last-resort income support to guarantee minimum subsistence. Although income support is confirmed as a benefit through law, criteria for eligibility are not clearly laid down. This means that agency personnel are required to exercise independent discretion. In social welfare offices, the client's right of financial support is established on the basis of certain set formulae.

In Nordic countries it long has been the practice that trained social workers meet clients applying for income support. In recent years, however, there have been efforts to delegate these tasks to staff involved with more purely administrative work. Seen from an international comparative perspective, the way in which trained social workers in the Nordic countries have been involved in managing this kind of financial support has been an exceptional arrangement.

Subsistence clients are required to meet their social worker about once a month in a face-to-face meeting to discuss their applications for income subsistence and/or how the former decision concerning their cases are going to be implemented. Clients are provided assistance on a means-tested basis: social workers examine the client's and her/his family's income and expenses and discuss relevant aspects of their daily living conditions. Often, many clients are long-term customers, which means that the relationship between participants may extend some way into the past.

As a gatekeeper in a street level bureaucracy (Prottas 1979; Lipsky 1980) the social worker implements the rules concerning financial help, which often is done very much on the basis of local practices and local knowledge of the "culture" of the municipal welfare-office. In practice, this entails often applying the procedure of means testing in relation to questions of client morality. This means that the assessment by the social worker of the extent of help required by the client is linked closely to representations of the client's moral character. Owing to this, research has often been focused on theories and problems involved with investigating the causes of the client's situation. These aspects have been especially central to the work of several welfare state researchers (e.g., Hydén 1994; Cedersund & Saljo 1994).

There is, however, another aspect of examining the client's situation, closely tied to the assessment of client's moral credibility, namely the implicit or explicit considerations concerning financial assistance as an investment in the client's future. An issue here is, of course, the credibility and the reasonableness of the client's plans and prospects for the future. This aspect of reasoning, conditioned by local financing and political considerations, has always been relevant, but has gained more even more importance today when the Nordic welfare state systems are being seriously challenged.

Apart from the bureaucratic, organisational and normative rules and obligations imposed on their job by local administration and the state, social workers also have obligations towards their professional values and practices. Most social workers engaged in customer service at social welfare offices have an academic education, and in defining client needs and problems in their encounters with clients, they often take into account professional criteria and principles. Central to these are ideals concerning respect for the client's individuality as well as the integrity of their own professional practices. In principle, the professional background of social workers makes them sensitive to many problems related to long-term or sudden poverty. Their concern extends to the personal dimension of client experiences of the need for seeking financial help and to the troubles connected to it, such as joblessness, divorce, heavy debts, being quite alone with one's troubles etc. In addition, social workers are in a position to practice social control of the deviant behaviour, such as heavy drinking, neglecting one's children or treating one's parents badly in their old age.

In this context of a mixture of often contradictory expectations and orientations, social workers tend to ask themselves whether what they do counts as "social work". For instance, they frequently describe their subsistence clients as "routine cases". Social workers often complain that they do not have any effective means or time to help their clients. In Finnish social welfare offices, social workers often express serious doubts about the applicability of ideal social work methods and procedures in their daily work: they complain that the classic procedure of problem-solving does not have much support. Many social workers, in fact, tend to speak more for modest and minor solutions they try to find together with their clients, rather than for a work based on a systematic analysis of client's problems.

In my research the encounters and relationships between social workers and clients are interpreted as negotiations between participants, conditioned by the above mentioned important co-ordinates of their everyday dealings with each other. Two points should be specifically noted: firstly, attending to her or his clients constitutes the hard core of the social worker's daily work for the foreseeable future, and secondly, the attainment of professionally more ambitious goals of social work requires co-operation on the part of the clients (cf. Lipsky 1980, 58-59). It may be argued that the psychological and professional meaning of interaction is essentially dependent on the client's participation, which is a matter of local negotiation from " below up" (cf. Drew & Heritage 1992, 23).

## The Data

My main data consist of tape-recorded discussions between eight social workers and their clients, i.e. a total of 32 encounters, in two different social welfare offices in a Finnish city. I also made, though not very systematically, numerous observations about these encounters and listened to what social workers said about the client or the encounter. This I could do before clients came, as well as after they left the office meetingrooms. Clients were mostly long-term customers, but some of the clients had met the social worker only once or twice before. There was thus a great variation in encounters in terms of the length of the social worker-client relationship. Also the encounters varied in length. Some of the meetings were over in less than ten minutes, while one-third took more than half an hour. Also the contents of the conversations differed, but may be crudely described as bargaining over benefits, providing information about other services, support and activation and general social talk (cf. Mäntysaari 1991).

## The Conversational Alignment

In everyday conversations, people normally understand each other and the flow of talk is relatively orderly. Yet sometimes problems arise. Participants occasionally misunderstand each other's actions. Perhaps they forget a word or lose track of what was being said, etc. But we also know that when problems arise, they normally are quickly taken care of. Participants are successful because they actually work at it.

Nofsinger (1991, 111-144) describes these processes that keep conversation "on track" under the title "alignment". In defining these processes, Nofsinger refers to "aligning actions" (1991, 111-112). He distinguishes two senses of alignment, the first being "the process of resolving discrepancies between people's conduct and cultural expectations" (1991, 112). The other sense of alignment refers to talk used to frame messages for purposes of clarifying, interpreting, and managing conversational meaning and communicator roles (1991, 112). Nofsinger uses the term alignment in this latter sense. Interpreting the term "alignment" rather broadly he focuses on "those activities through which participants achieve interaction by aligning their individual actions" (1991, 112, emphasis Nofsinger). Different participants' utterances and conversational actions are lined up, straightened out or laid out in an orderly way in order to achieve intersubjective understandings rather than separate understandings.

Nofsinger examines how this aligning work is done in ordinary conversations through a wide variety of conversational practices, from recipients' routine responses to repairs of conversational problems. Adjacently placed second actions, as well as second pair parts, convey to other participants a sense of how that second speaker interprets the prior utterance. In analysing the conversational alignment, Nofsinger emphasises that one should focus on how various conversational practices are used to display exactly what sorts of alignment (Nofsinger 1991, 114).

Things get more complicated when we begin to focus on so-called institutional talk. From a CA point of view, we then begin to address issues of which institution is relevant to a particular conversation and how participants "know " (Schegloff 1991, 1992). Drew and Heritage (1992, 33) give a dramatic example about how participants, in selecting an activity that a turn is designed to perform, locally construct in the same "context" two different relevant contexts. In the example from health-visitor studies, a father and a mother respond to a remark from the health visitor by performing quite different actions. When the visitor remarks "He's enjoying that" the mother responds "He's not hungry..." She treats the remark as implying that the baby is "enjoying" whatever he is sucking or chewing because he might be hungry - the mother's response is a defence against something which she treats as implied in the health visitor's remark. The father, by contrast, simply agrees with the health visitor. Thus, in designing their responses quite differently, the mother and father elect to perform alternative activities. Both actions have a "logic": the father treats the health visitor's remark as an innocent "conversational" one, but the mother, who is oriented to the visitor's advisory tasks in the visit, employs a different inferential schema. Her response is oriented to the institutional role of health visitor as an evaluator of baby care and to her own responsibility for that care.

Maynard (1992) and Heath (1992) have analysed interactions in circumstances where there may be different alignments between professionals and clients as regards "what next". Maynard (1992) has studied how with the use of the so-called perspective-display series, clinicians and parents may collaboratively establish an alignment regarding the existence of a child's problem and the expertise of the clinic in dealing with it. This he describes as exhibiting "accord on the existence of a problem also implies an alignment as lay and professional participants with regard to expertise for understanding the problem's exact nature" (Maynard 1992, 336).

Clienthood and the understanding of the problematic situation is not a given social context but rather a joint, collaborative achievement of the parties involved, a "framework of accountability" (Heritage 1984; Marlaire & Maynard 1993). This provides the general setting for the participants' actions. Establishing this common framework in social work seems to be rather problematic. In their ethnographic study, Baldock and Prior (1981) paid attention to the obscurity of verbal communication in social work. It seemed that social talk and task-oriented speech intermingled so much that it was difficult for the analyser and the client to distinguish between them. The clients did not seem to have an idea about the agenda of the meeting and what was expected of them in the course of the meeting (cf. Drew & Heritage 1992).

Implicative for the overall structure of a conversation is its opening as well as its closing (Schegloff & Sacks 1974). The opening is a key moment in negotiating of topical structure of the conversation. In the early part of the conversation, both participants need to address the question why they are meeting again, or to select a specific topic, which assumes the status of the "first topic" (Schegloff & Sacks 1974). On the other hand in the closings, participants can display their understanding about which kind of conversations they are closing. I use this observation from the domain of ordinary conversations as a methodological recommendation. This provides a focus for concentrating in this social welfare setting of various interpretations on the openings, on the one hand, including the ways of getting the money matter started as a topic, and, on the other, on the closings of the encounters. The participants' orientations to the conversational event as a whole are probably present both in the openings, as well as in the closings of the encounters. An interesting question is then: what kind of homology or similarity in terms of an activity-type (Drew & Heritage 1992) can be found?

Sometimes the participants' aims and strategies in the social welfare may fit each other in such a way that they are aligned with each other in the manner they display their understanding of the encounter (cf. about goals and institutional talk, see Drew & Heritage 1992). This raises, however, an empirical question. What kinds of understandings about "what is going on here" participants are able to construct?

## Doing "Bureaucracy" Co-operatively

In many encounters the conditions of the client were taken up by the social worker in a report about the previous encounter, as illustrated in lines 20-21, 23 of extract 1. This transcription is of course translated from Finnish and is a slightly simplified version of a more precise translation of the transcription used in previous articles (Rostila 1995, 1997).

*Extract 1*

R1a1 (opening)
((permission for tape-recording and using these extracts has been received from all parties))

| | | |
|---|---|---|
| 14 | | (5.0) |
| 15 | S: | Let's get you on this machine first. Now what was here. |
| 16 | | (2.0) |
| 17 | C: | ((coughs)) |
| 18 | S: | Tellinen Tuomo ((reads the whole name of the client)) |
| 19 | | (4.0) |
| 20 | S: | Yes that was what we put in here last time. You were then (.) and now |
| 21 | | it is the foot. |
| 22 | C: | Yes. |
| 23 | S: | with your affair (and) |
| 24 | | (.) |
| 25 | C: | and now it happened to me that I went to work and |
| 26 | | (.) |
| 27 | | they said there is no more work that |

The client filled in the report, which was initiated by the social worker, with what he had in mind (see lines 22, 25-27 above).

Those encounters, which were begun by this report-pattern, were regularly closed using "a shutting down a topic" method, where the statement "alright" or "OK" is met with a similar statement (Schegloff & Sacks 1974, 306). In the following example (extract 2) that is done in lines 315-316:

*Extract 2*

Pj5a1 (closing)

```
307 S:   your rent vouchers hand them [in]
308 C:   [yeah]
309 S:   and (.) then we have to make a new appointment.
310      ((some lines omitted, social worker examines calendar))
311 S:   so let's say (something in a low voice)
312      (2.0)
313      ((telephone rings and social worker answers the phone))
314 S:   aha you have got your (turns to the client)
315      yeah this is [OK]
316 C:   [yeah OK] yeah so thanks bye
317      (.)
318 S:   yeh bye
```

It is a common practice to close the subject of a monotopical conversation on mutual agreement by using "shutting down a topic" technique (Schegloff & Sacks 1974, 306). Then the "yeah" that follows can be heard as a possible pre-closing, as here in lines 316-318.

These encounters seem to begin, as well as end, in mutual alignment, so that both participants in their co-ordinated actions display a sense of the encounter being a monotopical encounter. Here, the focus has been on the client's financial condition, even though some interesting variations in these opening and closing-practices were found (see details in Rostila 1995). In this conversational environment, all the facts, statements, etc. about the client's causes of having to come to the welfare office, as well as all the details concerning his or her everyday life and future plans, are embedded within this sense of the encounter. Whatever the participants have been talking about, the client's conditions in between these openings and closings, they leave behind the impression of being a part of a conversation which primarily concerned the client's money matter.

Formally the structure of the encounter can be presented like this:

Opening the money matter
Talking about aspects of the client's life as part of the overall topic "money matter"
Closing the money matter

The report form can be seen as a device to begin the business at hand in a co-operative way, where the social worker proposes a narrative footing for the client to use. In so doing, the participants can smoothly sail over the rocky waters of the client being under a pressure to tell why he or she has come into the office. Thus other more risky alternatives, such as, for instance, asking for help, which might be face-threatening for both of them, can be avoided. The social worker's initiation of this report-pattern, which is much used in bureaucratic settings (a "reporting practice", Shotter 1984; Cedersund & Säljö 1994), can be seen as an act of professional power, as well as, cautiousness.

This "professionality", however, does not seem to have much to do with social work, but is rather a way of casting both participants in roles that fit better in the bureaucracy. The same can be said about the closings. This argument, I think, becomes clearer in the next section, when we look at the other type of encounter which is accomplished co-operatively.

**Doing "Social Work" Co-operatively**

It is important to note that the participants in the "bureaucratic" encounters like those above had met only perhaps a couple of times, or even just once before, so that the clients can be characterised as more or less "new". On the other hand, the clients that I describe in the following as participants in "social work" encounters seemed to be at least a bit more long-term acquaintances with their respective social workers.

In many cases a conversational topic, which seemed to have nothing to do with applying for money, could be introduced and discussed at length in the beginning of an encounter. Here, in extract 3, participants talk about the client's minor trouble concerning her chances to get enough sleep (lines from 6 onwards), a matter which seems to be closely connected to her duties as a mother, which comes out in line 16:

*Extract 3*

J1b2 (opening)

```
4          (5.0) ((tapping the keyboard of the computer))
5    S:   (so how have you been doing)
6    C:   (yeah) (        ) I was (.) I haven't been sleeping very well.
7          (.)
8    C?:  (for) a while
9          (.)
10   S:   (      ) what, what is it with us. I mean have you too
11         not been sleep[ing
12   C:              [no
13         (.)
14   S:   you shouldn't
15         (.)
16   C:   my girl's not been very well (and everything)
```

The client in the case happens to be a single mother, and she thus is approaching circumstances that are important as well as challenging in her daily life. As such the topic seems to be also relevant for the social worker, who gives some sort of support through becoming a sympathetic recipient of the trouble (displaying his similar kind of trouble, making participants a bit like co-partners in this trouble).

The same topic rather surprisingly is reintroduced as a final item after talking nearly half an hour about other topics at the end of the encounter (extract 4). This occurs immediately prior to the social worker making a move towards closing the encounter by starting to make an arrangement (arrangement as implicating closing, see Schegloff & Sacks 1974; Button 1991):

*Extract 4*

J1b2 (closing)

```
606  C:   I don't know (.) if I could just get some sleep mhh (smiling)
607        (.)
608  S:   Mm (smiling?)
609        (.)
610  S:   well (.) Mary'll look after the children for you
```

611    won't she if you (.) take a nap
612    (.)
613    (    )
614 S:  if only you don't (s[tay) there
615 C:  [would it be alright hehh ((laughs))
616    (.)
617 S:  would would it be alright to take a [nap
618 C:  [hhh ye
619    (.)
620 S:  yeah
621    (.)
622 C:  (hh) have to go and (see if me mum)
623    (.6) ((papers shuffled))
624 S:  hey, I'll phone you and be in touch about this club things if
        (lines omitted, discussion about community work in the club)
675 C:  but do let me know then
676 S:  I'll be in touch
677    (.)
678 C:  OK (.) yes well
679    (.)
680 C:  [thanks and bye
681 S:  [(bye)

In these "social work" encounters, the money matter was taken up as a separate topic. In the following case (extract 5), a male client has talked for a while about his problems with drinking too much alcohol and being absent from his work. As the client is dwelling on his future options in holding on to his job (from line 43 onwards), the social worker takes up in line 59 the money matter with a straightforward question:

*Extract 5*

Pj5b3

43  C:  we agreed with the boss that I
44      can work on Saturday as compensation
45      (.)
46  S:  yes
47      (.)
48  S:  yes

```
49          (.)
50   C:     it would have been possible to do so.
51          (.)
52   S:     yeh
53          (.)
54   S:     yes
55          (1.4)
56   S:     (I think it was left)
57          (0.6) ((rustle of paper))
58   S:     well how are your now just these (.) money matters
59          going so erm you said something on the phone
60          that you were in dept
61   C:     yes (.) (I am) (          ) in dept (.) and that's why
62          I actually again so//
```

On closer inspection, why is it we can say that the money matter is taken up as a separate topic, and why it is so important? To answer the latter question first, it is important that we can show that the participants make this difference, because it is on the basis of their orientation that we can also argue, that this encounter differs fundamentally from the previous monotopical bureaucratic encounter-type. This, because the encounter consists of several conversational topics, that are talked as separate topics. This cannot have, in any meaningful way, structures similar to previous encounters, with similar phases. I hope also that by showing this in detail, I can underscore again that in many social worker-client encounters participants do seem to have a shared understanding of what they are aiming at.

The details in what happens before the social worker asks about money matter, and the question itself, construct the money matter as a separate topic of conversation. In this sense of organising the structure of a conversation as "topical talk" (Schegloff & Sacks 1974), the money matter becomes a topic in the same way as did the previous topic of (misuse of alcohol). As a conversational object it thus gets its separate attention, and is focused on as a particular topic in this conversation. Participants construct this understanding in their mutual alignment with each other.

The details of what happens before the social worker asks about money matter show that the participants have talked the previous topic into its end; the topic is jointly closed by "holding over a prior activity" (Button 1991, 252-3). By continuing an ongoing activity, the client repeating the option to work on Saturday as a compensation (lines 44 and 59) and the social worker repeating her tokens of receipt of this information (lines 46, 48 52, 54), participants have displayed to each other that the topic is at its end.

Also the social worker's question itself constructs the money matter as a separate topic of conversation. The change of topic is marked by a pause, change in orientation (rustle of paper) and the word "well" (lines 56-58). This taking up of the client's possible money problem as a distinct topic treats money as a separate area of concern, disconnecting it explicitly from the previous topic and other matters of interest. In fact, we may claim that the words "just those" express that money was a less serious matter, compared with the evidently more serious issues in the previous talk.

An interesting issue, which, I think, emphasises the "social work" character of this exchange of words, is why the social worker at this point did not try to continue the topic about the client's future plans to compensate his absence from the workplace. My interpretation is that the participants were oriented to the possibility that the client was moving close to the financial aspects of his absenteeism. And it was precisely for this reason - and a handy place for that - that the social worker took up the money matter before the client did. The client's initiation of this could have been a face-threatening act, which could have threatened the sense of "social work". By bringing up the money matter by herself the social worker had a chance to present her perspective on the money matter, as a relatively minor thing, and quite distinct from the client's future plans and matters of greater importance for "social work".

The participants thus managed to construct a shared understanding that the money for them was only a single separate thing in respect to the client's life and his future plans in general.

The same sense of a co-operatively accomplished order and understanding, which was present in the details of openings and closings, was characteristic for the taking up of money matter in these encounters. We can thus argue that there was a sense of a common, shared agenda.

Formally, the rather complicated structure of the encounter could be presented as follows:

Opening the encounter by talking some "social work" - relevant topic and closing it
Opening possibly other topics and closing them
Opening and closing the money matter
Opening and closing the same topic, which was talked as the first topic and closing it

Closing the whole conversation by making arrangements for future meeting

On the other hand, it seemed, however, that no ideal social work procedure of problem solving was implemented in these encounters. It was thus hard to identify a clear-cut pattern of different phases, by which participants would have executed the tasks of description, assessment, planning and follow-up (see e.g. Egelund & Halskov 1986). I had the feeling that social workers preferred to improvise, together with their client, an encounter that they felt fit better their style and the individual contingencies of the client's situation. Important subjects, however, reflecting the client's particular vulnerabilities, could be talked about in a comfortable and supportive atmosphere and a conversational environment thus was created for discussing, at perhaps another time, more details about the client's plans for future.

**Non Co-operative Encounters**

The following extract (extract 6) shows how, after the issue of permitting the recording had been settled, a young mother starts applying for her monthly financial support (lines 32-34) and how her social worker responds (lines 35 and 37):

*Extract 6*

R1a1

```
32   C:   right the. Here is first of all this (.)
33        ((hands some bills onto the social worker's desk))
34        [medicine]
35   S:   [noo]  yes wait a minute
36   C    [yeaah]
37   S:   [did] you s(ay that) he actually now already got one
```

Firstly, it should be noted that the client (see lines 32-34) violates the norm that it is the social worker as a professional, and not the client, who is in charge of the agenda (Heath 1981; Cedersund 1992; Baldock & Prior 1981). The non-alignment of the social worker can be seen in her request to stop the course of action taken by the client (line 35). In fact, the social worker does not align at all as the recipient of the papers. The extract ends as the social worker hurries to pose a question, in an effort to recover from the attack and take a more active, examining role. Here, she hints about the client's husband's unemployment benefits. The overlapping speech (from line 4 onwards) indicates how the participants are actually competing with each other in order to get the turn of talk and eventually persuade the other in their different preferable courses of action. The client here focuses on the expenses while the social worker focuses on the family's income. From this point of view, the client's turn of starting can be seen as a carefully "planned" activity, where she presents her bill as the first in a series ("first of all this") thus building a means of keeping her turn of talk (cf. Jefferson 1990).

The opening is very non-co-operative: it is a result of both participants' planned, active and in this sense, conscious strategies of action. These planned acts can be understood as reflecting the particular experiences and interests of the participants. In general the participants in this type of encounter without mutual alignment, know each other well in a social sense, but in negative terms. This can be seen in the comments made by the social worker to the researcher asking about this client: "she does not trust me, so I don't trust her," "she lied to me several occasions", and "without any appointment they come barging in". It was common that social workers complained that some clients had a bad habit of dumping a heap of their bills on the social workers desk. Quite possibly, this may have been seen by social workers as an indicator of poor or too much "clientification" and deficiencies in clients' planning of their economies. Of course, in this exemplar, we do not have any access to the client's opinion about her social worker.

The different orientation of the two parties to the conversation is also reflected in the closing (extract 7):

*Extract 7*

7R1a1 (closing)

```
622  S:   [they don't] count here
623  C:   [oh yes]
624  C:   ok
625       (0.4)
626  C:   [right]
627  S:   [it's like with] these children's
628  C:   yeah (.) I'll pick up these toys now (.)
```

629         ((there are some children's toys on the floor of the office, that she starts
630         to pick up))
631 S:     erm (.) you want to go down there (.) take the lift
632 C:     yeah [I'd pick up these things now
633 S:         [I
634             (.)
635 Researcher:    I can help and pick these up
                          ((collecting toys and some talk about them))
643 C:     right (.) see you
644 Researcher:    bye
645         (1.0)
646 S:     it's not
647         (1.0) (tries to open the door: some problem with it)
648         (a bang)
649 S:     (bye now)

The client had asked previously about her expenses from buying clothes for the children (not shown), but the social worker says, as a counter-argument that child allowances are not counted as income (line 622). Speaking simultaneously (line 623) the client indicates, that she was aware of that, and thus in a way empties the social worker's information as an argument. The client's "ok" (in line 624) and even more strongly her "alright" (line 626) can be heard as a possible pre-closing. The social worker still orients to explaining the rules concerning the expenses of children's clothes (see line 627). The client begins, however, to prepare her departure (line 628), providing her justification for the closing in a have-to-go manner. The initiation of the closing brings to an abrupt end the social worker's information. By refusing to receive this information, the client is refraining from providing any approval by her to the conversation (for a detailed discussion about approving of conversation in the closings, see Rostila 1995). The participants' misalignment seems to continue until the end of the encounter: it seems that not even "bye-byes" are exchanged between them. The researcher is involved in a practical activity (picking up toys after line 634), where the exchange of these terminal greetings between the social worker and the client seem to be no longer relevant.

# Conclusion

Under the constraints of social welfare bureaucracy, as well as those of professional goals of social work, social workers and their clients in Finnish social welfare offices seem to have constructed rather different types of encounters. The participants thus display different roles in the encounters. And by skilfully co-operating or refraining from co-operation, they construct the meaning of the encounter around the two main alternative options: those of "social work" and "bureaucratic" or administrative work. The participants can thus present their relationship either as participants in a smoothly going and co-operative examination or as participants in a helping relationship. Both participants, however, are required to accomplish this.

As shown in the openings and closings of these encounters, the participants often do succeed in rather skilfully organising their talk together in such a way that a shared understanding of the main agenda of the talk for them is displayed and preserved in the course of the interaction.

The patterns of talk that I found emphasise the structural differences between the encounters, and different options that the participants have in negotiating the way they talk about the client's situation. The picture is different from the picture given in many other studies, but fits well to the results of Marianne Ranger's ethnographic study of social worker-client meetings at a social welfare agency in Norway (1986, 1993).

The study draws attention to the everyday-life capabilities of the participants in interaction. It seems that often the inequality built into the situation and the control exercised in it by the social worker as a representative of the institution is often skilfully transformed into collaboration by social workers and their clients.

The display of participants' different mutual alignment or non-alignment also leads us to see how and in what sense social workers meet clients as persons and thus individualise them. They make relevant their own as well as their co-participants particular identities. These often are based on a long common history, and sometimes defined in terms of what for us appears as hidden agendas involving treatments of client and their financial concerns in particular ways. As we have suggested here, participants actually are able to construct very different kinds of understandings about "what is going on here".

This is important in practical terms. Research findings about these different forms of communication and the interactional work taking place in the microlandscapes of the welfare state put us in a much better position to evaluate unrealistic policies, instructions and training (cf. Silverman 1997). Thus what can be learned about the quality of communicative work at this level of the welfare state can help us identify different types of communication patterns and perhaps in this way provide leads about how shifts occur from one pattern to another.

Our perspectives and values are, of course, decisive for the evaluation of the encounter-types. In Finland, as well as in other Nordic countries, a shift of emphasis has been taking form concerning the principles of social welfare. In this gradual, and hotly debated development, a new balance is being sought between universal social rights and citizens' duties. Concomitant with this development, new ideas and practices of individually tailored welfare-contracts between public authorities and social welfare-clients have been promoted. There also are efforts being made to include in these practices new agencies, such as non-governmental organisations or the so-called third sector. These changes, especially those involving activation policies, have met much criticism. Yet, no matter which policies are pursued by the administrators of the Nordic Welfare State, it is important that we examine in depth and in detail how these are implemented in the face-to-face interaction between social welfare agencies and their clients.

The benefits of different encounter-types can be discussed against this background. Surely the co-operative encounters seem to be preferable. But which type of mutual alignment is better and for whom? Even though on the one hand the encounter of the "bureaucratic" type may be suitable for contractual relationships, "social work" encounters, on the other hand, may provide a better environment to talk openly enough about the client's personal feelings and difficulties. But critical questions, too, have to be asked. Does the "social work" talk at the 1 welfare office, based on the personal familiarity of the participants with one another and perhaps a shared view of problems offer enough professional and/or therapeutic possibilities? And how suitable is a conversational practice based on familiarity for a contractual client relationship? Should not the interactional practice be neutral rather than confidential? It may be that there are not any general answers to these questions. Even prima facie poor communication can be functional in its context. From the perspective of social work, encounters without participants' mutual alignment can be sometimes defended as efforts to offer professional help to those who have not recognised that such a service exists for them?

# Notes

Symbols used in transcription:

[ ]     indicates talk that has been overlapped by someone else's talk
(0.4)   numbers in brackets indicates silent, lapsed time, in tenths of a second
(.)     indicates a tiny gap
(yes)   words in parentheses or empty parentheses indicate the transcriber's difficulty in
        hearing what was said
(( ))   contains author's descriptions

# Bibliography

Baldock, John and Prior, David (1981) Social Workers Talking to Clients: A Study of Verbal Behaviour. *British Journal of Social Work* (11) 19-38.

Button, Graham (1991) Conversation-in-a-Series. In Boden, Deidre and Zimmerman, Don (eds.) *Talk and Social Structure: Studies in Ethnomethodology and Conversation Analysis.* Cambridge: Polity Press.

Cedersund, Elisabet (1992) *Talk, Text and Institutional Order. A Study of Communication in Social Welfare Bureaucracies.* Linköping University, Linköping Studies in Arts and Sciences 78: Motala.

Cedersund, Elisabet and Säljö, Roger (1994) Running a Bit Low on Money. Reconstructing Financial Problems in the Social Welfare Interview. In Sprondel, Walter M. (ed) *Die Objektivität der Ordnungen und ihre kommunikative Konstruktion.* Suhrkamp der funktionalistischen Vernunft. Frankfurt am Main 1987: Suhrkamp Verlag.

Drew, Paul and Heritage John (1992) Analyzing Talk at Work: An Introduction. In Drew, Paul and Heritage, John (eds.) *Talk at Work.* Cambridge: Cambridge University Press.

Egelund, Tine & Halskov, Therese (1984) *Praksis i socialt arbejde. Vilkår och udviklingsmuligheder i social-og sundhetsforvaltninger.* Kobenhavn: Munksgaard.

Eräsaari, Leena (1995) *Kohtaamisia byrokraattisilla näyttämöillä.* Helsinki: Gaudeamus.

Fredin, Erik (1993) *Dialogen i Socialt Arbete. En studie av socialbyråsamtal i ljuset av modern dialogteori.* Linköping: Motala.

Heath, Christian (1981) The Opening Sequence in Doctor-Patient Interaction. In Atkinson, Paul and Heath, Christian (eds.) *Medical Work. Realities and Routines.* Farnborough, Hants: Gower.

Heath, Christian (1992) The Delivery and Reception of Diagnosis in the General-Practice Consultation. In Drew, Paul and Heritage, John (eds.) *Talk at Work.* Cambridge: Cambridge University Press.

Heritage, John (1984) *Garfinkel and Ethnometodology.* Cambridge: Polity Press.

Heritage, John and Sefi, Sue (1992) Dilemmas of Advice: Aspects of the Delivery and Reception of Advice in Interactions between Health Visitors and First Time Mothers. In Drew, Paul and Heritage, John (eds.) *Talk at Work.* Cambridge: Cambridge University Press.

Hydén, Lars-Christer (1991) *Moral och byråkrati. Om socialbidragsansökningar.* FoU-rapport 7/1991, Stockholm: Stockholms Socialförvaltning.

Hydén, Lars-Christer (1994) The Social Worker as Moral Worker: Applying for Money - the Moral Encounter Between Social Workers and Clients. In Gunnarsson, Britt-Louise, Linell, Per and Nordberg, Bengt (eds.) *Text and Talk in Professional Contexts*. Uppsala: The Swedish Association of Applied Linguistics.

Hydén, Lars-Christer (1996) Applying for money: The Encounter Between Social Workers and Clients - A Question of Morality, *British Journal of Social Work* (26) 843-860.

Jefferson, Gail (1990) List Construction as a Task and Resource. In Psathas, Georg (ed) *Interaction Competence*. Lanham, Maryland: University Press of America.

Kullberg, Christian (1994) *Socialt arbete som kommunikativ praktik. Samtal med och om klienter*. Linköpings universitet, Linköping: Motala.

Lipsky, Michael (1994) *Street-level Bureaucracy. Dilemmas of the Individual in Public Services*. New York: Russell Sage.

Marlaire, Courtney L. and Maynard, Douglas W. (1993) Social Problems and the Organization of Talk and Interaction. In Holstein, James A. and Miller, Gale (eds.) *Reconsidering Social Constructionism. Debates in Social Problems Theory*. New York: Aldine de Gruyter.

Maynard, Douglas W. (1992) On Clinicians Co-implicating Recipients' Perspective in the Delivery of Diagnostic News. In Drew, Paul and Heritage, John (eds.) *Talk at Work*. Cambridge: Cambridge University Press.

Mäntysaari, Mikko (1991) *Sosiaalibyrokratia asiakkaiden valvojana*. Sosiaalipoliittisen yhdistyksen tutkimuksia 51.Tampere: Studies by the Social-Political Association.

Nofsinger, Robert E. (1991) *Everyday Conversation*. Newbury Park CA: Sage Publications.

Peräkylä, Anssi (1995) *AIDS Counselling. Institutional Interaction and Clinical Practice*. Cambridge: Cambridge University Press.

Prottas, Jeffrey M. (1979) *People-processing. The Street-level Bureaucrat in Public Service Bureaucracies*. Lexington: Lexington Books.

Ranger, Marianne (1986) *'Er det bare meg som roter sånn?' Klientsamtaler på et sosialkontor*. Oslo: Universitetsforlaget.

Rostila, Ilmari (1995) The Relationship Between Social Worker and Client in Closing Conversations. *Text* (15) 69-102.

Rostila, Ilmari (1997) How to Start to Talk about Money: Developing Clienthood in Interaction in a Social Welfare Office. *Scandinavian Journal of Social Welfare* (6) 105-118.

Schegloff, Emmanuel, A. (1991) Reflections on Talk and Social Structure. In Boden, Deirdre and Zimmerman, Don (eds.) *Talk and Social Structure: Studies in Ethnomethodology and Conversation Analysis*. Cambridge: Polity Press.

Schegloff, Emmanuel, A. (1992) On Talk and Its Institutional Occasions. In Drew, Paul and Heritage, John (eds.) *Talk at Work*. Cambridge: Cambridge University Press.

Schegloff, Emmanuel A. and Sacks, Harvey (1974) Opening Up Closings. In Turner, Roy (ed) *Ethnomethodology*. Middlesex: Penguin.

Shotter, John (1984) *Social Accountability and Selfhood*. Oxford: Basil Blackwell.

Silverman, David (1997) *Discourses of Counselling. HIV Counselling as Social Interaction*. London: Sage.

Sörensen, Torben Berg (1995)*Den sociale samtale*. Århus: Forlaget Gestus.

# Afterword: After Listening - Another Picture of the Nordic Welfare State and its Operations

SØREN PETER OLESEN

The data, analyses and conclusions presented in this anthology should in no way be understood as making claims for statistical representativeness. As noted in the introduction, these reports draw from research carried out at a handful of sites in the NWS. Consequently, readers should be extremely cautious about using these findings to draw conclusions about the workings of the welfare systems of Finland and the Scandinavian countries - at both micro and macro-levels. As this is being written, thousands of conversations are taking place at social welfare offices, child protection agencies, vocational advising offices, employment offices, treatment facilities of all sorts, probation offices and other welfare settings in Denmark, Finland, Norway and Sweden. Thus it has to be emphasised that those conversations serving as the focus of the foregoing chapters represent only a tiny slice of the total life of the NWS.

With this caution in mind, we may now pose the question: What is it that might be concluded from looking back at the chapters comprising this book? Clearly, one general conclusion to be drawn from the material presented and analysed - not least as found in the accounts from Sweden presented by Kullberg, Cedersund, and Hydén - is that there are some major problems involved in the proper effectuation of public policies within the welfare system itself. During recent decades, conservative politicians as well as political scientists (e.g. Rothstein 1994) have seriously questioned the legitimacy of public administration within NWS.

Central to their critiques have been processes of "clientification", disciplining and bureaucratisation. Theoretically, these writings may be understood as lending support to highly critical views of the state in general as formulated by Foucault and other post-structuralists and of the welfare services in particular as developed by Goffman, Prottas and Lipsky. These writers and others have produced Weberian-like, heavily pessimistic theories about the mechanistic and "people-processing" tendencies built into the bureaucratic apparatuses for meeting human needs developed in modern societies.

As noted in the introduction, these views are very much part of the intellectual climate influencing research on authentic conversations in the welfare systems. Thus, one conclusion readers might draw from certain chapters here is that the Nordic welfare systems do not work as effectively as policy-makers have intended, and in some respects the welfare systems work at cross-purpose to the policy goals of public service. Another conclusion might be that the NWS in some respects does not live up to the high standards that policy-makers and the professions have envisioned for it. In either case, this means that certain of those activities within the public welfare system described in the foregoing do not make as big a difference as presupposed when it comes to the "moment of truth": the final delivery of services to citizens/users/clients.

This understanding, however, must be tempered by the very important fact that none of the foregoing chapters were originally designed to be evaluations of how the public policy is implemented within the NWS. Therefore, they lack the kind of methodological considerations, concerning, for example, how to measure goal-achievement, normally applied in evaluating policy-implementation. However, most of the accounts presented here can be considered as fairly thorough case studies of ongoing processes within agencies belonging to the NWS and for that reason might be suitable for such purposes.

Furthermore, since political science literature in the Nordic countries contains relatively few empirical micro-level studies (Rothstein 1994), there is some value in relating these findings to a more general discussion of social policy implementation and other aspects of work being done within the NWS. This, too, must be done with caution since there is no automatic way of interpreting data and results in qualitative studies. Instead, such findings must always be considered as being inherently ambiguous. Therefore, the interpretations to be drawn from this research are heavily dependent on political and ethical considerations of both interpreter and reader. What one reader might consider as actions from the social worker leading to reproduction of a repressive order, another reader might consider as supportive acts leading to empowerment.

As one concrete example of this we might refer to the findings in the chapter by Vehviläinen. She shows how the vocational counsellor in a subtle and smooth way is trying to get one of her clients to go back to a job that the client herself has excluded as a possible site of future work.

This exemplifies the different interpretations that could be made while looking at the interactions within the agencies of the welfare system. Is the counsellor disempowering or empowering the client? And in the theoretical frame of Goffman (1983): Are structural traits simply being reproduced through the interactional order in this meeting or are such structural traits somehow being loosened and softened through the interaction?

Leaving aside further discussions of data interpretation and representativeness, there are three things needed to be said here to clarify own position regarding the kinds of implications readers may draw from the studies presented in this anthology.

*First* of all, many of the patterns described by this book's contributors and other researchers as well are not specific to Nordic public welfare bureaucracies. A number of these reflect dilemmas found among actors in those specific orders comprising "people-processing-organisations" located throughout the world - not just in the Nordic countries. This means, for example, that the kind of prevailing categorisations and identity constructions identified by Kullberg, Cedersund, and Hydén in their accounts of welfare agencies in Sweden can be expected to be a part of any organisation, public or private, having "people-processing" objectives - no matter where in the world these organisations may be found.

*Secondly*, as indicated by many of the contributors, social workers and other "street-level bureaucrats" in welfare bureaucracies possess considerable relative autonomy in relation to the goals and the policy of NWS. This, for example, is very well illustrated by the descriptions Forsberg and Vagli provide of child protection workers and the decisions they are required by law to make for the best interests of the child. Some researchers have raised the issue of relative autonomy as an important question in terms of a claimed legitimacy crisis of the welfare system (Rothstein 1994). Put in plain terms, these researchers maintain that the legitimacy of the welfare system is being jeopardised if policy makers are unable to control those who are to implement political reforms. However, problems involving autonomy, implementation and steering exists within all complex organisations, and are not specific to the organisation of the Nordic welfare systems. Furthermore, the rational model of organisational theory informing such views has been seriously questioned in recent writings on organisations - especially those referred to collectively as the new institutionalisation.

*Thirdly*, even though Hydén, Kullberg, Cedersund, Forsberg and Vagli expose obvious insufficiencies within these systems, such shortcomings represent only one side of the coin. This might be understood as the *bureaucratic aspect* of or *agency-orientation* to how public policy is effectuated within the public welfare system. On the other side, for instance, the findings by Olesen, Rostila and Vehviläinen display a different picture. These investigators show what might be called the *professional aspect* or *client-orientation* to the work being done. Their findings provide evidence of a well-developed role assumed by professional helpers giving much-needed public service to the individual help-seeker. In their chapters, these researchers present pictures of welfare state professionals handling problems of varying complexity with a high degree of individual competence.

Taken together, these and similar findings contained in the foregoing pages represent the other side of the coin. Clearly, there exists a body of evidence showing the NWS actually making a difference in the lives of citizens/users/clients seeking ways to improve the conditions of their lives. Vehviläinen and Olesen, of course, draw their conclusions on the basis of listening to encounters between the counsellors at welfare state offices and client groups made up of students and unemployed union members. Since both this clientele and indeed counselling services have only recently appeared in the mosaic of the NWS, this raises the possibility the relative newness of these operations may account for the overall positive assessments these authors have drawn from their research results.

With respects to this possibility, Lipsky, though fundamentally a sceptic, mentions three preconditions contributing to "keeping new professions new": sticking to policy goals on behalf of management, adherence to professional standards and ethics by front-line workers and finally user influence (1980). Further, it may be that these counselling services are so new that the kinds of essentialist client stereotypes and accompanying negative traditions found in other areas of welfare state functioning, particularly in social work, have not yet gained a foothold among practitioners. Indeed, it may be that such constructions of clients may never gain dominance in professional discourse since trade union membership and student status are time-honoured elements of personal integrity and self-esteem in the Nordic countries.

Also, as Rostila points out in his chapter, the situation of even the most traditional clients in the Nordic welfare systems - those coming to social welfare offices seeking financial assistance - is no longer what it once was. As he points out, today's clients at social offices increasingly can make their own decisions in choosing co-operation or alignment as strategies for taking part in the interaction at the public encounter. In this new situation, the client thus becomes a co-operator in her or his own right, not merely as an object for manipulation "under the cover of kindness" or just another administrative category.

Along similar lines, Hydén's description of administrative identity as a construction of the welfare state system may be complemented by the concept of public identity. According to definitions advanced by Hetzler (1994), public identity refers to the legal rights (economic, political and social) and experiences people can gain as individuals encountering welfare state staff members. Her research on the welfare state has shown that there are different categories of identity, which she interprets as stages in a process of social change leading towards a fully developed public identity. It is at this final stage, where people claim their rights and attend to their interests as empowered individuals.

Similarly, Vagli, Jokinen, Juhila, Suoninen, Leppo and Arminen provide evidence of the dialectic of the welfare state's positive operations counterbalancing its more negative workings. Though to a lesser degree than Vehviläinen, Olesen and Rostila, these researchers show that the welfare state making a difference - even for those clients whose actions often work against their best interests. As Rostila suggests in his chapter, social workers possess the potential and positioning for functioning both as agents of stasis as well as change. Consequently, it is a critical task for research focused on client-helper interaction to identify those patterns working to promote change as well as those acting to neutralise or counteract change.

It is clear than that the slices of client-helper encounters presented and analysed in this volume provide two opposing perspectives on the NWS. Neither of these, we wish to maintain, should be seen as an unequivocal image of the Nordic welfare systems at the micro level. In one sense, the oppositions and contradictions presented here are not surprising since, as we earlier pointed out, the welfare states of Finland and the Scandinavian countries are a continually evolving product of struggle between opposing forces. Therefore, it should come as no surprise that the street-level arenas of the Nordic welfare systems are rife with conflicts, contradictions and paradoxes. This is so because the NWS itself has been a gigantic arena of ongoing struggles between a myriad of forces since its inception (Seltzer and Stjernø 1980).

Indeed, awareness of the ongoing contradictions and conflicts at the heart of the Nordic welfare state was central to the writings of Herbert Tingsten, one of the most vigorous champions of the Swedish welfare model. It is said that Tingsten often claimed that the most dangerous enemies of the welfare state were those proclaiming that the final victory had been won and that the welfare state had been achieved. Given these and related views of the dialectics and dynamics of the welfare state, there exists an obvious and continuous need for the development of critical as well as constructive perspectives, research, and analyses of its operations - at both macro and micro-levels.

This need has become ever more imperative in recent decades in the wake of the major attacks launched against the welfare state in Europe and the Americas. As one constructive critic of the welfare state has warned, there is a great danger that support by the general public for such attacks can develop in what he terms the "black holes of democracy" (Rothstein 1994). These, he claims, take root at the micro-level of welfare state operations where practitioners meet clients. In the worst case scenario, if too many people experience the system and its personnel as an order characterised by "support-giving" leading to disempowerment, the possibilities for welfare services to make significant and positive differences in the lives of their clients will be greatly diminished, if not eradicated. As a consequence, the democratic ideals and principles envisaged by the policy makers of the NWS will then disappear into this dark void.

Reading between the lines of even the most optimistic pictures of welfare state functioning presented in this book indicates that possibilities for these black holes to develop are ever present in the interactions between welfare state staff and their clients. Whether these risks are linked primarily to the micro-level of client-helper relations or whether they are more bound up with the meso- and institutional levels of system operations should be seen as an empirical matter. Taken together, the accounts presented in the preceding pages may be understood as a beginning toward providing some possible answers to these questions.

In concluding this anthology, it seems appropriate to emphasise that the findings presented here point to the need for developing public services incorporating a heightened awareness of professional standards and ethics. These accounts indicate, too, that citizens/users/clients must be better equipped to make demands when encountering front-line representatives of the NWS. Clearly, too, there is a pressing need for further research to clarify those factors and conditions both conducive and detrimental to the potentials for Nordic welfare systems to make differences in the lives of people seeking help and assistance from its varied agencies. If these systems are to function as planned by policy makers, the prime research goal in years to come ought to focus on identifying - through qualitative, comparative and even quantitative research - the differences making differences, as Gregory Bateson so aptly put it. What we have suggested here are some of the ways that investigators concerned with such key issues may begin to make such identifications.

In closing, it must be strongly reiterated that this book's many findings provide no single final conclusion about the NWS. However, we feel that the recent shifts in research described in the introduction represent a step in the right direction. By using these methods to investigate and identify what is necessary and sufficient to produce social justice and injustice at the micro-level of welfare operations, we have tried to make clear that policy goals involving these vital issues formulated at the macro-level are not automatically transferable. All this anthology's contributors here have tried to point out in various ways from their different vantage points, how the interaction ultimately taking place at the street-level of the Nordic welfare systems involves more than the key questions of equality and justice. In the final analysis, encounters between the professional helpers of the welfare state and those seeking services and help from it may involve far more basic questions of decency and dignity.

## Bibliography

Goffman, E. (1983) The Interactional Order, *American Sociological Review* (48)1-17.

Hetzler, A. (1994) *Socialpolitik i verkligheten. De handikappade och försäkringskassan.* Lund: Bokbox Förlag.

Lipsky, M. (1980) *Street-Level Bureaucracy: Dilemmas of the Individual in Public Services.* New York: Russell Sage.

Rothstein, B. (1994) *Vad bör staten göra? Om välfärdsstatens moraliska och politiska logik.* Stockholm: SNS Förlag.

Seltzer, M. and Stjernø, S. (1980) Et nytt sosialt arbeid. In Leonard, P. and Corrigan, P. *Kritisk syn på sosialt arbeid.* Oslo: Universitetsforlaget.